T0283265

DEEP POCKETS

DEEP POCKETS

Snooker and the Meaning of Life

BRENDAN COOPER

CONSTABLE

CONSTABLE

First published in Great Britain in 2023 by Constable

3 5 7 9 10 8 6 4 2

A CIP catalogue record for this book
is available from the British Library.

ISBN: 978-1-40871-777-6 (hardback)
ISBN: 978-1-40871-778-3 (trade paperback)

Typeset in Electra by Hewer Text UK Ltd, Edinburgh
Printed and bound in Great Britain by Clays Ltd, Elcograf, S.p.A.

Papers used by Constable are from well-managed
forests and other responsible sources.

Constable
An imprint of
Little, Brown Book Group
Carmelite House
50 Victoria Embankment
London EC4Y 0DZ

An Hachette UK Company

www.hachette.co.uk

www.littlebrown.co.uk

In memory of my father, Alan Alfred Cooper
Look ye also while life lasts

– Let it alone. Let's to billiards.
Antony and Cleopatra, II.5

Contents

BREAKING OFF

Undiscovered Snooker

At around 9 p.m. on 2 May 2022, at the Crucible Theatre in Sheffield, Ronnie O'Sullivan turned away from the table and hobbled towards his beaten opponent Judd Trump. The usual form, at this stage, would be a handshake. But this was something deeper, more eloquent. The two players met in a tight embrace. At the age of forty-six, O'Sullivan – who had been Trump's hero, muse and mentor – was, by rights, the father figure; but he was the one unsteady on his feet, weak and overwhelmed, vulnerable to the possibility of toppling to the carpet. Trump was not just hugging him – he was holding him up, while the audience clapped and roared.

As the embrace continued for over a minute, the pair whispered in each other's ears. There was no way of knowing what they said to each other in those moments. There were shades of the final scene of *Lost in Translation* – Bill Murray whispering to Scarlett Johansson on the whirring streets of Tokyo, words secret and inaudible, not meant for others, private truths no one else must hear. It was a scene of breathless emotion – and it conjured up old ghosts, lost icons. Forty years earlier, it had been Alex Higgins on the same stage, clutching the Crucible trophy to his chest, weeping freely as he called for his baby girl. Now, as Ronnie O'Sullivan turned to the crowd, his eyes were puffed and crimson, cheeks wet under the Crucible lights as his son and daughter raced into his arms.

The mood was fitting for such a historic moment. O'Sullivan had just won the World Snooker Championship for the seventh time, matching Stephen Hendry's record and securing his position at the very pinnacle of snookering greatness. All debates about the greatest of all time were finished. To any question about the best-ever player, there was now only one answer.

The final of the World Championship was watched by four and a half million people on the BBC. This made it the most popular programme on British TV that day, beating both *Coronation Street* and *EastEnders*. Record numbers had also watched on Eurosport, not just in the UK, but also in Italy, Poland, Spain, Germany and France. And it is far from the case that only the eyes of Europe were on the game: in China, viewing figures have regularly exceeded a hundred million. It might come as a surprise to many people that snooker has been listed as one of the top ten sports in terms of worldwide TV ratings. Snooker, in short, is huge. Snooker is big news.

Despite this popularity, though, the amount of literature on the sport is minimal. Beyond player biographies, pulpy 'greatest match' anthologies and the odd instructional guide, there has been very little written about the game since the 1980s. The great Clive Everton's *Black Farce and Cue Ball Wizards*, now over fifteen years old, remains the only serious effort at a history of the game in the entire twenty-first century. Column inches on snooker are slim, and almost non-existent beyond the World Championship fortnight. Other sports can boast vast libraries of books historical, analytical and political, exploring cultural significance from every conceivable angle; not so for snooker. The game hovers in a strange silence – it remains, to a large extent, an unwritten game, whose deeper meanings are a blank map, uncharted by the written word. The discrepancy is unique. Nowhere else in sport, culture and entertainment is there such a thinness of serious writing on something so widely followed.

And yet it is a game beloved of novelists, poets, thinkers and philosophers. A. S. Byatt has long been an avid fan, explaining that she relishes 'the narrative of it, the drama. I love it the way you love a Matisse.' Martin Amis, labelled by the *New York Times* as a 'hardened snooker addict', once confessed being on babysitting duty 'earning brownie points so I can play snooker later in the week'. He penned a memorable account of a match against fellow novelist Julian Barnes; Barnes himself used to have a full-sized snooker table in his house. As an English undergraduate, Pulitzer Prize-winning poet Paul Muldoon squeezed in his studies 'between games of snooker'. Lionel Shriver, whose novel *The Post-Birthday World* features a professional snooker player, has itemised what enthrals her about the game: 'I love the sound of it, that delicacy, subtlety and quiet.'

Another literary snooker fan, writer and *Pointless* star Richard Osman, surprised Radio 4 listeners with a left-field musical choice during his 2021 appearance on *Desert Island Discs*. Alongside tracks by Suede, Erasure, and Future Islands, he chose an obscure piece called 'Drag Racer' by The Doug Wood Group – better known, to most people, as the theme tune to the BBC snooker. 'One of the sports that has given me a huge amount of joy is the snooker,' he explained. 'I was sitting on the sofa about three or four months ago, the snooker started, I had a packet of Frazzles and I thought, I'm fifty, and the nine-year-old me was doing the exact same thing. And the rather lovely thing is the theme music to the snooker has not changed either. And the second I hear it, it brings me such great inner peace.' It is a sentiment familiar to millions of snooker followers – that feeling of calm brought on by snooker on the television at home; the engagement with something that is both quiet and exciting, a grand epic of drawn-out drama.

'We look at the world once, in childhood,' Louise Glück hauntingly wrote. 'The rest is memory.' When it comes to what we love, so much depends on early childhood epiphanies. I remember lying on the living-room carpet, five years old, with the snooker on the TV. Not quite my first memory, but one of the first. On the screen was the 1985 final between Steve Davis and Dennis Taylor. Many years later, I discovered this must have been a Christmas special repeat of the final, shown that same year; I remember the faces of Davis and Taylor boxed at the top of the screen, commenting on events. *If this be magic, let it be an art lawful as eating . . .* and there was magic in that moment. The secure dreamscape of childhood homeliness somehow fused itself with the game playing itself out in front of me, forming into a pearl of love for snooker that has lasted my whole life.

This book is an exploration of the deep meanings of snooker – a love letter to the game, and a philosophical journey into its soul. Clive James once said, 'Whoever called snooker "chess with balls" was rude, but right'; like many of snooker's greatest sales pitches, the phrase actually came from Barry Hearn, the mastermind of snooker's commercial golden era. And it is true: snooker *is* chess with balls, a game that combines the intellectual weight of chess with the visceral energy of the very best elite-level sport. It is time to unwrap its secrets. This book will tour the undiscovered territory of snooker's deep pockets.

Twenty-two chapters follow – one for each ball on a snooker table at the beginning of a frame. Each chapter casts its gaze on snooker through the lens of a particular philosophical idea, facet of humanity or cultural perspective. It is a journey that will illuminate the rich and intricate links between snooker and the world of ideas. Ronnie O'Sullivan said, 'I've tried a number of religions and gurus in my time . . . but ultimately they didn't do as much for my peace of mind as snooker.'

The comparison between snooker and religion is apt; for snooker, ultimately, is something more than a game. It is a belief set; a way of seeing; an entire philosophical system. Fanciful though it may sound, it may in fact be no exaggeration to say that snooker can help inform the nature of reality – that, in its interplay of colour and light in a void of surrounding dark, it can help to trace the meaning of life itself.

TIME

The lyf so short, the craft so long to lerne
Geoffrey Chaucer, *The Parlement of Foules*, 1380–83

Time. An all-powerful force, an inscrutable mystery . . . Chaucer's line, from the opening of his poem, redrafts a Hippocratic aphorism – best-known by its Latin translation, '*Ars longa, vita brevis*'. Life is short. But skill? Skill takes time.

By the time we have mastered whatever we are trying to master – perhaps long before – our brief appearance on the planet will be over. 'The cradle rocks above an abyss,' wrote Vladimir Nabokov, 'and common sense tells us that our existence is but a brief crack of light between two eternities of darkness.' We are trapped inside time, and the worst thing is we don't have much of it to work with.

In the light of this sombre truth, it is no surprise that there is a long tradition of downbeat reflections about our helplessness at time's hands. Poets across the ages have agitated about the inescapable reaper lurking at the end of the road.

It was a core concern for Shakespeare in his sonnets. 'Nothing 'gainst Time's scythe can make defence,' he wrote in the twelfth sonnet, 'Save breed, to brave him when he takes thee hence.' We might all be doomed, but at least if we have children, we can continue our life through someone else. W. H. Auden painted time as a kind of cartoon villain, lying in wait like the Child Catcher, looming over our brief flashes of pleasure:

> In the burrows of the Nightmare
> Where Justice naked is,
> Time watches from the shadow
> And coughs when you would kiss.

At every single moment, as we go about our lives, time and its talons are always there, lurking in the bland details of the everyday: 'the crack in the tea-cup opens/A lane to the land of the dead'.

Philip Larkin, the godfather of day-to-day gloom, read the dawn of a new morning simply as a dismal reminder of where it was, exactly, that time would be taking him:

> I work all day, and get half-drunk at night.
> Waking at four to soundless dark, I stare.
> In time the curtain-edges will grow light.
> Till then I see what's really always there:
> Unresting death, a whole day nearer now . . .

There it was, inching closer. Nothing more terrible, nothing more true.

In the modern world, time seems to be getting shorter. This speeding up of reality has been widely discussed; technology provides such rapid access to information that stretches of time are winnowed down to an instant. There was a time, perhaps, when time was slow; when it might have felt more gradual, incremental, an inch-by-inch shift from moment to moment. But the time that Macbeth described as 'creep[ing] in this petty pace from day to day' does not feel much like twenty-first-century time. Our time is much, much faster.

We live in an era of frantic speed, hostile to the possibilities of slow enquiry. Martin Amis has talked of the 'acceleration of history'. Things happen more quickly and we condition ourselves in response. A philosophy of 'accelerationism' has, in a variety of guises, intensified developments in technology and capitalism to speed up human progress. The *lyf so short* seems to be shortening – shortening fast.

On this fizzing circuit board of hurry and haste, snooker sits oddly. It resists speed. It is famous – even notorious – for being slow. It can be tempting to describe the game as an emblem of a different age, when fewer distractions imposed themselves on the lives and entertainment options of the public. Back in 1946, snooker's World Professional Championship final took place over an entire fortnight – a best of 145 frames. Even as it later emerged from obscurity into the national consciousness, many of the top players operated at a level of slowness that would be scandalous today. Ray Reardon, master of the 1970s, played a brand of the game that blended heavy break-building with grinding, ruthless safety play. Two-time world finalist 'Steady' Eddie Charlton practised a philosophy of gritty determination and extreme defensive attrition. This was the norm, for the era. Snooker time was slow time.

The essence of snooker slowness, though, was best embodied by Cliff Thorburn and Terry Griffiths – two timeless legends of the old guard. Born less than a year apart, the pair were in many ways very different characters. Thorburn had honed his craft in the pool halls of Canada, learning to survive on money matches and working as a rubbish collector to keep himself afloat. On one occasion, Thorburn won his match only to find himself staring at the barrel of a gun belonging to the losing party; he was certain he was about to die, until it became clear his opponent wanted to sell the gun for a bit more cash. It is a hair-raising story, that says something about his roots: abandoned by his mother as a toddler, Thorburn's had been a shockingly tough, brutal upbringing. He was streetwise and battle-hardened, his scars seeming to provide him with a kind of cold inner steel. At the table, he was broodingly serious, approaching snooker like a form of mortal combat – his watery eyes somehow both intense and melancholy, a smile rarely surfacing from under his Burt Reynolds moustache.

Griffiths, from the Welsh Valleys, was as cheerful as Thorburn was dour. His chirpy response to TV presenter David Vine, after his 1979 World Championship semi-final victory – *'I'm in the final now, you know'* – has entered the annals of snooker folklore, a cherished moment of eccentric, affable charm. But Griffiths' life had also been tough – working down the coal mines as a teenager, followed by various jobs to make ends meet as an amateur before turning professional in his early thirties. It might be reasonable to draw a link between the hard childhoods of Thorburn and Griffiths and the brutal, dogged snooker they both played, but this is too simple – too speculative to be satisfying. All that can confidently be said is that they were the supreme kings of slow snooker – risking little, delighting in prolonged tactical battles, steadily grinding opponents into the dust.

Both became world champions. Famously, Griffiths' march to the title in 1979 took place in his very first season as a professional. The following year, Thorburn overhauled Alex Higgins to take the trophy. 'As they say in Canada, he's the "Grinder",' Higgins said after the match. 'And he grinds very hard, I can promise you.'

It was a few years later, in 1983, that Thorburn and Griffiths met in the World Championships to produce a match that is still legendary in its levels of mind-numbing, sluggish grit – the ultimate late-night battle. It was the second round. The match was tight throughout; in the final session, little separated the players. Midnight came, and midnight went. Everything boiled down to a final frame, as the wee hours rolled on . . . Thorburn eventually triumphed, 13–12, at 3.51 a.m. According to Clive Everton, this was 'nearly two hours after the BBC had ceased recording': not only the cameramen, but most of the public had gone home, leaving an elite group of fans watching this savage high-water mark of endurance. Astonishingly, Thorburn survived two more final-frame encounters in the quarters and the semis before being crushed, exhausted, by Steve Davis in the final.

And the slowness of snooker is by no means just a thing of the past. As a new century dawned, Peter Ebdon – another world champion – developed a towering reputation for defensive play. The most notorious example was in the 2005 World Championship. His opponent was none other than Ronnie O'Sullivan – reigning champion, crowd favourite, and specialist in volatile brilliance. Temperamentally – and in practically every other respect – the two were diametrical opposites. In a characteristic example of his unpredictable ways, O'Sullivan had shaved his head just before the match. It gave him a look curiously similar to the bald Ebdon – making the contest appear a little like yin versus yang, Jekyll against Hyde, a fight between hostile twins.

O'Sullivan had been leading comfortably – 8–2, at one stage – before Ebdon pulled things back to 10–9. The snail-like approach Ebdon had taken throughout the game (at one point taking three minutes for a shot, prompting O'Sullivan to ask the audience for the time) reached new levels in the twentieth frame. After an opening long red, an easy brown occupied him for well over a minute, as he stalked round the table, scratching his brow, asking for the cue ball to be cleaned. The table, it seemed, presented nothing but problems – problems only he had the discernment to notice.

Slouched in his chair, Ronnie was getting increasingly agitated – looking up to the heavens, shaking his head in weary disbelief. Ebdon studied the reds as if they presented some curious scientific anomaly. He was down to play a shot – then he was up, changing his mind, scratching his head again, face fixed in the tight frown of Rodin's *Thinker*. After an easy pink went in, taking the break to twelve, he once more grimly inspected a variety of reds, all easy shots, as if each harboured some terrible or frightening truth. The referee was asked to clean the cue ball again. By this stage, Ronnie was laughing to himself, hand covering his eyes. At last, Ebdon selected a red, geriatrically settled himself on the shot, interminably lined it up, and missed it by six inches.

As the crowd sighed and whispered, Ronnie laughingly eyeballed his opponent, but Ebdon seemed to be on a different plane of reality, impassively sipping his water. The result of the match now seemed inevitable. Ronnie was just too frustrated to concentrate; Ebdon went on to win 13–11. Some said it was 'cheating' – that the slow play was a deliberate tactical move, designed to frustrate his attacking foe. But Ebdon didn't see it that way.

'When I'm trying my hardest, I seem to go slow,' he said afterwards. 'I don't do it intentionally.'

The following year, Ebdon played Graeme Dott in a breathtakingly long, colossally tedious World Championship final that ended close to 1 a.m. and was described in the *Mirror* as 'snooker's worst-ever final' and 'officially . . . the most BORING of all time'. In its wake, the *Guardian* was prompted to run a mischievous feature titled FIVE THINGS MORE BORING THAN DOTT V. EBDON.

The style of figures such as Ebdon, Rory McLeod, and Rod 'The Plod' Lawler led snooker authorities towards the feeling that something had to be done. 'We are very conscious of the need to entertain,' said Barry Hearn, then chairman of World Snooker, in 2015, 'and I have asked the senior referees to be more assertive.'

Slow snooker was making the game fragile, so the argument went, dragging it away from the essential demands of twenty-first-century entertainment. It was a school of thought also found in other areas of the sporting world. In cricket, the need for speed had led to the development of Twenty20, designed to 'grow and diversify' the sport's fanbase, encouraging young people towards the game and evidently providing a putative remedy to the five-day slog of test matches. In snooker, Hearn introduced average shot times, designed to 'name and shame' the slowest players. In 2017, the 'Snooker Shoot Out' was intro-duced, limiting shots to fifteen seconds and introducing a much more relaxed approach to crowd noise. Here was snooker reborn for a modern audience – a transmogrified Frankenstein's monster, bespoke for an impatient, hyper-accelerated world.

And yet snooker survives, and survives best, in its purest form. Amid the agitation over speed, the slowness of snooker seems to hold its own precious value. Even Barry Hearn himself was ambivalent about regulating time too tightly, commenting that he didn't believe 'in a shot clock for [the] major tournaments'. Steve Davis – a shrewd wit, chess enthusiast and under-acknow-ledged philosopher of the baize – has sagely pondered the 'slow-burner' spirit of snooker. According to Davis, any effort to make snooker *fast* actually pushes against what makes the game compelling. 'It's a bit of a red herring,' he observed, 'to think that you have to make snooker faster to be more entertaining. Snooker doesn't work that way, actually it works the opposite way to a lot of sports – it doesn't have to be fast to be entertaining . . . sometimes the tactics alone can create the enjoyment and the fascination.'

The point is a crucial one. It is in the slowness of snooker that the soul of the drama really shines – the complex drama of the epic narrative. The ebbing and flowing, the steady block-by-block build of plot, the passages of quiet, the flickers of tension, the flat periods, the little turning points . . . all of it facilitates the intensity of the dramatic climax, the sudden moments of explosive significance. The time scale and the leisurely pace allow the drama to breathe. Sports writer Barney Ronay has suggested that snooker is valuable because it 'remains essentially low-key and ponderous at a time when most of the stuff on television seems so frazzled and needy'. Perhaps, in its abrasive relationship to our precipitous reality, snooker teaches us something about time. Perhaps it is not *entirely* unreasonable to say that its ethics of gradualness and protraction can help us to understand how to flourish amid the frenetic energy and pace of modern life.

The fact that a snooker player does not have a time limit has a very particular, philosophical significance. 'This has been going on for over three minutes now,' said referee Ben Williams to Mark Selby, in the 2021 world semi-final. 'You do need to think about taking a stroke.' But, just maybe, this sort of warning is a mistake – a misunderstanding of the deep principles of snooker.

Faced with their next shot, a player may need several minutes or just a couple of seconds. In this space they are, in a sense, in control of time – or at least, for the player and for the audience, it feels that way. The pressure to complete the shot is outweighed by their temporal autonomy. They take whatever time they need. All of the burdens of the world outside the match are paused. Within the space of the shot, there is only the player and the table, the specific challenge they must face, or problem they must solve. All is still: time feels frozen.

In his monumental work of radical ontology, *Being and Time*, Martin Heidegger argued that the fundamental meaning of being was tangled up with time and our progression through it. 'Time,' he wrote, 'must be brought to light and grasped as the horizon of every understanding and interpretation of being.' The essence, the meaning of being hinges on temporality – our existence within time. It is not enough simply to say that being involves time . . . being actually *is* time. Standing at the table – contemplating the next shot – the snooker player is staging a form of resistance to time itself. The resistance, of course, isn't real; time watches from the shadows as always, for the snooker player as much as for anyone else. But it is a powerful idea, even if no more than a seductive delusion – the capacity to stop, to be in full control of everything, with godlike potential over the table in front of you. Walk round the table, sip your drink, chalk your cue. Take all the time that you need; you have all the time in the world.

There is a specific beauty to a television screen that features a snooker table; a beauty that goes beyond the elegance and the regularity of the multicoloured tableau. It is beautiful in part because, quite often, the image is still. Off-screen, the player might be waiting, looking, thinking, lurking, but on the screen, nothing is happening. The stillness of the image – a world placed on pause – embodies the transcendence of time which is perpetually denied us.

In his 'Ode on a Grecian Urn', John Keats observes that the beauty and wonder of art stems from precisely this transcendence.

The still images on the urn do not move and will never move; the scenes presented, and the emotions they convey, will last for ever:

> Ah, happy, happy boughs! that cannot shed
> Your leaves, nor ever bid the Spring adieu;
> And, happy melodist, unwearied,
> For ever piping songs for ever new;
> More happy love! more happy, happy love!
> For ever warm and still to be enjoy'd,
> For ever panting, and for ever young . . .

The beauty and meaning of art, for Keats, arises out of its permanence: 'When old age shall this generation waste,' he notes, looking at the urn, 'Thou shalt remain.' Art is significant because it is unlike ourselves – it embodies a transcendence we can recognise but cannot know; it will not fade and die.

However Einstein's theory might have complicated our understanding of time with its relativity, its capacity to be bent and warped, our helplessness at its hands remains clear. However slow we go, however much we pause, it doesn't matter; a pause is just a pause within time, not a pausing of time. Perhaps the significance of slowness is less about a resistance to time than about the creation of space to think, to reflect, and to be.

In his novel *Slowness*, Milan Kundera wistfully laments the disappearance of this sort of possibility from the modern world: 'Why has the pleasure of slowness disappeared? Ah, where have they gone, the amblers of yesteryear? Where have they gone, those loafing heroes of folk song, those vagabonds who roam from one mill to another and bed down under the stars?' With the phenomena of reality hurtling towards light speed, we need more than ever the space to be slow.

'Wisely and slow,' says Friar Lawrence in *Romeo and Juliet*, offering advice he might have usefully heeded himself. 'They stumble that run fast.'

Slowness is precious; slowness is something we need; a consolation pitted against the inevitability of our end. Slowness is the heart and soul of snooker.

2

Disorder

I desire the things that will destroy me in the end.
Sylvia Plath, journal, March 1951

Order versus disorder. Construction versus destruction. Darkness versus light. Countless thinkers have proposed that human civilisation is a battle between contraries such as these. Friedrich Nietzsche saw humanity as straddling two opposed forces of nature – the Apollonian (order, reason) and the Dionysian (chaos, emotion and madness). Sigmund Freud suggested that all individuals harbour two competing drives – *Eros* (the drive towards life and love) and *Thanatos* (the drive towards violence, destruction and death).

In every one of us, perhaps, there is some conflict between principles of harmony and darker, self-harming instincts. And one of the challenges we face, as we strive for some semblance of self-restraint, is that anarchy can be much more fun. As ex-Van Halen frontman David Lee Roth once said: 'We've all got our self-destructive bad habits . . . the trick is to find four or five you personally like the best, and just do those all the time.'

On the surface, sport is one of the last places you might look for examples of self-destructive behaviour. Sport, after all, is supposed to reveal the pinnacle of human physical capacity.

Sportspeople are perfected specimens – prepped and trained to perfection, every muscle toned and primed, athletic bodies pushed to levels of fitness way beyond anything a normal person might imagine. Ultra-ruthless tennis cyborg Novak Djokovic enjoys a daily routine along the following lines: twenty minutes of yoga or tai chi; a carefully controlled breakfast of water, honey, and fruit; ninety minutes of on-court practice; some cool-down stretching; a lunch of salad and gluten-free pasta; a one-hour workout in the gym; a protein drink; another ninety minutes of on-court practice; some more cool-down stretching. Dinner will feature more salad, perhaps with tuna, salmon or soup. 'In terms of winning,' he explained, 'there is nothing to choose between number one and a hundred. Instead, it's a question of who believes and who wants it more.'

At the same time, though, elite sport is an extreme experience – so extreme that it can have a disruptive effect on the individual. The stress of professional competition has led many to drugs, alcohol and mental health frailties. Fixated by the need to win, plenty of top athletes have fallen to the temptation of performance-enhancing substances. When Ben Johnson's steroid scandal shocked the world at the 1988 Seoul Olympics, he made it very clear that the real problem of drug use went far wider: 'Why should I do this clean,' he complained, 'when everybody else is cheating?' Over three decades later, hundreds of doping violations are still recorded in sport every year – despite the serious health risks involved, including heart disease, infertility, cancer and early death.

And sporting substance abuse is hardly limited to performance enhancement. After beating Wladimir Klitschko in 2015, Tyson Fury slipped into a spiral of drink and drug abuse, ballooning at one point to twenty-eight stone: 'Within a month of being crowned world heavyweight champ, I was an emotional wreck, on my way to a heart attack thanks to class-A drugs, junk food and alcohol.' In football, top-level players such as Adriano, Andy Carroll, Paul Gascoigne, Tony Adams and Paul Merson all battled hard against booze. The pressure, it seems, was too much to handle.

'I had no tools to cope,' Adams once explained.

Gascoigne routinely downed nine brandies plus cocaine before matches. 'I was on four bottles of whisky per day for three months,' he confessed. 'It took two bottles just to stop the shakes.'

It is not, in fact, hard to find these stories. They exist in every sport. They are a kind of shadow in sport's soul; a darkness at its heart. Sport, in other words, harbours a kind of paradox; at the same time that it models the highest possibilities of the physical body, it is also a hotbed of scars and self-harm. The drives of Dionysus and Thanatos thrive in its very highest ranks.

It is only fair to say that, at a physical level, snooker is in a very different place to most other sports. It's not that *none* of the players are in shape; some of them might just about make it into a competitive athlete category. Ronnie O'Sullivan – still frequently cited as the fittest player on tour, as he slides into his late forties – is celebrated for his dedication to running. He says it offers both a physical challenge and a means of mental health management. 'I've noticed I don't get so moody, there isn't the same self-loathing,' he explained. 'Running just makes me feel so much better about myself, which is good for everyone around me too.'

It's perfectly clear, though, that his level is that of a keen amateur rather than anything approaching a professional calibre: he once finished 189th at the Southern Cross Country Championships; in April 2021, he came ninety-eighth in the Chingford League 5k. 'I knew I was always going to have to be one of these untalented runners who has to work hard to get whatever he can out of it. Don't get me wrong, no matter what I do, I like to be at the front. But with running I knew I wasn't expected to win.'

Sure, in snooker it can be helpful to have good fitness. But being out of shape is no barrier to success. Elsewhere on the circuit, the bodies that bob round a tournament table come in a motley assortment of shapes. There are triple chins; love handles; bloated bellies bulging against waistcoats. Drops of sweat glisten on pink, pork-chop foreheads. Damp patches lurk in stale armpit crevices. Maybe, just maybe, this is one reason why self-destructive behaviour has been such a presence in snooker history – in some sense, one of its defining features. You don't *need* to live a puritanical lifestyle to win a snooker match. There is no need for Cristiano Ronaldo levels of bionic physical perfection. You don't need a six pack. You don't need to run. In snooker, in theory, you can booze, you can binge – and you can win.

The story of snooker is stuffed with excess; in looking for the spirit of Dionysus, it is hard to know where to start, since Dionysus seems to be everywhere. But there are few stories of intemperance quite as compelling as the story of William 'Big Bill' Werbeniuk. A talented Canadian cueman, Werbeniuk was one of the great characters of 1980s snooker – a fondly remembered cult figure from the TV golden age. Affable of eye, globular of build, he was an emblem of what the public wanted snooker to be. Snooker, after all, was a game drawn from the beer glasses and fag smoke of dingy working men's clubs, dens of infamy far from the right side of the law. The game was not supposed to be about self-restraint or ascetic dedication. The pencil-thin, mechanically focused Steve Davis was both the most successful player of the 1980s and also perhaps the decade's least popular competitor. Davis was determined, organised, and disciplined. The last thing people wanted was for *Davis* to win.

Werbeniuk's drinking habits during snooker matches were so spectacular that they still look like fantasy, a made-up joke, despite the countless sources for their truth. His key problem was an arm tremor. Whenever he tried to line up a shot, his cueing arm and hand would shake appreciably; for obvious reasons, this compromised his game. It just so happened, though, that booze – huge amounts of booze – was the perfect antidote. It was customary for Werbeniuk to sink ten pints of lager *before* a match began. Once the match was started, he would nurse roughly one pint per frame; across a long match, like a best of nineteen or a best of twenty-five, this could take him to the far side of thirty pints by its conclusion.

Stories of his warrior-like guzzling abound. In 1982, he challenged fellow professional Eddie Sinclair to a drinking contest. Sinclair managed forty-two pints before passing out; after sinking his forty-third, victory beer, legend tells that Werbeniuk declared, 'I'm away to the bar now for a proper drink.' In 1990, he knocked back not just twenty-eight pints of lager, but also sixteen whisky chasers during a match against Nigel Bond; after losing, he gobbled a whole bottle of scotch to 'drown his sorrows'.

In eyebrow-raising testimony to a bygone, more exotic age, Werbeniuk managed – somehow – to argue that the oceans of lager he consumed during tournaments were a necessary condition of his professional performance. So, for a period in the 1980s, he was able to claim money he spent on beer as a tax-deductible expense. It was not to be forever, though: his career abruptly ended in 1990, when the beta blockers he took to help his heart were deemed to be a performance-enhancing drug and outlawed by the authorities.

Werbeniuk may never have been an absolutely top player; he never made it past the quarter finals of a ranking tournament. But at the same time, in the story of snooker, he has become something more than a player – a folk legend, a myth, a Falstaff or Sir Toby Belch of mischief and roistering revelry. Werbeniukian stories radiate a cartoonish feel, like something from a comic book. In the 1980 World Team Cup, he was stretching across the table for a shot – an awkward business for a man of his proportions. A thunderous ripping sound sang across the arena. Big Bill had torn his trousers. He turned to look at the audience, a look of confusion on his face. 'Who did that?' he asked. Werbeniuk's place in snooker folklore is secure, and not because of any tournaments he won.

While Werbeniuk remained largely a journeyman profes-sional, dissipation can be found just as dramatically in some of the greats of the game. In the 1980s, Jimmy White became one of the true stars of snooker; he remains, probably, the most popular player in the history of the sport. There are plenty of reasons why he became so beloved among snooker fans; he was charismatic, he was humble, he played a risky brand of snooker, and, very often, he didn't win. But it is impossible to avoid a sense that some part of this popularity stemmed from the life-style he led. Stories of chaos and indulgence run throughout his career. Jimmy White was a brilliant player . . . but Jimmy White was a wayward boy; Jimmy White was wild.

A snooker prodigy of unusual brilliance, he was tipped for success from an early age. At the age of eighteen, he was the youngest-ever winner of the World Amateur Championship. He was clearly the Next Big Thing, a talent so extraordinary that the World Championship would inevitably be his. Except, notoriously, it never was. White is the most celebrated nearly man in the sport's history – a six-time world finalist whose inability to win it is forever shaded with a sense that, with a different way of life, there would surely have been a different outcome.

'I was a big drinker,' White has said. 'I came from a drinking family. Even at twenty, I could drink all night.' And drinking was a feature of his life throughout the 1980s, when snooker was at peak popularity and top players were some of the country's best-known celebrities. White's first autobiography, *Behind the White Ball*, tells a vertiginous story of late nights, blackouts and bedlam of every conceivable kind.

'You really had no chance, Jimmy,' lamented Harvey Lisberg, his one-time agent. 'You don't allow yourself a level playing field.' White's own mother saw such deeply self-destructive peril in his lifestyle that, in her view, it was actually a good thing he never became world champion.

'According to my mum, losing saved my life. She didn't tell me how she felt at the time . . . she thought I was so wild that she feared for my survival.'

In the late nineties, White followed his autobiography with *Second Wind*. It transpired that the first volume had missed out some things – quite a lot of things.

There was a darker tale beneath the darkness already revealed. It hadn't been just booze that had taken a hold of Jimmy. He had been a regular cocaine user too – the 'Devil's Dandruff', as he fondly termed it. Coke, it turned out, proved to be a perfect foil for the booze – a counterweight and a complement, opening up new pathways of even greater abandon. With coke, he could keep the binges going for longer – much longer. It meant, he discovered, that he could drink all the way through the night – before a snifter of cocaine would haul him back to normal. When a clear head had returned, there would only be one plan on the menu – to get completely hammered once more. Cocaine provided White with a kind of magical stamina, delivering him godlike reserves of energy; a late night on the booze could dramatically balloon into several sleepless days of uninterrupted pleasure.

What is particularly striking, in these tales of carousing and capering, is the way White talks about embracing the self-destruction. There was hedonism at work, for sure: it was all a heap of fun and he enjoyed himself aplenty. But there is something darker, too, in his yarns – a conscious awareness of the self-damage, of the cost at play. He knew how much harm he was doing to himself, but he just didn't care. Along with fellow player and wildman Kirk Stevens, he had launched himself into a nihilistic mission of boundless indulgence: 'We were two mad kids doing the best to kill ourselves . . . we were flirting with death and we didn't give a shit. Everything else went out of the window – our self-respect, our families, our money and our snooker.'

For a period of several months in the late eighties, coke addiction became crack addiction. In Jimmy White's story, there is a complicated blend of pleasure-seeking and a yearning for oblivion. 'I had such fun,' he says, 'even though I can't remember much': the way he tells it, he embraced the very ghosts of addiction by which he was plagued. And they affected his career, without doubt, but not so much that he was denied success. 'Have you ever been drinking before matches?' a journalist once asked him. 'I used to drink all the time, big time, before matches,' he replied with a grin. 'And, erm . . . in between matches, during matches . . . many times, I've played under the influence – and won.'

White himself was the premier protegé of the all-time grand master of snookering self-destruction, Alex Higgins. The legend of Higgins looms over snooker history like little else; his charisma, unpredictability and wild behaviour were at the very core of the game's popularity explosion in the late seventies and eighties. '*Pot Black*, colour television and Alex Higgins' were the three reasons why snooker got big, according to ex-player, commentator, and erstwhile waistcoat-flaunting *Big Break* co-host John Virgo. But while White managed, perhaps surprisingly, to survive his days of indulgence, the Alex Higgins story evokes a more tragic feel, since Higgins did not escape his demons.

They were not just there at the end, but all the way through his life – imperishable ghouls of alcohol, drugs, gambling, depression and violence. He attempted suicide in 1985, just three years after famously winning the World Championship for a second time; after downing a bottle of pills in front of his wife and daughter, his words were, 'If you want to go and get a doctor, do so. If you don't, that's up to you – I don't care.' The attempt was very nearly successful; according to his wife Lynn, he had been just ten minutes from death.

By the end of the eighties, Higgins' career was in freefall. At the 1990 World Championship, he lost 10–5 to Steve James in the first round and remained in the arena long after the match had ended, a sad and dejected figure ordering multiple glasses of vodka and orange, slumped and twitching in his chair. After punching an official backstage – an act that would earn him a one-year ban – he announced his retirement in a drunken press-conference rant. 'You can stick your snooker up your jacksy,' he slurred to the crowd of assembled journalists.

Higgins did, in fact, return – but he was never more than a shadow of his former self. In his very last years, enfeebled by a battle with throat cancer, he cut a heartbreaking figure; gaunt, skeletal and unsteady, able to speak only in a sore, scratched whisper.

'I was crying all day. I'm devastated,' said Jimmy White after Higgins' death in 2010 at the age of sixty-one. 'I was in awe of him. I didn't always agree with what he did but I loved him. I have lost a friend and I will remember him for ever.'

But what, in the end, should we make of these tales of indulgence and damage? It is not as if they are unique to snooker. Wherever one looks, in sport and elsewhere, it is certain you will find countless stories of chaotic lives, of wasted talent, of wilful self-destruction. Could there, though, be some truer, more meaningful connection between disorder and the game of snooker?

On the face of it, the game seems actively to resist disorder – almost to be its antidote. It offers a geometrically ordered, rectangular table, with coloured balls positioned at regular intervals; a fully set-up snooker table has a kind of mathematical grace, a purity and a neat symmetry. Not only this, but the game itself is both played and watched in silence – with the players themselves locked in wordless concentration and the audience respectfully, reverentially hushed, like a congregation in a church.

But to *play* snooker is, of course, immediately to disturb the regularity. Clusters of balls are broken up and knocked into odd positions; the opening order is instantly destroyed. A snooker table in the middle of the frame is a fractured, postlapsarian spectacle. A kind of complicated chaos reigns, a bespoke, unrepeatable mess, unique every time – until the table is finally restored, at the end of the frame, to the order of emptiness itself.

Perhaps, just possibly, a frame of snooker mimics the entropy of our lives, the sense of failure we struggle with, of drifting away from order and sense. Perhaps, in fact, there is something more unstable in the silence of the snooker player. Perhaps it is not so much about calm but, rather, about volcanic possibility, trauma or pain. 'My grief lies all within,' observes Shakespeare's Richard II. 'And these external manner of laments/Are merely shadows to the unseen grief/That swells with silence in the tortured soul.'

3

GENIUS

Geniuses are people who dash off weird, wild, incomprehensible poems with astonishing facility and then go and get booming drunk and sleep in the gutter.

Mark Twain, journal, 1866

What does it mean, precisely, to be a genius? It is a word that demands some careful handling. Julian Barnes wisely wrote of the words, 'I love you,' that, 'We'd better put these words on a high shelf; in a square box behind glass which we have to break with our elbow; in the bank. We shouldn't leave them lying around the house like a tube of vitamin C.'

The word 'genius' perhaps belongs on a similar such shelf, protected from misuse. Aimed properly, it should only ever evoke something rare, precious, a fire of brilliance dizzyingly beyond the ordinary. The concept seems to go beyond mere excellence towards an actual reconfiguration of what can be achieved: a genius, in other words, is someone who is capable of things that seem, or seemed, impossible.

Here is critic Harold Bloom on Shakespeare:

The more one reads and ponders the plays of Shakespeare, the more one realises that the accurate stance toward them is one of awe. How he was possible, I cannot know . . . The plays remain the outward limit of human achievement: aesthetically, cognitively, in certain ways morally, even spiritually. They abide beyond the end of the mind's reach; we cannot catch up to them. Shakespeare will go on explaining us, in part because he invented us.

It is not simply that Shakespeare had a great mind: his creative output constitutes the impossible made real. Physicist Brian Greene has explained how Einstein's theory of special relativity was something much more than an advance of scientific understanding. It was a kind of intellectual earthquake, disrupting and rearranging the ground beneath our feet – obliterating previously acquired thought and yielding something radically, astonishingly new:

> Upon turning the final page of Einstein's manuscript, the editor of the journal, Max Planck, realised that the accepted scientific order had been overthrown. Without hoopla or fanfare, a patent clerk from Bern, Switzerland, had completely overturned the traditional notions of space and time and replaced them with a new conception whose properties fly in the face of everything we are familiar with from common experience.

If to be a *genius* is to revolutionise our entire understanding of reality itself, then it is evident that the bar is set pretty high.

For reasons that are not difficult to identify, the concept of genius has an uneasy relationship with sport. It is difficult – maybe even harmful – to apply profundity where profundity isn't welcome. From a certain angle, the point of sport is precisely its lack of significance; the philosopher Noam Chomsky opined sport 'has no meaning and probably thrives because it has no meaning, as a displacement from the serious problems which one cannot influence'. Sport is an escape from the substantial: whatever meaning it contains in people's lives arises directly from its inconsequentiality. Identifying genius across this shallow plane feels skewed, improper, even embarrassing. In the shadow of figures like Shakespeare and Einstein, it can come across as an indecent act to ascribe genius to a footballer, a cricketer or someone who knocks snooker balls around a table.

And yet, in sport – in snooker – the word 'genius' does quite often get used. What can it mean, in a snookering context? Even if deploying the word really is just absurd misuse, interesting things revolve round where it is directed. It is notable, for instance, which players do not get labelled as geniuses. Some of the finest and greatest in the sport's history – Steve Davis, Stephen Hendry – are rarely awarded the term. Something about consistency and control gets in the way. Davis and Hendry were too composed; too rational; too ruthlessly and reliably successful. The word's gravitational pull is centred elsewhere – towards something darker and more unstable. The spectre of disorder looms over genius. And there is no doubt, at all, about the original genius of snooker history.

In the textbooks of snooker technique, there is very little that looks anything like the technique of Alex Higgins. Beset with twitches, sniffs, and odd jerks of the limbs, Higgins would approach the table like a battered boxer trying to stay upright. His drunken stagger reflected the fact that he was, quite often, drunk. Any snooker coach will confirm how crucial it is to stay still on the shot: unless still, a player has no chance of lining the shot up properly and no chance of potting the ball. Alex Higgins confounded this philosophy – playing with a reckless, angry heave of the cue, seeming to jolt his head up at the very moment he struck the ball. His whole body would twist and capsize; sometimes it looked like he was playing the shot without looking. Technically, it was a catastrophic cue action – the sort that would promptly be corrected in a rookie teenager. It was a curiosity, and a miracle, that he ever got close to potting anything at all.

But pot things he did. And at his best, he could be capable of the seemingly impossible – a level of snooker beyond the mind's reach.

In the 1982 World Championship semi-final, he was the author of what is still, probably, the most legendary break in the history of the sport. His opponent was Jimmy White – already touted, at the age of twenty, as Higgins' rash and riotous successor. White was on the cusp of victory: 15–14 ahead, with just one frame needed, and fifty-nine points up. Just a few more balls from safety.

He was having to lean across the table, lining up the next red with the rest (over his career, White was to become famous with the rest, often cited as one of the great rest-wielders to grace the game). This shot, though, would not go to plan. White played at such a speed that, when balls were going in, everything oozed with the fluency of ocean waves; but when he missed, it often looked like he had rushed it. Perhaps he was stretching a bit; perhaps he was impatient about the winning line. In any event, he snatched the shot and missed by a fraction, shoulders sagging instantly in frustration. But he was almost there – he'd get another chance. His opponent's hopes were very close to zero.

Higgins eased towards the table, moments away from producing the closest thing to genius that snooker has seen. The pressure was extreme: he had to clear the table. If he missed anything, he was finished.

The first red was easy; in general, though, the balls were not favourably placed, with two of the reds welded tight to cushions.

And almost straight away, he got himself into trouble – over-hitting the first red and sliding clumsily into the pink. This is the moment that the fireworks began – a blitzing sequence of phenomenally improbable pots, throughout the course of which he was, more or less, never in a good position. A brilliant long green allowed him to nudge out one of the awkward reds. After watching a long black travel the length of the table and drop into a corner pocket, he took a moment to look up at the crowd, where his wife sat watching with their baby daughter. Chalking his cue, he smiled up at them. It was a wry acknowledgment of the pressure, but it was something else too – a signal that confidence and momentum were building.

After another red, he was out of position again – stuck in a grim no man's land, midway between blue and pink, one of the bleakest districts on a snooker table. As he eyed up the unappealing prospect of the blue, he leaned on the table with an irritated sigh. 'He must get .it,' observed Jack Karnehm in commentary, 'or else it could be the end of the match.' What followed is perhaps the most famous, arguably the best shot in snooker history: awkwardly leaning over pink and reds, he blasted the blue into the corner pocket, the cue scything the air like a javelin, white ball spinning back off the side cushion at a far-fetched angle back towards the reds. The crowd applauded with an ecstatic, changed air; faint hope was morphing into awed expectation.

Higgins should not have been able to do this. The difficulty of the clearance, the strain of the setting, was too much. Except, shot by shot, the balls were disappearing. All of a sudden, moments later, the remaining pots were simple. Just the colours remained. 'All easy shots these, normally,' worried John Spencer in commentary. 'But every one a pressure shot, in this situation.' From yellow to black, though, the balls were cleanly potted: the clearance was complete. The crowd erupted. As he swaggered back to his seat, Higgins pointed at the crowd, lit himself a cigarette, and commenced a strange sequence of shoulder exercises, as if he were about to be asked to chop up some firewood. He seemed now to be twenty feet tall, an Olympian God preparing to devour his callow victim in the opposite chair.

It is impossible to disentangle the brilliance of Alex Higgins from the disorder of his personal life, and there is something very troubling about the connection. If genius and volatility are so deeply linked, then to venerate one is, arguably, to venerate the other – with all the sadness and tragedy this might involve. But things happened in the career of Higgins that were simply different – the compellingly out-of-the-ordinary talent was matched by a compellingly out-of-the-ordinary lifestyle. Triumph and tragedy, for Higgins, always seemed so intimately connected – the light and the dark whisked into one, his career always contradictory, Janus-faced, an unstable collision of contraries.

His 1982 World Championship victory came after a year of depression and breakdown – in which a typical day, according to his biographer, 'would almost inevitably involve a couple of pints of Guinness before noon and then half a dozen vodka-oranges in the back of the Kenilworth public house'.

In a 1995 World Championship qualifier, Higgins got himself into an argument with veteran referee John Williams. Higgins had asked him to move; when Williams refused, pointing out he was actually standing behind Higgins, the latter retorted he was standing not in his line of sight, but 'in his line of thought'. What ensued was a peculiar distillation of radiance and grief: to the astonishment of his opponent, former Buddhist monk Tai Pichit, Higgins burst into tears as he compiled a brilliant break of 137, his highest-ever break at the World Championship – his 'tears falling onto the cloth as he went through the colours'. The sadness was always right there, in the eyes of Alex Higgins – eyes that were restless and distant, as if constantly waiting for the next calamity. 'If we see a light at the end of the tunnel,' wrote Robert Lowell in his poem 'Since 1939', 'it's the light of an oncoming train.'

Higgins, the archetypal maverick, was always defined by his hostility to convention and his externality to the mainstream. In describing John Berryman's relationship to American poetry, Michael Hofmann called Berryman a 'sort of one-off comet that approached that cosy solar system, lit it up for a while, and then exited'. Higgins tends to get imagined similarly – as a kind of temporary visitor from a different universe, capable of unique things because he was in fact his own distinct species. 'He was one of a kind,' fellow Northern Irishman Joe Swail has said. Welsh player Mark Williams believes, 'There is no one like him any more, the style he played with.'

But it is a dangerous business to decontextualise, or to think that a particular kind of brilliance, just because it seems extraordinary, will never be seen again. Even as Higgins compiled his fêted 1982 break, the presence of Jimmy White opposite him was a hint that new generations of youthful virtuosity were waiting. And sitting at home watching Higgins' break was a six-year-old boy who would take notions of snookering genius further than anyone had ever dreamed possible.

'Ronnie is the best genius any sport has ever had – pure genius,' claims Steve Davis. They are strong words, from a figure of Davis' stature. And there can be little doubt that Ronnie O'Sullivan has stolen Higgins' mantle as the closest thing to genius that snooker can muster. The word 'genius' might well be fantastically inappropriate in snooker – but if it *is* appropriate, it needs to be attached to O'Sullivan.

The title Peter Ebdon once bestowed on him, the 'Mozart of snooker', evokes not just his brilliance but his precocious beginnings; O'Sullivan was a child prodigy of Mozartian proportions. He made his first century break at the age of ten; at fifteen, he made his first maximum. When he entered the professional ranks, his levels of talent were so spectacularly far ahead of his peers that he won seventy-four of his first seventy-six professional matches. In 1993, at the age of seventeen, he won his first ranking tournament, the UK Championship: he still holds the record as the youngest winner of a ranking event. Ronnie's journey towards greatness seemed both easy and inevitable, written in the stars.

But darker clouds had already gathered. In 1992, Ronnie's father was given a life sentence for murder. There had been an altercation in a Chelsea nightclub. A man – one of the drivers for Charlie Kray – had been stabbed to death. Ronnie Sr pled not guilty: but away he went for eighteen years. It was, unsurprisingly, an event that had a profound effect on the young O'Sullivan:

> When Dad went down I was devastated . . . I was seventeen, I was professional, I'd qualified for the World Championship, so all I felt I could do was get on with stuff. I was a young man, independent, so I tried to put everything to the back of my mind. But, of course, that was impossible. It was tough.

Given this yawning catastrophe at the very outset of his career, Ronnie's accomplishments are all the more extraordinary – seven-time world champion, most ranking-event wins, most Triple Crown wins, a thousand-plus century breaks and comfortably the winner of most prize money in the sport's history. And yet his story is characterised by danger, doubt and caprice, vertiginous shifts from high to low. In assessments of his achievement, a bizarre sense remains that the game's most successful player has somehow fantastically underachieved.

Over the years, many fans and followers of the game have wondered what is to blame for O'Sullivan's mood swings, his sporadic struggles with substance abuse and depression. A product of trauma – the acute pain of his father's imprisonment – or something innate in his disposition, a volatility in his DNA? Ultimately such questions are both unanswerable and unseemly. In interviews, he can be impeccably, even cartoonishly, cheerful – bantering away with breezy, boyish charm. There is always, though, a lurking sense that anger or impatience might emerge at any moment. His uncommonly expressive, caterpillar-eyebrowed face seems gymnastically capable of glee, gloom and menace. And, over time, alongside his tales of success, he has accumulated a darker set of tales – a ghost trophy cabinet of misdemeanours and meltdowns.

In 1996, he was slapped with a ban for punching an official backstage. Two years later, he was stripped of his Irish Masters title after testing positive for cannabis. Later, he would reveal cannabis to have been a persistent temptation, especially in the early years. And, in a clear echo of Higgins' career, the professional success and personal turbulence seem to have been deeply intertwined, as if the latter actively fed the former:

> ... that brilliant year professionally was when I was having my weekly benders and my private life was in bits ... I remember getting to every World Championship and thinking, I can't wait till this tournament is over 'cos then there's no more drug tests, there's nothing for three months, so I can go out and smash it. I'd got caught once, early on in my career, but that's all. I'd get tested between events, and I was trying to judge it perfectly so there'd be no drugs left in my system, but I was pushing my luck ... I loved

a joint. The only problem with a joint is that one spliff follows another, and another.

Just as for Higgins, just as for White, the lure of excess shone brightly. On a typical bender, he would get through fifteen pints of Guinness a night. 'I was the king of sabotage,' he confessed.

On the table, O'Sullivan is an alchemist, a conjurer of the impossible. At his best, the cue ball moves as if telekinetically controlled. No ball is safe: hopeless, ugly positions lead to frightening, wizardly clearances. In the light of this brilliance, it can seem perverse to focus on the episodes of controversy. Maybe too much attention has been given to moments like the 2005 UK championship – when he stuck a towel over his head in a match against Mark King, perched in his chair like a crudely fashioned Halloween ghost; or the following year, when he abruptly conceded mid-match against Stephen Hendry, marching out of the arena with his hand over his eyes.

But O'Sullivan has also courted controversy on many an occasion. In interviews, he has repeatedly claimed a lack of interest in snooker, threatening to retire countless times. His off-the-cuff criticisms of venues, policies and players were a source of regular frustration for Barry Hearn:

Ronnie O'Sullivan is a lovely, lovely person . . . he's also a genius, and therein lies the problem. A genius is not normal, they don't say normal things and they don't act normally, that's one of the reasons they are a genius and we have to allow for that. Ronnie comes out with some outrageous things and I allow for it, in the same way that I allowed for Alex Higgins because he was a genius, Jimmy White, genius, Phil Taylor, I don't expect normality from geniuses. The sad thing, for me, is sometimes the errant ideology of a genius is counterproductive to their own personal welfare.

The strength of Hearn's suspicion towards O'Sullivan is all too evident here. A brilliant player he might be; but clearly he is not to be trusted.

It was the Roman philosopher and dramatist Seneca the Younger who ascribed to Aristotle the line, 'No great mind existed without a touch of madness.' It is a vivid link, deep and ancient. The reason Davis and Hendry have *not* generally been viewed as geniuses has nothing to do with any failing in their ability or in what they achieved. It is, in short, because they were steady and stable: servants not of Dionysus, but of Apollo. Davis and Hendry steadfastly kept to the sunlit path that led towards success. Genius, in contrast, prefers to be out of the sunlight, somewhere in the shadows. *He's also a genius, and therein lies the problem.* In Hearn's comments, reverence merges awkwardly with dismissal. It is precisely *because* O'Sullivan is a genius that we shouldn't listen to him. The age-old notion survives: the genius and the madman are one and the same. As such, it is fitting for them to be both revered and ignored.

Perhaps it is the inevitable curse of genius to be viewed with distrust and confusion; perhaps this is simply what must happen when someone operates beyond the mind's reach. History shows quite clearly that, as much as we might admire genius, very often we are frightened by it, we are repulsed and we fail to understand it. It was not until a long time after his death that William Blake became recognised as one of the monumental creative geniuses of human history. In 1805, Robert Hunt reviewed an exhibition of his work: 'The poor man fancies himself a great master and has painted a few wretched pictures ... These he calls an Exhibition, of which he has published a Catalogue or, rather, a farrago of nonsense, unintelligibleness and egregious vanity, the wild effusions of a distempered brain.'

4

VICTORY

If one lives long enough, one sees that every victory sooner or later turns to defeat.

Simone de Beauvoir, *All Men are Mortal*, 1946

'How important is it to you, to win it?'

It was the spring of 1981, and the World Championship was approaching. For the interview, Steve Davis was sporting a plain green jumper – the green, one might even say, of a snooker table, as if the jumper itself had been tailored from a sheet of baize. He was smiling at the question.

'It's the most important thing in the world to me,' he replied. But a moment later, the smile vanished, and his face seemed to darken as a new thought occurred. 'It's a *disaster* if I lose,' he added, before falling silent.

According to Plato, victory should not involve a focus on external things – it must be directed inwards: 'The victory over self is of all victories the first and best, while self-defeat is of all defeats at once the worst and the most shameful.'

William Faulkner avowed, 'The field [of battle] only reveals to man his own folly and despair, and victory is an illusion of philosophers and fools.'

The concept of 'victory' is a fractious one. It has sharp edges.

Victory is freighted with the consequence of inflicting pain and defeat on another. It seems to appeal not to our higher instincts, but to traits of selfishness and egotism.

At its worst, a ruthless desire for winning pushes us towards pure malignity – a disposition emptied of the kindness that, we hope, make us truly human. Lurking in the dark is the malice of Shakespeare's Richard, Duke of Gloucester, grotesquely seducing Lady Anne after having killed her husband – motivated not at all by romantic sentiment, but by a pure revelry in the twisted implausibility of the victory: 'I nothing to back my suit at all/But the plain devil and dissembling looks/And yet to win her, all the world to nothing!/ Ha!' In Milton's *Paradise Lost*, hubristic pride drives the armies of Satan as they rashly seek victory over God:

> The banded Powers of Satan hasting on
> With furious expedition; for they weened
> That self-same day, by fight or by surprise,
> To win the mount of God, and on his throne
> To set the Envier of his state, the proud
> Aspirer . . .

Philosophy and literature warn us that a cold desire for victory is a moral dead end – a dangerous, delusive will-o'-the-wisp. It leads to hostility and nastiness. It is where pride and foolishness dwell. It is the antithesis of the moral goodness towards which we all should strive.

These ideas do not seem to have been much of a concern for Barry Hearn, who in the mid-1970s stumbled across a snooker player who would change both his life and the course of the entire sport. Hearn had already made a pile of money from a string of snooker halls: for Hearn, the consummate tycoon, snooker began as a business interest | more than a personal passion. One day, he found himself watching a 'skinny ginger kid' at one of his halls – the Lucania snooker club in Romford, east London – a kid who was, with a cool, robotic certainty, in the process of clearing the table, setting the balls up, and clearing the table again. It was a fork in the road: a dollar-sign Damascus moment. 'All I saw was someone who was young, very dedicated . . . totally devoid of personality,' he later quipped. As a player/manager duo, Steve Davis and Barry Hearn were to become unstoppable – Davis's gauche introversion and one-eyed focus perfectly complemented by Hearn's brash swagger and salesmanship.

At the time Davis turned professional in 1978, snooker still wore its heritage on its sleeve. The atmosphere of working men's clubs hung powerfully in the air, and the game's fags-and-booze ethics were clearly discernible in the lifestyles of many of the players. It was simply normal, during a match, for a player to keep himself company with a pint or three of bitter – often, at the same time, working through a pack of Marlboros. In old footage of seventies matches, the action is unfailingly bathed in a visible, ambient haze of cigarette smoke, through which players floated like ghosts in fog. It is no coincidence that tobacco became the major sponsor of snooker in the television boom. Snooker, one might say, was from a rough background. It was not the place for health or restraint. 'Booze,' noted sports journalist Desmond Kane, 'was already part of the culture of working men in billiards halls before the TV cameras shone a light on it.'

But with Davis, absolutely everything was different. He approached the game with monastic discipline and psychotic levels of obsession. A shy, awkward child, snooker had been pretty much the only thing in his life from an early age. 'If you're ugly with no personality, why would you go to a nightclub to get knocked back? "No thanks," I'd tell mates, "I'm going to practise for eight hours." And that was how I became good.' With his father as mentor, he studied everything about snooker and its history – obsessing about strategy and tactics, agitating about technical perfection. The smooth, upright elegance of his technique is still seen by many to be the most flawless the game has seen. Even the dimple in his chin was sometimes griped about as an unfair advantage, helping him to cue straight – as if Davis was not a human, but an android exclusively designed to play snooker.

In stark contrast to his wild contemporaries, his routines were marked by careful self-restraint: 'My personal schedule was dinner, bed and a good night's sleep . . . I developed a new slant on the "work hard, play hard" ethic. Work was practice, play was tournaments.' While others may have enjoyed the celebrity and the attention, Davis often seemed interested in nothing beyond the game itself. Even the fans were a kind of inconvenience – an intrusion on his neurotic focus: 'I don't interact with the fans. I can't interact with them. I don't even acknowledge them. All I want is to be left alone in my own little shell and prepare for my task in hand.'

The result was absolute domination. Steve Davis did not simply succeed in the 1980s: he owned the 1980s. The mere statistics – half a dozen world titles; half a dozen UK championships; seven consecutive years as world number one – do not begin to explain the towering levels of snooker supremacy he sustained.

Quite often, Davis would not simply win – he would obliterate. Intimidated by his superior technical ability and his aura of mournful, intense concentration, other players would just collapse. Scorelines would read like embarrassments, massacres. He won his first UK Championship against Alex Higgins 16–6.

The following year, he retained his title by disembowelling Terry Griffiths 16–3. In 1983, the World Championship final was over by the end of the afternoon, Davis winning 18–6 with a session to spare. Until 2020, there had only ever been two whitewashes in two-session finals, and Davis inflicted both of them – against Mike Hallett, in the 1988 Masters, and against Dean Reynolds in the 1989 Rothmans Grand Prix. These are just a few samplings from a decade of almost ceaseless power. In many cases, it felt like his opponents had lost the matches before they had even begun. Against Davis, it was difficult to maintain belief. It was like playing against God himself. The adversary – envier of his state, proud aspirer – was plainly doomed to fail.

The psychology of Davis is of interest here. He consciously gloried in the demolition of his rivals: 'If ever I have my foot on somebody's neck in a match, I never ease up the pressure. Once I have him reeling, I keep applying the pressure – not offering him a glimmer of hope – and, eventually, he will crumple under the relentlessness of it all.' It is characteristic of champions, elite performers, to embody this kind of ruthlessness – recognising weakness, attacking wounds, tearing others to pieces without any hint of misgiving or mercy. 'Play it tough, all the way,' as cricket legend Don Bradman counselled. 'Grind them into the dust.' It was a very helpful quality for a winner, one Davis was well aware that he possessed to an unusual degree. 'One of my greatest strengths was being able to inflict this type of annihilation on an opponent. I could comfortably keep up the mental pressure and never think of easing up. My focus at times was extraordinary.'

Listening to the post-retirement Davis – specialising, as he does, in dry wit and affable self-deprecation – it is easy to lose a sense that he was such a cold-blooded deity of the baize. Davis was a savage winner: he was ruthless and brutal. His intimidating air was partly a natural consequence of winning so much, but it was also, in part, cultivated – he would deliberately remain aloof from the other players, keeping to himself during tournaments, ignoring those around him if it seemed beneficial to do so. He was a complex, quietly eccentric character – his reputation for coldness sitting oddly with elements of the anxious and the neurotic.

He harboured some obsessive-compulsive habits; *Daily Mirror* correspondent Tony Stenson quipped, 'Many believe he even counted the beans on his toast and chalked his cutlery.' Davis once, in an interview, complained that biscuits have 'got far more poisons in them than they used to have', and that skimmed milk is to be avoided, since 'the process they use to skim it produces very small fat globules, which are more dangerous than proper fat'. Here he is disclosing a paranoiac approach to drinking water:

> I would always smell the glass beforehand as well – to make sure there wasn't the smell of any cleaning fluid left over in there. By the end of the decade, I also recall thinking how easy it could be for somebody to spike my drink during a tournament. That may sound a little paranoid but it was a genuine concern. As a result, I only had bottles of unopened water during matches.

Vague echoes emerge here of piano prodigy Glenn Gould and his oddball needs, refusing to play concerts unless he sat on his father's rickety old chair. Steve Davis is typically painted as the absolute polar opposite of Alex Higgins: the ultimate, clean-cut, dedicated professional who could not have been any more unlike the ultimate, hell-raising, unpredictable wild man. Antithetical as he so obviously was to his nemesis, though, there was a definite sense that – however strange Higgins might have been – Davis wasn't quite normal either.

But despite his dominance, it is not for any of his countless victories that Davis is most vividly remembered. It was the destiny of Davis to be involved in snooker's very greatest moment; and it was not a moment to end as he would have wished.

By the middle of the 1980s, Dennis Taylor had been around the snooker scene for a long time. His had been a good career – he had even made it to the world final, back in 1979. As he entered his late thirties, though, there was a clear sense that his best days were behind him. He was just about hanging on as a player – surviving as a canny specialist in tough, tactical play, but limited in terms of ability. To the public, he had become best-known for his preposterous-looking spectacles, perched upside down on his nose, giving him the outlandish look of a wigless circus clown. A likeable chap he may have been – but he clearly was not a champion.

Taylor's much-mocked goggles, though, were crucial to a resurgence in his career. Short-sighted for most of his life, he had worn conventional glasses in his early playing years. But – as any bespectacled cueist will confirm – wearing glasses for snooker presents some problems. The curvature of the lenses warps angles and the frames get in the way. For a time, Taylor tried contact lenses, but that was no good at all; they burned his eyes. He turned to former player and commentator Jack Karnehm for help. The product was a pair of upturned glasses that looked absurd, but brilliantly served their purpose – allowing Taylor to line up shots through the very centre of the lens and cancelling out distortions. The benefits were rapid: in October 1984, he thrashed Cliff Thorburn 10–2 to win the Grand Prix, his first-ever ranking-event victory.

Despite the breakthrough, he was still something of an outsider going into the 1985 World Championship – a dark horse, perhaps, but far from a favourite. He started the tournament well and, with each round, his form got better – in the quarter final, he comfortably despatched the adamantine Cliff Thorburn; in the semis, he eased past world number two Tony Knowles. Against Davis in the final, though, it seemed his goose was cooked. It was a shameful mismatch: he had no chance. And to begin with, this is exactly how it seemed to be panning out, as Davis impassively sprinted to an 8–0 lead. The match was turning into an embarrassment; the result was inevitable, and there was almost no point in watching.

The Olympian drama of the game's climax has displaced attention from a moment in frame nine that Davis has long identified as being a hauntingly critical turning point. Ahead in the frame, he was faced with a tricky green. It was close to the cushion, and he was having to stretch across the table to get to the white. If he had not been so far ahead, he may well have been more cautious – but he went for the pot and left it dangling over the hole, allowing a grateful Taylor to clear up. 'I would love to know what would have happened,' Davis later mused, 'had I played a safety shot on the green.'

Momentum, now, was with the challenger – Taylor had his tail up, he found some form from somewhere and, by the end of the evening, he was only 9–7 behind. The reigning champion's mood was thunderous: 'I left the Crucible shell-shocked. I wanted the earth to swallow me up . . . I had steam coming out of my ears as I walked back to the hotel.'

Taylor's fighting qualities remained with him the next day. Davis kept on pulling ahead – it was 13–11; it was 15–12; it was 17–15. Each time, though, Taylor managed to claw things back. And, just after 11 p.m., the scoreboard declared a buttock-clenching seventeen frames each. For the first time ever, the Crucible final was down to the final frame. Both men left the arena, to gather thoughts and offer prayers; they came back to a standing ovation and crashing applause. 'And so the lights go down,' whispered Ted Lowe in the commentary box. 'The players shake hands.' A message appeared on the TV screen for viewers at home, confirming that episode three of *Bleak House* had been postponed. Jarndyce v. Jarndyce could wait. This was Davis v. Taylor time.

In terms of quality, the sixty-eight-minute final frame is one of the worst sporting displays you are ever likely to see. By now, Davis looked like a corpse. His skin had turned a horrible shade of greyish blue, the colour of chicken freshly out of the freezer. His opponent, in contrast, had gone purple as a plum, the eyes behind the glasses seeming to bulge dreadfully, like a haddock. They were not in a state to produce good snooker, and they did not. Everything was missable: everything was missed. The players grimly potted the balls more or less one by one, ineptly inching towards the frame's conclusion like two drunken amateurs down the local club after closing time. After an endless series of crude blunders, missed chances and constipated safety shots, Davis managed to cobble together a break of twenty-five – the highest of this hellish frame – and only the colours were left. Davis was nine points ahead. Endgame was imminent. The zenith of snooker history had arrived at the door.

Taylor found himself trapped in a snooker: after spending an age shaking his head and studying the angles, he missed the yellow by over a foot and gave away a foul. Davis sank the yellow and outrageously fluked the green. *Eighteen* ahead now . . . on the very brink of triumph. In the annals of snooker, it is a neglected point that Davis actually had a clear shot on the brown, one that would have taken him safely to glory. A pretty decent chance, it was, too: mid-range, the brown trickily close to the cushion, but also quite near the corner pocket. He only missed it by a fraction. As he sat back down in his chair, he looked up to the heavens and produced a deep, yogic sigh. 'I think a ... *breathing* exercise,' wondered Ted Lowe in commentary.

Thus far, Taylor had been cueing like Mister Magoo, hitting the ball so badly that it seemed to be travelling at random angles entirely detached from his intentions. He was, though, about to produce what was not only the best shot of his career, but one of the greatest pressure shots in the entirety of snooker history. Whole continents seemed to separate the white ball, stuck at one end of the table, and the brown, marooned at the other. The pot was so formidably difficult that it seemed a deranged option at this stage of the match. But there was no obvious safety ... Taylor lined it up and – to the surprise of everyone, perhaps including himself – he hammered it straight in. In any context, it was a brilliant shot: in this context, it was a miracle.

More than that, he was just about on the blue. It wasn't a perfect position – a bit of a thin cut. Watching from his chair, Davis licked his lips, as if contemplating a kebab. There was a kind of electric hum now coming from the crowd – the sound of vast, distant swarms of bees. The hum died away; silence, as Taylor descended into the shot.

The blue went into the heart of the pocket, but the cue ball was coming to rest by the cushion: Taylor performed a brisk Tom Jones hip thrust, in a bid to will it back out into the table. The thrust didn't work; the pink was difficult. Time, at this stage, was doing strange things, seeming to twist and stretch. Taylor hesitated for a few seconds that felt like several hours, building himself up to a gamble he knew he had to take. He went for the pink – and very nearly missed it, overcutting it slightly and watching it chillingly wobble in the jaws before it dropped. Drop, though, it did. *Bid me run, and I will strive with things impossible.* Something unthinkable had happened. After thirty-four frames, over two

44

days, the World Championship final had come all the way down to the final black.

'Are you sure/That we are awake?' asks Demetrius in *A Midsummer Night's Dream*. 'It seems to me/That yet we sleep, we dream.' The late-night black-ball drama at the end of the 1985 final has this kind of dream-like, unreal quality. It all seems fantastical: a fairy tale of improbable wonders. These moments, so often replayed, are so much more famous than anything else in snooker history that they have transcended the sport – becoming a kind of shimmering televisual national treasure, an endlessly repeated Christmas holiday treat to watch nostalgically with a tray of chocolates and a glass of Old Peculier.

Part of the enchantment results from the infinitely unlikely odds of the whole match boiling down to this precarious, atom-thin knife-edge. Part of it results from it all happening after midnight on a Sunday – the point of the week most supposedly hostile to drama, with everyone usually tucked up in bed, glumly braced for work or school the next day (still, nearly four decades later, the final holds the record for the highest post-midnight viewing figures on British TV). But part of it, too, is the actual result of the match – the fact that, this time, it really would all be different; this time, for once, the loser would become the winner.

At the table, Taylor was staring at a risky double. The white was stuck to one cushion – just above the middle pocket – and the black stuck to the opposite cushion, just below the middle. As he pondered the shot, he appeared to have become nothing but a pair of giant disembodied eyes behind the spectacles. 'What do you do with this one, Dennis?' asked Jim Meadowcroft in commentary, voice treacly with tension. Taylor chose to go for it. There were some strangled yelps from the crowd, who thought at first it was in, then realised it was not, missing by a millimetre, slamming against the pocket's upper jaw and easing away to the top cushion. By this point, Davis had developed a sinister, translucent, alien glow. As he edged to the table, he looked like he was about to be sick.

It was now his turn, though, to produce a pressure shot of superhuman excellence – impeccably knocking the black from one end of the table to the other, a safety shot of coaching-manual perfection. Taylor went for another double, this one reckless and implausible – a cavalier shot that could have left the balls anywhere, and that he was lucky to see run safe. Next time round, Davis botched his effort: an ugly double kiss. For the very first time, in this final-ball exchange, a player was left with a realistic chance to win. Taylor had a long shot – almost straight – diagonally across the table. It was easier than the brown he had potted, but it was, still, a nasty one. It never looked likely, it never looked right, as he creakily lined it up. He missed it by so far that he almost hit the wrong side of the ball. As the crowd breathed a vast sigh of sadness, commentator Jim Meadowcroft offered some poignant words of sympathy: 'That was the biggest shot of his life.'

In life, an awful lot comes down to details. So much depends on tiny particulars that perhaps, at the time, look too small to matter. 'The happiness of life,' wrote Samuel Taylor Coleridge, 'is made up of minute fractions – the little, soon forgotten charities of a kiss, a smile, a kind look, a heart-felt compliment . . . and the countless other infinitesimals of pleasurable thought and genial feeling.' Sometimes, the fine details that life throws us matter a great deal; sometimes, the fine details are every-thing. As Taylor went back to his chair he pinched his brow, inflicted with a sudden migraine of anguish. In missing the pot, he had sent the black ball hurtling back towards the opposite corner, leaving Davis with what initially seemed to be an easy

46

victory shot – a simple tap-in. The game was done. It was all over.

But as Taylor, and the crowd, and the insomniac audience at home all focused in on the scene in front of them, it became evident that the ball was not *quite* over the hole. The white was on the cushion. The black had drifted just a little bit further from the pocket than had initially looked likely. The upshot was a just-very-slightly-tricky thin cut – and into a 'blind pocket', too, where the player cannot directly see the pocket as they line up the shot. Two inches closer to the pocket – maybe even one inch – maybe even half an inch – and a player of Davis' class would not have been able to miss it, irrespective of any surrounding pressure. But this was a shot perfectly pitched in the shadowy wilderness between simplicity and difficulty. It was unlikely that the reigning world champion would miss a pot like this . . . but it was not impossible.

The cadaverous ghost formerly known as Steve Davis came to the table for the most famous shot of his career. He got down to play it with surprising speed, perhaps impelled by nerves or a desire to get things over with: maybe, in retrospect, he got down too quickly. He knew he needed to hit it thin; Davis has always been clear about what was going through his mind in these moments. To hit it too thick would be to bottle it. 'To my credit, I didn't undercut it. When a club player misses a cut they are usually too afraid to catch it thin enough so, in my defence, I did play it better than a club player.' He made sure, then, that he hit it nice and thin. But he hit it too thin. He'd missed it.

In the commentary box, Ted Lowe produced the most eloquent 'No' in the history of television, injecting at least three shocked syllables into a one-syllable word: 'No' became something more like 'no-*oh!*-ohhh'. A bemused Davis mimicked Taylor's brow-gripping migraine gesture. The crowd moaned and muttered in astonishment, before bursting into a savage roar as they saw that the black was sliding invitingly over the pocket. *'This is really unbelievable,'* were Lowe's understated, accurate words. The shot Taylor now had was unmissably easy. The crowd were hushed. Time was on hold. Taylor breathed; he aimed; and he knocked it in.

Taylor's celebrations are, of course, the stuff of legend. He held the cue aloft, shaking it in both hands like some triumphant samurai or swashbuckling hero of ancient times. He thumped the cue into the floor. He pumped his fists. He wagged his finger – a sassy gesture of *I told you so.* His face, rouged with tension just moments earlier, had dissolved into a glorious, smiling Penfold of happiness. In immortal footage, he folded his arms, marched over to the trophy, and kissed it. 'A fabulous picture,' said Lowe, 'of a very happy and popular man.'

This, here, was a different kind of champion – the script, this time, had been ignored. It was not the invincible machine, but the affable everyman who had come out on top. You might say it gave everyone a sense of hope. As David Vine materialised for the mandatory post-match interviews, it was unsurprising to see that Davis was not very keen. He had the look of Oedipus discovering his wife was in fact his mother.

'Steve, it's a pretty tough moment this one, isn't it?' Vine asked.

'Yes,' he replied.

'Can you believe what's happened tonight?' Vine continued, hoping for something.

And then, out of the infernal depths of misery, a moment of dagger-sharp, Wildean wit. 'Yeah,' said Davis. 'It happened – in black-and-white.'

Brutalised as he was by the 1985 defeat, Davis remained the dominant force in snooker. He did suffer another shock the following year – outgunned by the unfancied Joe Johnson – but he ended the eighties mightily, with three consecutive World Championship wins. The consistency of his success did lead, though, to something of a popularity problem. 'People were bored of me winning all the time,' he has said. 'They became so bored that apparently I became boring.' *Spitting Image* memorably lampooned him with the ironic moniker Steve 'Interesting' Davis. He had started 'to receive odd things in the post' – threats; hate mail; even, on one occasion, a soiled nappy. It would be convenient to assign all this bad feeling to tall poppy syndrome – but there were perhaps other, more political reasons for such pockets of antipathy.

Hard-working, serious, successful and rich, Steve Davis was the perfect living embodiment of Margaret Thatcher's Britain. This was, to say the least, an opinion-splicing tag in a divided era of miner's strikes, social unrest and mounting inequality. Davis served as a conformist icon of the establishment. It came at a price, as authors Luke Williams and Paul Gadsby have perceptively explained: 'For a substantial number of fans who did not approve of Davis's dominance on the table and his commercial activities off it, the way he embodied Thatcherite ideals led to him being seen as something of a hate figure.' In an unusual move for a sportsman, he even appeared at a Conservative Party youth rally in 1983, alongside Kenny Everett and Jimmy Tarbuck. There were times, as he lifted up his trophies, when he could actively hear the boos from sections of the crowd.

Throughout all the years of domination, though, he never really seemed to mind. Boos from the crowd, he maintained, were a kind of compliment – a testament to the fact of his superiority. Davis' job was, quite simply, to win. And it was something he did very well indeed. As he violently dismantled a demoralised John Parrott 18–3 in the 1989 Crucible final, inflicting the heaviest such defeat of all time, few people could have predicted that his reign was soon to end. He was to be deposed by a young Scot who would take the mentality of ruthless competition to an entirely new level.

'It's a place,' Stephen Hendry frankly mused, 'that is hard to describe. Everything else seems to fall away and suddenly you're faced with a kind of tunnel vision in which you can almost see events happening even before you've set them in motion. It's just you and the table. Anything could be happening around you; there could be a murder in the auditorium and you wouldn't notice. You're there solely to win, and that knowledge somehow makes you unstoppable.' Hendry ruled the 1990s with a cruel authority that had never been seen before in snooker. He had, of course, learned from the master: in his early years, he paid meticulous attention to everything about Steve Davis, not just technically, but also in terms of his demeanour. Davis stalked round tournaments like a winner: Hendry did the same. Davis remained distant from other players: Hendry did the same. But he developed his own ethos, too, taking things beyond the Davisian paradigm and managing, somehow, to become a more lethal assassin.

Hendry was the Hannibal Lecter of snooker: he would kill you and eat you if it meant winning the match. Davis had always favoured a balanced approach, blending the big breaks with bouts of wily safety play. Hendry did not like safety at all. He opted for extreme attack, all the time, always. He tore to pieces the old wisdom that all-out attack was too risky by demonstrating that, if you pot everything, nothing is risky. It was a volcanic shift in the game of snooker, centred around a devastatingly simple philosophy: pot a long red, make a century break, win the frame. Repeat until destruction is accomplished.

The comparison between Davis and Hendry is an appealing one, the pair ruling consecutive decades. And, as with all comparisons, one discovers a knotted mixture of overlap and contrast. Both shared a capacity to keep their emotions in check to such a remarkable extent that it seemed, often, as if they had no emotions at all. But there was always a more sadistic intensity to Hendry. His eyes, set on victory, seemed to burn with a manic fire. His need to win was a thrilling spectacle: he was murderous, cut-throat. When asked if he ever felt sad about Jimmy White not winning a world title, he reacted with astonished disdain: 'No! No, no, no. This is sport. If you haven't got what it takes to get over the line, then that's your fault.' The milk of human kindness did not complicate Hendry's ambitions for the throne.

In his obsession with the art of mastery, he gave just as much weight to psychological strength as he did to technique. 'I think temperament is a very hard thing to teach,' he has said. 'You have to have that. In any individual sport, I think everyone could be the world champion in anything: it's the fact that so few can do it under pressure. It's the difference between being the best and being an also-ran.' This closely echoes Novak Djokovic's line about what separates the best from the rest. The answer is not about your ability; it is about what is inside your head. Inside Hendry's head was a picture of his opponent's head stuck on a spike.

Macbeth would never have made it to the ill-starred crown on his own; he needed Lady Macbeth's insults and encouragements to do that. 'Screw your courage to the sticking-place,' she told him, 'And we'll not fail.' Snooker records suggest that the acquisition of victory requires support from outside the self – a winner cannot be expected to win alone. For all their innate strength and steel, both Davis and Hendry received the crucial help of a mentor figure. Barry Hearn allowed the reclusive Davis to manage both the pressures of competition and the trials of stardom. Davis has always been emphatic about the importance of this bond: 'Having Barry in my corner was quite astonishing, because he had the bravado that I didn't have. So while I could quietly go about my job – and not put myself under pressure by saying *I'm going to win* – he was saying that for me . . . It gave me a confidence that we were a team.'

For Hendry, it was the presence of Ian Doyle as his manager that focused his drive and hardened his work ethic. Doyle made sure that as a young teen he understood the sort of discipline and toil required for success. 'From now on you'll practise at my club seven days a week . . . Your dad will drop you off at half past nine and you'll be ready for practice by ten a.m. You'll finish at six p.m. and then you will be taken home. Got that?' The way Hendry tells it, the level of control Doyle exerted was obsessive, bordering at times on the menacing. He would not just police schedules and veto girlfriends, but tell Hendry what to wear, what to say and how to sit during interviews: 'He controlled my life. I have to counter that by saying that without him I wouldn't have got to where I did. But there were times I resented the things he made me do.' The results, in any case, were undeniable.

On the evening of 29 April 1990, a twenty-one-year-old Stephen Hendry – bedecked with gruesome Jason Donovan mullet – lifted the World Championship trophy for the first time. It felt like a changing of the guard, and it was. He would win another five world titles over the next six years. He won the Masters on his first attempt and for the next four consecutive years. Not a single season passed when he didn't win something. The standard of snooker was rising rapidly, but Hendry was streets ahead again, wiping the floor with his victims. 'It takes selfishness and a bit of unpleasantness,' he has said, 'to be able to bully, harass and psych out opponents. I have all that in spades.'

He, too, suffered popularity issues; on one occasion, referee
Alan Davidson had to calm a jeering crowd in a match against
Jimmy White. Just like Davis, he was the reluctant recipient of
abominable anonymous gifts: 'There was an occasion when shit
(dog or human – we never delved too deeply) was sent through
the post.' But he took it all in his stride. Davis' tally of six World
Championships was threatened, equalled and surpassed. As
Hendry capped the decade with a record-breaking seventh
world title in 1999, he was able to look back on an epoch of
domination even more complete than Davis'. In snooker history,
the 1990s are quite simply Hendry's property: the entire decade
is a boar's head, hanging on his living-room wall.

In a letter to his brother in 1819, John Keats wrote about the
importance of suffering in life. 'Do you not see,' he wrote, 'how
necessary a World of Pains and troubles is to school an
Intelligence and make it a Soul?' It is a typically Keatsian view;
in his 'Ode on Melancholy', he stresses the value of the 'wakeful
anguish of the soul', conceiving of melancholy and joy as equally
necessary, mutually dependent states. The notion of pain as not
just inevitable, but useful, is uncomfortable but compelling.
History hints that pain and achievement are perversely linked at
the root, the latter spawned by the former. Edvard Munch said
that 'Art emerges from joy and pain. Mostly from pain.' John
Berryman went as far as he could with the line that suffering
brings generative possibility: 'The artist is extremely lucky,' he
claimed, 'who is presented with the worst possible ordeal which
will not actually kill him. At that point, he's in business.'

An obsessive need for extreme success is a rare thing: it is
reasonable to describe it as a kind of abnormality in a person,
marking them out from their milder, more placid peers. For
most people, snooker is no more than a hobby, a pastime. Only
for a small number does it become a passion. And for someone

like Stephen Hendry, it was something further still – a solution; a redemption; a means of escape from the strains he faced as a child. In the wake of his parents' divorce, the game developed a kind of therapeutic value. He recalls his mindset during these teenage years in terms of this avoidance of reality: 'Now, more than ever, snooker is a fixation. I discover that the physical and emotional disturbance caused by the split can be pushed away into a corner when I'm at the table.'

Hendry, of course, is just one example; but his is not a unique case. In more recent years, the closest we have seen to Davis or Hendry levels of drive is in the fist-pumping passion and glacial grit of Mark Selby. And Selby has been explicit about how the tragedy of his father's death both took him to the edge of darkness and also inspired his achievements: 'For months after that, I just wanted to curl up in a ball and snooker was the last thing on my mind . . . As time went on, I had a different mindset and did it for him. He drives me on.'

Once again, we are in familiar territory. In snooker, you are never far away from the dark. Beyond the light of the table lives an abyss of nothing. The table becomes the universe: a place of safety, light and colour. Nothing else matters, nothing else needs to matter; but the dark, nevertheless, is always there. The words of T. S. Eliot in *Four Quartets* come to mind: 'Wait without thought, for you are not ready for thought:/So the darkness shall be the light, and the stillness the dancing.'

5

Loss

The art of losing isn't hard to master
Elizabeth Bishop, 'One Art', 1976

We tend to be taught that losing is somehow good for us. 'What is defeat?' asked the American abolitionist Wendell Phillips. 'Nothing but education – nothing but the first step to something better.' An admirable sentiment, it may be, but it does not automatically make losing any easier to bear. Losing can be a very difficult business.

In Edith Wharton's *The House of Mirth*, Lily Bart loses her money at bridge to a handful of society women who hardly need the cash:

Her head was throbbing with fatigue, and she had to go over the figures again and again; but at last it became clear to her that she had lost three hundred dollars at cards . . . It was the sum she had set aside to pacify her dress-maker – unless she should decide to use it as a sop to the jeweller. At any rate, she had so many uses for it that its very insufficiency had caused her to play high in the hope of doubling it. But of course she had lost – she who needed every penny, while Bertha Dorset, whose husband showered money on her, must have pocketed at least five hundred, and Judy Trenor, who could have afforded to lose a thousand a night, had left the table clutching such a heap of bills that she had been unable to shake hands with her guests when they bade her good night.

Under the dread of debt and surreptitious poverty, it is difficult for Lily to find much educational value in the loss. To argue that losing is the 'first step to something better' assumes the possibility of a constructive response that isn't always available. 'The art of losing isn't hard to master,' runs Elizabeth Bishop's acidly ironic line, as she unpicks the idea that the struggle of losing all depends on what, precisely, has been lost. Losing your keys may be easy enough to accept; losing a loved one, though, is a very different matter. The art of losing isn't hard to master? *Au contraire* . . . it very much is.

'In the death it's all down to one shot. In fact, it's always down to one shot. Everything is down to one shot, if I'm being philosophical for a minute. Luckily, it's one shot at a time.' These are Jimmy White's sanguine reflections on the bitterest loss in a career that has, fundamentally, been defined by losing. White is snooker's most popular, most eminent loser. It is a curious destiny for one of the most successful players in the sport's history. His haul of ten ranking titles still puts him in the top ten players of all time. In total, he appeared in no fewer than six World Championship finals – a stat that, on its own, makes him one of the very greatest ever players at the Crucible. Between 1990 and 1994, he made it to five world finals in a row; only Davis and Hendry have matched this feat. The problem, of course, is that he lost all of those finals. White is a black belt in defeat; a grand master in the solemn art of loss.

Is there such a thing as a *natural loser*? Is it a phenomenon of temperament? If the building blocks for a ruthless winner are so rare, are there some people, by the same token, who are simply wired up to lose? White's fate has often been put down to a lack of bottle. He lacks the *killer instinct*, so the argument goes. He is famed for being a notably – even a miraculously – good loser: gracious in defeat, kind and philosophical, keen always to suggest there are more important things in life than winning. It is a perspective violently absent from the worldviews of Davis and Hendry. 'I was rarely interested in a tournament once I got knocked out,' reflects Davis. 'I dare say that, as a breed, all the top players sulk. I know Stephen Hendry is similar to me. Once he was out – nothing; once I was out – nothing. BBC2 didn't exist and that was it.'

White, in contrast, always seemed to accommodate himself to defeat with otherworldly ease. His generosity is one of many things that made him so popular; as his legions of fans saw it, Jimmy White was simply a great bloke. Something else was perhaps at work, too; in becoming, as he did, emblematic of noble failure, he was a sort of consolatory mascot for the nation. It's OK to fail, because look at Jimmy White – he fails, too, and he never seems to mind so much. JIMMY BOTTLES IT, ran a head-line in the *Belfast Telegraph*, showcasing the bizarre story of his temporary name change from White to 'Brown' in order to promote HP Sauce. *Bottling it* shaped itself as the central Whitean motif. As the tragic failures of his career piled up, he became an ambassador for temperamental fragility; a perfect exemplar of how to lose, and lose well.

Five consecutive finals, five consecutive defeats . . . a quintet of tragedy without equal; a whole half-decade of hurt. In 1990 White lost comfortably to Hendry, a figure who would evolve into a familiar nemesis. The following year he faced John Parrott. Although Parrott had been playing well, this time White was the clear favourite. He was the more experienced campaigner; he had the finer credentials. Parrott had been flattened by Davis in his previous final appearance – many thought he might not handle the pressure. But the opposite occurred. Parrott turned up and played godlike snooker, winning the first seven frames. 'I don't think he even missed a safety shot, let alone a pot,' White later complained. The People's Champion had been bulldozed: he never recovered and ended up losing the match by a seven-frame margin.

In 1992, White's opponent was Hendry again. Throughout the tournament, White had been in the form of his life, making a maximum break in the first round against 'The Tornado' Tony Drago. And it seemed – for a while – that, this time, it would all come good. He began the final with starbursts of brilliance, racing to a 14–8 lead. A helpless Hendry had been largely wedged in his chair, glum and pouting. It really looked like it would, at last, be Jimmy's year . . . but in the mind of Jimmy White, things were beginning to buckle and stray. 'My head was racing,' he later explained, 'not with what I needed to do to beat Hendry, but with what I'd say afterwards in my speech. In my mind's eye I'd already lifted the trophy, I'd already shaken David Vine's hand, I'd read the back page of the next day's papers, I'd given my dad a hug, I'd thrown the biggest fucking party of all time.'

At 14–9, White was mid-break – over fifty points up, the balls all pleasantly placed. He was leaning over the table to play a red with the rest – an easy red this one, though, right by the pocket, more or less unmissable . . . except, of course, nothing is unmissable. He jabbed at it; the red wobbled in the jaws and stayed out.

As Hendry came to the table, he had a deadly look in his eye. The clearance facing him was critical: life or death. He despatched the first few balls with jaw braced tight, as if trying to sever his tongue with his teeth. Halfway through the break, there was a pot on the brown that has entered into legend – a quintessential moment of ice-cold Hendry guts. He had lost position badly on the final red; the white was precariously poised on the event horizon of the middle pocket, an ugly spot. Some sort of safety shot was the easiest option: this, though, was rarely the Hendry option. Instead, he produced what John Virgo lauded as the bravest shot he's ever seen – nervelessly sinking the brown with no thought for the dangers of missing, leaving himself perfectly on the yellow. With the clearance completed, White was still 14–10 up, but this was the beginning of the end.

For neutrals, the final session was difficult to watch. For fans of Jimmy White, it was a living nightmare, a slow descent through the circles of Dante's *Inferno*. White quickly morphed from a cool, swaggering artiste into a jumble of sweaty panic. Frame after frame went by. Hendry won them all. The truth is, though, that Hendry was by no means playing perfect snooker. In the session's opening frame, he missed an easy red and gave White a good chance to clear; but when it came down to frame ball, White bungled it. At 14–14, the match saw a joyless half-hour frame of spurned chances and prolonged tactical play . . . in it, Hendry made an array of errors, butchering safeties and missing a couple of simple pots.

Again, though, White failed to take advantage. It all felt less like a show of invincibility from Hendry and much more like a mortifying Jimmy White meltdown. Hendry stretched ahead . . . 15–14 . . . 16–14 . . . 17–14 . . . and then it was all over. Jimmy White had somehow managed to lose ten frames in a row. In the post-match autopsy, David Vine endeavoured to offer him some sympathy, but White wasn't having any of it. 'I even feel good now,' he insisted, a comment that brought a huge cheer from the crowd. It was also – as an insight into his mindset – very telling; it was hard to imagine a beaten Hendry saying such things.

In 1993 White made it to the final for the fourth year in a row. Might his fortunes be different this time round? The answer was a resounding no. His opponent in the final was a certain Stephen Hendry, who had been in particularly pitiless form, dropping only twenty frames across the four previous rounds. Not only that, but all was far from well in the world of White. Before the final started, he knew he had no chance. 'There was no way I could beat Hendry in the final and I knew it before I'd even put my dickie-bow on,' he explained. 'I'd not picked a cue up for a month before I made the trip to Sheffield that year. My private life was a shambles again . . . I'd spent months on the piss and coke, running around like a madman and generally just forgetting about snooker.' In the circumstances, it was a miracle that he'd made it to the final.

And on the night before the final started, believe it or not, he was out on the tiles. 'I got in at 7.30 in the morning. I'd ended up in a place called Pinky's . . . before staggering back to the Grosvenor House Hotel to try and get some kip. I had a mate with me . . . and by about 7 a.m. he was crying. "Jimmy, what are you doing?" he kept saying, but I just carried on partying and drinking screwdrivers.'

In the wake of such chaos, against a peak-powers Hendry, there was only one outcome. Hendry demolished him 18–5, the second-heaviest Crucible final defeat in history. White was thankful, relieved. 'If you watch the replay, when I shake his hand at the end, you see me smiling. That was because he'd just put me out of my misery.' For the myriad supporters of snooker's most popular player, these world-final beatings were becoming uncomfortably familiar and increasingly painful. Nothing, though, would ever be quite as painful as what was to happen in the final of 1994.

It was a year when Hendry's hopes seemed to be in tatters. On the night before his second-round match, he had slipped over in his bathroom. When he woke up in the morning, he couldn't move his arm. A scan revealed a one-inch fracture. It was the sort of injury that would have immediately clobbered most play-ers' hopes. Upon testing it, though, Hendry found that he was still able to cue a shot – the pain was severe, but easily outweighed by the dark threat of having to surrender his title. Pain was noth-ing: pain could be endured.

Whenever he wasn't playing, his arm was in a sling. When he was playing, though, he was brilliant. It is a testament to the unmatched steel of Stephen Hendry that more is not made of what he managed to do with a badly fractured arm. First, he squashed Dave Harold 13–2; then, in the quarters, he beat the dangerous Nigel Bond; and in the semis, he comfortably swept past a rejuvenated veteran player by the name of Steve Davis. Hendry – the agony-stricken, broken-elbowed invalid – had made it to the final once more.

His opponent: James Warren White. *Surely*, this year, on his birthday of all days, White would be able to do it? Hendry might previously have gripped him in a voodoo curse, but White could beat a Hendry with one arm. Hendry himself had noticed that White was 'more alert, more focused' this time round. This was a sharper, hungrier Jimmy White. This year, he had been more careful; this year he actually believed he could win.

Although the very start of the match hinted at the same old story – with Hendry moving into a 5–1 lead – it quickly devel-oped into an edgy, close, nip-and-tuck affair. It is a curiosity in the metaphysics of snooker that certain matches just feel destined to go right down to the wire . . . and this was one such match. Neither player was able to pull away. At 17–16, White seemed to defy all prior claims about a lack of bottle by assem-bling a superb clearance of seventy-five. For the first time since Davis v. Taylor, the final had come down to the deciding frame.

'Probably the two coolest people in the arena – well, in the country – are going to be the two players out there,' claimed

Dennis Taylor in the commentary box. When the frame started, though, it certainly didn't look that way. After a disastrous Hendry safety, White was in; he managed a break of eight before running hopelessly out of position. White then played an equally poor safety: Hendry put together a twenty-four before leaving himself with a delicate, thin red – he went for it without hesitation, of course, playing it characteristically Hendry-style, with no element of safety in mind. He left it dangling over the pocket. This was it: Jimmy White had his chance.

Who seeks, and will not take, when once 'tis offer'd, Shall never find it more ... what could White do, with this opportunity bathed in gold? The balls were nicely spread. The title was right there for him, teasingly hovering before his eyes, a winking succubus. His cue power was fabled; he was a master in the art of arcing the white off the black into the reds in order to burst them open. He had one such shot, here: a crucial one ... and he was unlucky. The balls had spread well, but he had been left with a horrible pot on the next red, requiring him to stretch all the way across the length of the table with extensions on both cue and rest. 'He's got to the final taking these difficult reds,' mused Ray Edmonds in commentary, 'and he's in the last frame of the final. So, who's to say he's not right?'

Well, he looked wrong. This was a shot beyond bravery: it was a suicide shot, a hemlock tea option. All of White's reputation for fragility had come down to this. Here it was: not just a bottle shot, but *the* bottle shot. The ultimate test of his nerve and mettle. He took his time on it, which was fair enough. The crowd watched on in expressive silence. He was awkwardly leaning between the baulk colours; his hyper-extended cue looked more like a fishing rod; he had to clip the red so very thin ... and the roars of the crowd revealed the outcome before the ball even dropped. Not a problem. Right in the heart of the pocket.

It was a pot that should have been match ball. Everything else on the table, now, was easy. All he needed to do was keep it together. A close observer might, perhaps, have been able to detect some ominous signs during these moments – the way his skin had changed to the colour of wet concrete, the way his brow was leaching a gel of damp under the Crucible lights. A few pots later, he left himself with a simple black off the spot and down he got to line it up . . .

In the death it's all down to one shot. Even watching it now, it is hard to work out precisely what he did wrong. Did he rush it? This is what has often been claimed, including by White himself. But it doesn't look that way, watching back; not really. His shot preparation was pretty much the same for the black as for everything else he had been potting. It is hard to pinpoint the precise nature of the malfunction. There must have been something, somewhere, in the machine of his action, some glitch of tension, that spasmed everything off target. He didn't just miss the black . . . he missed it by miles.

The moans from the crowd sounded like something from the depths of a medieval torture chamber. 'Dear me,' said Dennis Taylor, 'that was just a little bit of tension.' There was a grim sense of inevitability surrounding Hendry's return to the table. The pockets seemed to suck the balls into themselves, as if via giant magnets. A few minutes later it was all over. Jimmy White had lost. Again. And here was David Vine, the pontiff of the post-mortem, dangling his microphone and tendering the necessary consolations.

'Jimmy,' he said, 'what can I say, apart from "Happy birthday"?'

White's response was the definitive distillation of the Jimmy White temperament; a philosophical archetype of the capacity to lose, and to lose well. 'He's beginning to annoy me,' he said simply, with a beaming smile.

In the hall of fame of snookering loss, Jimmy White is unquestionably the showpiece, the main attraction. But he is far from the only member. Throughout the history of snooker stardom, its scenes of triumph and glory, there is a more melancholy tale running alongside, a tale of tragic losses. Certain players are associated not so much with lifting trophies, but more with instances of throwing it all away.

Willie Thorne – snooker-ball bald and walrus-whiskered – was one of the most fondly cherished players of the 1980s; he built himself a reputation for being one of the smoothest break builders in the game, notching up well over a hundred maximum breaks in an era when such things were still quite rare, even in practice. But he never won very much. The reason was often said to be located in his mind: something weak there, something brittle, something that left him vulnerable. Famously, he was once 13–8 up against Steve Davis in the UK Championship final, and missed a blue that must still rank as one of the easiest balls ever missed by a professional snooker player. Davis cleared the table and went on to win the match 16–14.

'To say it was an injustice is an understatement,' Thorne said later. 'I had completely outplayed him and should have won by a hundred yards.'

In the 1991 final of the Masters, Mike Hallett led Stephen Hendry 7–0 and 8–2 before more or less instantly transforming from a razor-sharp potting machine into a sculpture of burgundy blancmange. Hendry launched his counterattack; Hallett had nothing left to give. Frame after frame fell under Hendry's murderous gaze. 'Has anybody got a rope?' Hallett at one point asked the crowd. Hendry ended up beating him 9–8 – one of the very greatest comebacks in snooker history – or very greatest collapses, depending on your point of view. 'It is a great art,' runs a Danish proverb, 'to laugh at your own misfortune': when he got home that night, Hallett discovered that his house had been burgled.

One might expect the winners to become our heroes. They, after all, are our models to follow, apprehending the realities of achievement about which the rest of us dream. Why, then, is it so often the losers who receive the bulk of our love and support? Maybe, just maybe, it relates to what we see in the losers. 'Try again,' wrote Samuel Beckett. 'Fail again. Fail better.' It is the losers, not the winners, who are our doppelgängers; the losers who are ourselves. It is so much easier to understand the losers in life, because we see them in the mirror each morning . . . the winners are foggier, murkier, making less sense to us. If, as Eric Cantona claimed, life is a game, it is one that we know we will all ultimately lose. The essence of life is an accommodation of ourselves to this fact.

The second part of T. S. Eliot's *The Waste Land* is titled 'A Game of Chess' – an allusion, at least in part, to Thomas Middleton's *Women Beware Women*, in which chess becomes a metaphor for corruption, seduction and life's transience. Eliot presents women talking in a pub about their friend Lil, who is waiting for her husband to return from the war. The chatter is bleak, banal. But it's closing time:

What you get married for if you don't want children?
HURRY UP PLEASE ITS TIME
Well, that Sunday Albert was home, they had a hot gammon,
And they asked me in to dinner, to get the beauty of it hot—
HURRY UP PLEASE ITS TIME
HURRY UP PLEASE ITS TIME
Goonight Bill. Goonight Lou. Goonight May. Goonight.
Ta ta. Goonight. Goonight.
  Good night, ladies, good night, sweet ladies, good night, good
night.

Time, death, loom over the scene; the goodbye calls blur into the poignant words of Ophelia before she drowns herself. 'HURRY UP PLEASE ITS TIME': life is our game of chess, and its ineluctable endgame yawns in front of us. There is no other destination: winning is not available.

The same irony can be found in Ingmar Bergman's filmic masterpiece *The Seventh Seal*, in which the main character, Antonius Block, proposes a game against Death in a bid to win his freedom from death's clutches:

Block: You play chess, do you not?

Death: How do you know that?

Block: I've seen it in paintings, heard it in the songs.

Death: I really am a rather skilful chess player.

Block: Even so, you can't be more skilful than me.

Death: Why do you want to play chess with me?

Block: That is my business.

Death: You are right about that.

Block: My condition is that I may live as long as I resist you. If I checkmate you, you set me free.

If I checkmate you, you set me free . . . the point, of course, is that such a victory is impossible. The game against death is a game he cannot win. In the end, what connects all of us is loss. Perhaps, in the light of all this, it is no great surprise that it turns out to be the losers whom we love; it is the losers who soothe us with the recognition that we are not alone, as we try and fail to master the impossible art of losing.

6

FRAGILITY

I have been one acquainted with the night.
I have walked out in rain — and back in rain.
I have outwalked the furthest city light.
Robert Frost, 'Acquainted with the Night', 1928

In the 2006 UK Championship, Ronnie O'Sullivan was playing against Stephen Hendry in the quarter final. There had already been some signs that Ronnie was not in a good psychological place.

'I knew he wasn't right today,' said John Parrott afterwards. 'I've bumped into a couple of people today who said his demeanour wasn't correct.' Throughout the tournament, he had been remote and withdrawn, refusing to give any post-match interviews – although this, for O'Sullivan, was not unprecedented. The match against Hendry had begun badly: Hendry was in good form and moved into a 4–1 lead, sharply exploiting his opponent's mistakes.

In the sixth frame, O'Sullivan was on a break of twenty-four. As he moved round the table, there appeared to be something misaligned about him, a kind of absent or cancelled expression, as if his eyes weren't fully alive. He was faced with a black off the spot – pretty much as easy as it gets – but he botched his cueing, potting the black but failing to screw back as he wanted. 'Well that's one of the worst positional shots I've ever seen Ronnie play,' observed Dennis Taylor in commentary.

O'Sullivan, though, immediately got down to play a dicey cut on a red. And after getting absolutely nowhere near it, he did something inexplicable. He was shaking Hendry's hand. 'I've had enough,' he could be heard to say, before rubbing his eyes and marching out. 'This is quite incredible, I don't believe what I'm seeing here,' said Taylor. After just five frames in a best of seventeen, Ronnie O'Sullivan had conceded the match.

In *The Bell Jar*, Sylvia Plath graphically pried open the depths of mental illness. At the end of the novel, Esther Greenwood contemplates the prospect of getting out of the mental asylum to which she has been committed and returning to college, returning home:

> My mother's face floated to mind, a pale, reproachful moon, and her last and first visit to the asylum since my twentieth birthday. A daughter in an asylum! I had done that to her. Still, she had obviously decided to forgive me.
>
> 'We'll take up where we left off, Esther,' she had said, with her sweet, martyr's smile. 'We'll act as if all this were a bad dream.'
>
> A bad dream. To the person in the bell jar, blank and stopped as a dead baby, the world itself is the bad dream.
>
> A bad dream.
>
> I remembered everything.

Blank and stopped as a dead baby. Few phrases could more chillingly capture the violence and the desolation of depression. Throughout the novel, Plath uses the metaphor of the bell jar as a motif for Greenwood's sense of hopelessness. Impossible to avoid, the bell jar haunts and harrows. It is always there, inescapable, suffocating: 'Wherever I sat – on the deck of a ship or at a street café in Paris or Bangkok – I would be sitting under the same glass bell jar, stewing in my own sour air.'

The emptiness of depression lives in a desert place, out beyond where language can reach. Perhaps an inevitable destination, in the light of this, is the work of Shakespeare, language's most extreme edge. Here are the words of Hamlet:

> O, that this too too solid flesh would melt,
> Thaw, and resolve itself into a dew,
> Or that the Everlasting had not fix'd
> His canon 'gainst self-slaughter. O God, God,
> How weary, stale, flat and unprofitable,
> Seem to me all the uses of this world!
> Fie on't! Ah fie! 'tis an unweeded garden,
> That grows to seed; things rank and gross in nature
> Possess it merely.

Only fear of divine punishment stops Hamlet here from suicide, or so he claims. The language, 'weary', 'stale', 'flat', conjures a tableau of blandness and monotony; Hamlet sees around him a world drained of colour and purpose. He yearns for a kind of self-dissolution that would allow him to escape himself. In some early quarto versions, 'solid' reads as 'sallied', a variant of 'sullied'; to be alive is to be unclean, tainted, requiring the purification of oblivion.

Sport can be a brutal place when things are going badly; but it is not always brutal in the same way. In a team game, for instance, there is always the rest of the match to come – and with it, perhaps, is the possibility of redemption. In an individual sport, such prospects can be more limited. In snooker, they often do not exist at all. There are few images of sporting helplessness quite as complete as the snooker player, stuck in his chair. In tennis, golf, squash, cycling, boxing, the individual participant is always active, engaged. They always have something to do; they are, at every moment, in some way part of the contest. It is a particular condition of snooker that this is not the case. When a player is at the table, their opposite number can quite simply do nothing but watch.

At the sharp end of the professional game, even breaking off is a risky business; it is common for a player to watch their opponent immediately sink a long red and clear the table. *All they've done in this frame is break off* has evolved into an established commentator refrain. By extension, it is perfectly possible for a player to have no meaningful opportunities throughout an entire match. Here is one of the reasons why demons can hover over snooker; the game has a toxic, psychologically unhealthy quality. It is not good for the mind.

O'Sullivan's mid-match concession was the first incident of its kind in the history of professional snooker. A baffled Hendry was interviewed straight afterwards: 'I don't know what to say. Ronnie's obviously got his reasons . . . he knows what he feels inside . . . you can't criticise someone else for the way they feel . . . but it's bizarre.' The BBC studio was a hive of confusion as Hendry, Parrott and Hazel Irvine tried to make some sense of what they had just seen. The following day, Ronnie released a statement that combined an explanation of his actions with an element of apology for letting people down:

> I wish I could have given Stephen a better game and I'm sorry I didn't stick around to sharpen him up for his semi-final. I'm also really sorry to let down the fans who came to see me play – it wasn't my intention to disappoint them and for that I am truly apologetic . . . I am feeling disappointed with myself and am hurt

and numb, but I am a fighter and I will be back on my feet fighting stronger and harder than ever very soon.

The requirement for an apology highlights a troublesome tension: the protection of a player's mental health collides with the expectation that they satisfy a duty towards the paying public. O'Sullivan's language, 'I am feeling disappointed with myself,' seems both to express negative feelings about his performance and also a sense of guilt about the fact that he had failed his fans.

When his autobiography was published, a fuller explanation of O'Sullivan's frame of mind emerged. His description of precisely how he felt, in the moments leading up to the concession, is instructive:

> It was about 4 p.m., and I was thinking, I've got a couple of my jockey mates up here, they like a good booze-up. I'm going to get smashed tonight, absolutely wasted. Even though I was still running well, I didn't feel good in myself. It's funny: to the outside world I looked in great nick – healthy, trim, fit. Everybody was saying, you're looking well, but I was in pieces. I wasn't eating my way out of my depression, but I was running my way out of my depression. But even the running didn't always do the trick. And now I just wanted out.

The overpowering hunger for a binge is manifest. It was an oblivion-itch: a need to melt the solid flesh. *I'm going to get smashed tonight, absolutely wasted.* Throughout his autobiography, O'Sullivan references a desire to 'numb' himself – a need for escape that he was sometimes able to resist for days or even weeks at a time, but which nevertheless would always be there, a siren beckoning him away from the pressures of the real.

Against Hendry that day, O'Sullivan was clearly in a depressive state; very publicly, on BBC afternoon television, he was battling a breakdown in his mental health. He had been in no condition to play snooker. The only remedy had been for him to get *out* – out of the match, out of the building.

The general mood of response, though, was not supportive. Newspapers pondered whether or not he would 'face disciplinary action' in the light of 'the embarrassment he has heaped on their second most prestigious ranking tournament.' And disciplinary action is indeed what came his way; he was fined almost twenty-one thousand pounds and had nine hundred ranking points removed. The public also appeared to take a somewhat hostile view.

'The fans turned against me a bit,' O'Sullivan said. 'I got a couple of boos when I played a match in Preston, then when I played in the Masters at Wembley, which was the very next tournament.' It is not a moment in snooker history that reflects well on the sport's level of mental health support.

Should O'Sullivan have simply ploughed on that day, suffering through the darkness? What are the limits to such things? At what point, exactly – at what precise concentration of psychological distress – does it become OK for a player to say that actually they cannot go on, they are ill, they are in no position to continue? The official statement from the WPBSA was alarmingly machine-like – a Big Brother confirmation of procedural transgression that had very little to say about empathy: 'A Disciplinary Hearing took place on Thursday 31 May 2007 before the Disciplinary Committee of the WPBSA to establish whether Mr Ronnie O'Sullivan, a member of the Association, was in breach of the Association's Disciplinary Rules following reports concerning his conduct during the Maplin UK Championship in December. Mr O'Sullivan attended the hearing. The Committee found that Mr O'Sullivan's behaviour constituted a breach of the Association's Disciplinary Rules.'

And O'Sullivan is far from the only player to have battled with mental health fragilities. Graeme Dott is one of the more fascinating characters in snooker's history. Lacking the fluency and high scoring of many top players, he pushes a more old-school style – a gritty battler with little flash but plenty of fight and bottle. Despite his technical limitations, he has managed to forge an impressive career – especially at the Crucible, where the longer matches always seemed to suit his grinding approach. He reached the World Championship final three times, and in the epic Ebdonian tussle of 2006, he slugged his way through to the title.

For a former world champion, though, he has always been an under-appreciated figure, seldom given serious time in discussions of the game's elite. Part of the reason for this can be found in his resolutely unsexy method of play. Part of it, too, lies in his inconsistency. Alongside the World Championship victory, he has only ever won one other ranking tournament. Over the years his fortunes have varied wildly; his ranking has zigzagged repeatedly back and forth, into and out of the game's top sixteen.

A key source of this volatility has been his struggle with depression. 'One day my wife was going to college,' he has said, 'and I was in the living room. The TV wasn't even on but I was just staring at it. She went away, came back at two in the afternoon and I'm still there. Just staring.' His father-in-law's death, combined with his wife's cancer scare and miscarriage, created a whirlpool of trauma that shattered his mental health. Snooker was all he had; but his game was in ruins. He lost seventeen matches in a row. On one occasion, while playing in China, he was in tears in his chair; he had to put a towel over his face so that no one could see.

The one player who made a point of reaching out to help was none other than Ronnie O'Sullivan, who touched base with him in a crucially supportive phone call. 'I thought it was really nice of him. He doesn't really speak to me, it's not as if we're mates, but it was nice of him to do that . . . I looked at him in a different way after that.' An underrated, singularly pugnacious talent, Dott could well have claimed a secure place alongside the game's immortals, if it had not been for the troubles he faced. 'I had dark thoughts,' he explained. 'Whether you would do it or not, but definitely, there's no point lying about it. I had the thoughts.'

It is not hard to find further examples of mental health trauma elsewhere. Martin Gould is another player with the kind of jaggedly uneven career that might have more to do with illness than his level of ability. He has opened up about his depression: 'Quite a few bits and pieces started to really get on top of me. The more it got on top of me, the worse it started to feel. It got to a point where sometimes you wanted to say something, but just bottled it. You start to feel a bit ashamed . . . snooker is one of the sports that can be very lonely.'

In the 2021 Championship League, an emaciated-looking Gary Wilson stunned the audience by slamming the white ball with his cue after missing an easy red. In the frame that followed, he missed a black off the spot before saying out loud, 'I'm absolutely gone,' as if to himself.

'I've got no motivation to play snooker, to get out of bed, I'm struggling to see a purpose or an end goal,' he later explained. 'I don't know what the experts would say, but it sounds like depression and that's what I've been going through.'

With help – and thanks to their own brave openness – both Gould and Wilson found their way to avenues of support. Others, though, have not been so lucky. In October 2016,

Belgian player Steve Lemmens was found dead; he had walked in front of a train near his home town of Wezemaal.

The game's mental health awareness was dramatically lifted in early 2022 by the case of Mark Selby. A four-time world champion and contemporary great of the game, Selby's form has nevertheless fluctuated over the years and he has alluded at various times to battles with depression. In January 2022, after crashing out of the Masters, he opened up in a tweet that was widely praised for its bravery and impact: 'Just want to apologise to all my friends and family for letting them down. Mentally not in a good place at moment, had a relapse and trying to bottle it up and put a brave face on is not the way. I promise I will get help and become a better person. #mentalhealth'

The message immediately led to a torrent of support from the public, with well over a thousand people writing back to wish him well. Such was the response that Selby posted a follow-up the next day: 'I can honestly say all the matches I have won as a professional, the biggest match I have overcome was yesterday speaking out and finally admitting I need help . . . Finally feel a huge weight lifted off my shoulders.'

The sense of relief was palpable. 'It's testament to how far we've come,' said Hayley Jarvis, head of sport for the mental health charity MIND, 'that more and more people from the world of sport feel comfortable talking publicly about their own experiences.' Selby's candid messages, and the responses to them, feel like a door to a brighter future – one that involves a fuller, much more compassionate understanding of players and the pressures they face.

It would, of course, be foolish to conclude that depression is somehow a risk unique to snooker. There is plenty of evidence to suggest that all elite-level sport can potentially be perilous for mental health. But is it possible, at some obscure or deep-set level, that there could be a connection between particular sports, and the kind of people that choose to play them? Could it be that certain sports attract certain mindsets – certain kinds of person?

Journalist Mark Rice-Oxley has examined the issue of mental health in cricket. 'Sometimes you might have to wait hours, days even, to bat,' he noted. 'And then you might just get the one terrifying delivery of the match that leaves you with zero while everyone else has filled their boots. So that next time you go out there, that notion of failure is never too far away from the back of your mind.' Once again, inaction is the enemy; inaction provides time to think, and thinking can be dangerous. Perhaps sports with greater space for thought invite the growth of dark, self-analytical rabbit holes. 'Cricket is a mental game,' Rice-Oxley continued, 'and not enough is done to prepare players for that.' The list of recent England cricketers who have struggled with depression is remarkable: Marcus Trescothick, Jonathan Trott, Phil Tufnell, Graham Thorpe, Steve Harmison, Monty Panesar, Andrew Flintoff and Ben Stokes. Current England batsman and World-Cup winner Jonny Bairstow lost his father, former England player David, to suicide. The more psychological the game, perhaps, the greater the vulnerability. Perhaps thinking really is the enemy. And sitting in their chair, thinking, is all that a snooker player can do while their opponent plays.

One snooker player who does believe the game is harmful for health is Ronnie O'Sullivan. 'It's a bad sport,' he has said. 'It can cause you a lot of damage.' Part of the problem is that, outside the very top players, the rewards can be limited – certainly not large enough to justify or offset the pain of repeated defeats. Part of it, too, is the nature of what the sport involves, every single day; hours and hours of practice in the dark, away from others, with just the table itself for company. 'Snooker's just a really,

really tough sport . . . Stuck indoors, no natural light, draw the curtains, in there for five or six hours, you don't talk to anyone. That's not healthy, that's not a good way to spend your life. Look at a lot of snooker players, they don't know how to have a conversation, because they don't talk.'

Snooker players, in other words, are isolated figures – some of the loners in life. Detached from the rest of the world, they subsist too often in the toxic space of their own head. The individual nature of the sport means no one else is there to help; no one can offer comfort or consolation when things go badly. 'At least in football, you have your mates to lean on. They know when you are not having a good time and know what to say to pick you up . . . but in snooker you don't get that.' The picture O'Sullivan paints is gloomily clear. Snooker is a lonely game. It is a game of silence and dark. 'I always say to young kids, their parents, "Don't let them play,"' he concluded. 'My own kids, I say, "You're not playing snooker."'

7

TRUTH

To love truth for truth's sake is the principal part of human perfection in this world and the seed-plot of all other virtues.

John Locke, letter, 1703

There is no more formidable philosophical problem, perhaps, than the nature of truth itself – philosophy's most unanswerable riddle, and also its central concern. Aristotle saw all philosophy as a form of science focused on the exploration of truth. Many thinkers, though, have articulated less than full confidence in our ability to access the unfiltered facts about the world.

Immanuel Kant stressed the unknowability of the '*Ding an sich*', the 'thing-in-itself'. In a late notebook entry, Friedrich Nietzsche made an oft-quoted, oft-contorted claim that 'facts is precisely what there is not, only interpretations'. It was, in truth, not some manifesto for denying truth, but more of an observation that we can only ever interpret facts subjectively. 'We can establish no fact "in itself",' he explained. Truth, felt Nietzsche, might well be out there, but it is not going to be easy for us to find. The subjective reaches in vain for the objective. Truth is not easy to see. Truth, as Shakespeare reminds us, hath a quiet breast.

Sport is the supreme challenge of the physical. But it is also something much more; sport wears the garb of philosophy, and it treads in the temple of virtue. When top sportspeople are asked about what sport means to them, they generally do not peddle its physical challenges. Much more often, they stress its moral qualities: its capacity to educate and to edify.

Billie Jean King claimed sport 'teaches you character, it teaches you to play by the rules, it teaches you to know what it feels like to win and lose – it teaches you about life'. The notion of sport supplying a kind of moral code is commonplace among the sporting elite. Basketball icon Kobe Bryant declared, 'Sports are such a great teacher. I think of everything they've taught me: camaraderie, humility, how to resolve differences.' No less a figure than Lionel Messi said, 'I prefer to win titles with the team before individual prizes or outscoring everyone. I'm more concerned with being a good person than being the best footballer in the world.' These statements all circulate around a common theme. The meaning of sport does not consist in its physical properties. It is about something deeper; something more philosophical, instructive, moral. At its best, sport helps to guide us towards truth.

In the 2018 World Snooker Championship, Matthew Stevens was up against Kyren Wilson in the first round. It was a contrasting moment in the careers of the two players: Stevens, a classy operator and under-achiever, had developed a superb Crucible record back in the day – twice a finalist – but by this stage he was sliding down the rankings, his best years behind him. Wilson, in contrast, was a rising star. Stevens had been battling a cold; the match had been going badly. He was 8–3 down in a best of nineteen. He was, though, nicely in among the balls – in the middle of a great chance, with the reds well spread. He had slipped into a vaguely awkward spot for his next shot – the red itself was easy, but with the pink in his way, he had to squeeze his bridging hand over to one side.

All of a sudden, without warning, he was up – aborting the shot and walking back to his chair. What was happening? The crowd's sigh of sympathy morphed into admiring applause. 'There is a great example of why our sport is so good,' cooed John Parrott in commentary. 'Matthew Stevens, in a World Championship, with a chance that he's been looking forward to, has just touched the pink, stood up and said foul shot on himself. And that's why I'm so proud of this sport.' The referee hadn't spotted the foul: only Stevens knew. He could easily have got away with it. But the idea did not occur to him. His admission had been instantaneous.

Amazingly, something similar happened in the very next frame. Now Stevens was 9–3 down: on the precipice of defeat. He was in again among the balls. This time – bridging over one red to pot another – he had to skew his cue upwards as he played the shot, almost at right angles to the table. He potted the red – but immediately whispered something to the referee. 'He's fouled again,' noted Parrott, as the crowd groaned and clapped. Once again, the referee hadn't spotted the foul; Stevens had called it on himself. As he sat down, though, his face fell into gurns of uncertainty. He aimed a doubtful hand-wobble at his friends in the crowd. He wasn't sure he *had* actually touched the red. Television replays did not show any evidence that the red had moved. Stevens had called the foul out of an instinctive loyalty to truth – and then, on reflection, was far from convinced that he had committed a foul at all.

Snooker is replete with such specimens of sportsmanship. In the same tournament, the very next day, Barry Hawkins feather-touched a red and immediately told the referee. This time Joe Perry provided the commentary box approval: 'He's owned up to a foul there. That's one of the great things about our game.'

Liam Highfield had qualified for the Crucible for the very first time that year. In the process of getting squashed by Mark 'The Pistol' Allen, he accidentally touched the white while lining up a shot and turned straight away to tell the referee, whose view had been blocked by Highfield's body. 'He touched the white,' said Dennis Taylor in commentary. 'No one's seen it . . . that is one of the great things about this game of ours.' Moments such as these in snooker possess a quiet beauty. They are not the scenes of greatest glamour or renown; they are, though, exquisite instances of the honour of honesty sparkling amid the clouds of competition.

The concept of 'sportsmanship' is an intriguing one, in which the word *sport* shifts across into the territory of its second meaning. To be a sportsman, to be sporting, means not necessarily to be involved in sport, but to be an exemplar of ethical integrity – a role model for others to note and to follow. The principle of truthfulness lies at its heart. All sports revere its presence, constructing prominent, complex mythologies around it. In its finest form, sportsmanship manifests as a noble self-sacrifice, a show of pure human selflessness resonating far beyond a sport's horizons, acquiring an almost religious significance.

In cricket, the paradigm is the batsman who walks without heeding the umpire's decision. In the 2003 World Cup semi-final, Adam Gilchrist famously did precisely this. After a mistimed sweep roused a Sri Lankan appeal, umpire Rudi Koertzen gave him not out – but Gilchrist turned and walked off anyway, knowing he had hit the ball. 'Everything in my body just said go . . . walk,' he said afterwards. 'You've got to go. That's out.' It was, interestingly, a divisive move – he was the target of criticism, in some quarters, for an act of sportsmanship that was paradoxically condemned as unsporting, improper and even unpatriotic.

In football, Paulo di Canio's overall record of conduct on the field was, to say the least, something of a mixture. But in a December 2000 match against Everton, he astonished the footballing world with a moment of compassion so legendary that, over twenty years later, it is still talked about as one of the greatest acts of sportsmanship ever witnessed in the game. The scoreline was poised at 1–1. There were five minutes to go. As usual, West Ham badly needed the points. The ball was floated into the box, where di Canio was waiting . . . but instead of shooting, he just reached up and caught the ball.

The Everton goalkeeper, Paul Gerrard, was lying in a heap over on the edge of the penalty area after twisting his knee. Instinctively, di Canio had rebelled against the idea of firing the ball into an empty goal. It didn't seem truthful. It didn't seem right. The crowd at Goodison Park gave him a standing ovation. FIFA gave him their Fair Play Award. 'We wanted to kill him, really,' manager Harry Redknapp later said.

In snooker, it is perhaps not a surprise that the player with the most formidable reputation for honesty is Jimmy White. If there is anything essential, anything *echt*, about White's approach to the game, it is this. As Luke Williams and Paul Gadsby have noted, integrity is one of the reasons so many people loved him: 'His appeal transcends all boundaries of age and class largely because, for all his rough-around-the-edges behaviour away from the table, on it he is a gentleman who always calls his own fouls and never makes excuses in defeat.'

In the 1993 world final, he was in the process of being pulled to pieces by Stephen Hendry. In with a chance, he was lining up his shot – but pulled away sharply, signalling to the referee before pacing back to his chair, shaking his head. 'That is Jimmy White,' observed 'Whispering' Ted Lowe in commentary. 'Immediately he fouled the ball, he walked away.'

It is typical of Lowe, snooker commentary's immortal master, to get things so perfectly right. This was not just an instance of sporting behaviour from White – it was an unadulterated manifestation of his whole identity. *That is Jimmy White.* Jimmy White is not just a sportsman. He is the archetype of sportsmanship itself.

'Christmas was close at hand,' runs a passage in Dickens' *Pickwick Papers*, 'in all his bluff and hearty honesty; it was the season of hospitality, merriment, and open-heartedness; the old year was preparing, like an ancient philosopher, to call his friends around him, and amidst the sound of feasting and revelry to pass gently and calmly away.' It is an ancient thing to associate honesty with warmth, happiness and home. In the light of this, one might have thought we would always gravitate towards it. Truth, it seems, is good for us. It is better to be honest. It is better to be truthful. The path of honesty is the path of wisdom. But it is often not the path we actually choose.

8

FALSEHOOD

I WON THIS ELECTION, BY A LOT!
Donald J. Trump, Twitter, 7 November 2020

We live, it is often said, in a world beyond truth. A world where lies are indistinguishable from facts; where real news rots into fake news. And it is not just that false information exists along-side factual information in a damaging way; false information actually wins. A 2018 study in *Science* noted that 'False news reached more people than the truth; the top 1 per cent of false news cascades diffused to between 1,000 and 100,000 people, whereas the truth rarely diffused to more than 1,000 people.'

In this post-truth information fog, any utterance acquires a degree of substance. The more frequently it is uttered, the more apparent substance it gains. This has been described as the 'illu-sory truth effect'. The process goes well beyond mere influence; the repetition of information chemically alters our brains. As we hear information time after time, some snag or fault is triggered in the mind and, as if by magic, fiction morphs into fact. 'Repetition increases truth,' explains Lisa Fazio of Vanderbilt University, 'even when it directly contradicts what you already know.'

These, in other words, are dangerous pavements. The spectre of falsehood haunts us in new, precarious ways. Is truth a dying art?

Can we trust the words we hear? There is such a thing as purely toxic speech . . . we encounter it in Shakespeare's *Othello*, where Iago's machinations are motivated by one overwhelming urge, to bring about the ruin of Othello's life. The desire is so all-consuming that it becomes the single purpose behind everything he utters. 'I am not what I am', he offers in the play's opening scene: what Iago speaks does not reflect him, in any true sense, at all.

Iago detaches himself at a fundamental level from verbal authenticity. He speaks not in ideas, but in an unrelentingly toxic series of manipulative fictions. 'Nothing can exceed Iago's power of contamination,' writes Harold Bloom, 'once he begins his campaign.' It is only at the very end of the play that things are different. With Desdemona dead, and the devastating plan successfully complete, Iago no longer has any need for speech at all. Uninterested in offering any explanation for his actions, he lapses into a permanent silence:

Othello: I do believe it, and I ask your pardon.
            Will you, I pray, demand that demi-devil
            Why he hath thus ensnared my soul and body?
Iago: Demand me nothing. What you know, you know.
            From this time forth I never will speak word.

To many observers, Iago's actions seem to be beyond the human – devoid of empathy or remorse and incomprehensible in terms of human motivation. But even Othello himself is able to see it differently – tempted as he is to explain Iago away as a 'demi-devil'. The malevolence of Iago's purpose is, in fact, neither supernatural nor satanic. It is an all-too-human evil: 'I look down towards his feet, but that's a fable.'

Snooker, in so many different ways, is a game of contradic-tions. At one level, it is the quintessential gentleman's game:

smart, restrained, formal, decorous. At another, it is a delinquent hive of rascals and rogues. The game's ancestry is a story of smoky men's clubs, spiv haunts and gambling dens. Betting, one might say, is in snooker's blood.

In the snooker halls of seventies Canada, Cliff Thorburn made a living hustling against characters with names like 'Suitcase' Sam, 'Oil Can' Harry, and the 'Whale'. Stephen Hendry wryly recalls how, as a youngster in the eighties, he was rinsed by Jimmy White and Willie Thorne in a Hong Kong members' club. 'Jimmy and Willie invite[d] me to play "points" with them. This is a game in which you allocate a pound to every point scored, and you pay whoever follows you . . . Sadly for me, my attacking style of play meant that every time I missed a shot, Willie and Jimmy would be rubbing their hands with glee and at the end of the practice I had to ask Ian [Doyle, his manager] for the six hundred pounds I owed them.' For White, this kind of carefree approach to winning and losing money was just a natural part of life: 'I had one sneaky account with Natwest that had thirty thousand pounds in it – a massive amount of money back then, but the kind of sum I could burn in five minutes flat at the racetrack.'

There are clashing elements of feelgood fun and disquieting shadow in the way White won and burned his millions. The story of Willie Thorne, though, is much more glaringly bleak. Throughout his career, and after it as a commentator, he was well known as a big-time gambler. There is a famous story of Thorne betting £38,000 on John Parrott to lose, after hearing his cue had been stolen, only to watch Parrott miraculously fight back to win the match. To make things worse, Thorne was commentating while it happened. 'All of a sudden he's winning 5-4,' he later said, 'and I'm having to close the commentary by saying it's unbelievable, spewing up as I say it.'

He was never able to beat his gambling demons. During betting sprees he would stuff piles of cash in the lining of his coat: 'I would have forty to fifty thousand pounds wrapped around me in cash. I had twenty-odd accounts.' In 2002, he attempted suicide – overdosing on sleeping pills before his stepson rescued him. In 2014 – by this time over a million pounds in debt – he was on the verge of suicide again, taking a knife up to his hotel room before being stopped by his wife. In his late years, struggling with cancer, he was spotted in a Sheffield casino in the middle of the World Championships, grimly glued to the betting machines. The gambler's yearning haunted him till the end. 'I can understand that a man might go to the gambling table,' wrote Honoré de Balzac, 'when he sees that all that lies between himself and death is his last crown.'

It is one thing to gamble on sporting outcomes; but it is quite another to gamble on yourself. The most fundamental expectation we have of any sportsperson is that they will try. The spectacle of sport is a spectacle of effort and struggle, at the extreme end of dedication and skill. To stop trying is an unforgiveable sin – but the worst sin of all is to stop trying for the sake of money. This is the lowest circle: the darkest in all sport. Drug cheats like Lance Armstrong, Ben Johnson and Justin Gatlin might well have been justly vilified for their crimes against honesty – but at least they were trying to win. No sporting stigma quite has the noxious potency of match-fixing.

It is a vice with a long and murky history. Way back in 1919, eight members of the Chicago White Sox threw the World Series against the Cincinnati Reds. Disillusioned with bad contracts and low pay, the players were an easy target for Arnold Rothstein's New York crime mob. Although they were eventually acquitted in a public trial, they were permanently banned from the sport. The purity of baseball had been tainted forever.

The connotations of innocence in 'White Sox' were no longer appropriate. The story became known as the Black Sox Scandal.

Since then, every major sport has been blighted somewhere by match-fixing. Scandals have taken every kind of shape – some of them obscure, some of them unforgettable. In boxing, dozens of fighters over the decades have taken a fall for the sake of a suitcase of cash; question marks have even hovered over some of the sport's most iconic moments, like the Mohammad Ali v. Sonny Liston fights of the 1960s. In 1980, Italian football was rocked by the *'Totonero'* – an infamous betting scandal involving a host of top Italian clubs, and leading to bans for over twenty players, including Paulo Rossi; a second *Totonero* followed in 1986. Cricket has suffered a whole swathe of match-fixing cases – none of them more notorious than that of Hansie Cronje, the South African captain, who orchestrated a string of fixed matches in league with an Indian betting syndicate between 1996 and 2000. 'In a moment of stupidity and weakness,' he later said, 'I allowed Satan and the world to dictate terms to me. The moment I took my eyes off Jesus my whole world turned dark.' Conspiracy theories still float around Cronje's sudden death in a plane crash two years later, aged just thirty-two.

And snooker, sadly, has not been a stranger to match-fixing troubles. Alongside his tales of gambling woe, Willie Thorne also openly told of a time he was asked to throw a game – a line that, despite all his difficulties, he simply refused to cross: 'I was offered to go bent once in a match in the Benson & Hedges championship. But, even at my lowest ebb, I would never have given in to that. There have always been games that you knew the result of before they began, everyone in snooker did – and I know that a couple of my matches were bent from the start.'

Jimmy White tells a parallel tale – of receiving an approach from a shadowy, briefcase-carrying character before a match against Thorne. This was also in the Benson & Hedges championship, and it is tempting to conclude that both players are describing an approach from the same person.

White had never seen the man before. He was an edgy and nervous figure, with restless, twitchy eyes. He began by asking if he might have a quick chat, in private; he didn't explain the reason for the request. In one hand he gripped a small briefcase. Jimmy agreed to give him five minutes of his time.

Once they had entered the safety of the dressing room, the stranger flipped open the lid of the case. It was stuffed with piled up wads of cash. Thirty-five thousand pounds in total, the man explained.

He offered White the opportunity to count it. Out of instinct, he reached out and thumbed through the notes. There was no denying that it was an awful lot of money. He asked the man what on earth this was all about.

The answer, it turned out, was simple. The money would all be his . . . but only if he contrived to lose the match against Thorne by five frames to two.

White told him where to go. Sure, it was a lot of money. But it simply wasn't worth it. 'You can't live with being bent,' he summarised, 'not if you love the game.'

Not if you love the game . . . it is a response typical of White, snooker's foremost ambassador of honour. But not all players have found it quite so easy to keep to the virtuous path.

Silvino Francisco and his nephew Peter both joined the professional ranks in the early 1980s. They were the first top players to emerge from South Africa since Perrie Mans, who had made it to the 1978 World Final. Both Franciscos found a degree of success in the game – Silvino won the British Open in 1985 – but neither performed consistently. And controversy, of various flavours, loomed over both their careers. After his

British Open win, Silvino accused his opponent Kirk Stevens of playing under the influence of drugs – a divisive claim, which earned him a fine and a fair amount of unpopularity, although in the light of later revelations regarding Stevens, he may have had a point. In 1989, there was unusually heavy betting on a match between Silvino Francisco and Terry Griffiths at the Masters. The *Daily Mirror* splashed the scandal over its front page. Scotland Yard investigated; Francisco was arrested and interviewed, but ultimately released without charge.

Six years later, Peter Francisco was up against Jimmy White in the first round of the World Championship. Once again, unusual betting patterns preceded the match: this time, it was for White to win by the precise scoreline of ten frames to two. After the first four frames were shared, White won eight in a row. The final score – *see what a ready tongue suspicion hath* – was 10–2. These were the frank observations of Clive Everton:

> I commentated on the entire match with [John] Virgo as my summariser in the first session and Dennis Taylor in the second. All three of us were puzzled at times by Francisco's shot selection. Dennis said, 'I can't figure out what's going wrong with Peter,' and, 'His thinking doesn't seem to be there. He hasn't got his thinking boots on today.' I said, 'He's just not thinking straight.'
>
> I was so used to players trying their hardest, particularly at the Crucible, that the explanation took some time to break clear of my subconscious.

The crucial clue came from a shot played by Francisco in the seventh frame. Blessed with a host of easy options to clear the table, Francisco opted for a bizarre positional shot to get on the yellow, leaving himself needlessly cueing over the black. 'Even so,' Everton noted, 'his attempted yellow should at least have hit the jaws. Instead, it missed by what I described as "a vast margin".'

The penny had dropped. The reason Peter Francisco was playing so badly wasn't because he didn't have his 'thinking boots' on; it was because he was deliberately trying to lose. There was an investigation. Francisco was found guilty, not of match-fixing per se, but of 'not conducting himself in a manner consistent with his status as a professional sportsman'. He was banned from snooker for five years.

Over the years that followed, match-fixing allegations would rear their ugly head every now and again. Sometimes it would come to nothing; Peter Ebdon, Jamie Burnett and Stephen Maguire were all investigated, at different times, before being cleared of any wrongdoing. In stark contrast, erratic Aussie maverick Quinten Hann was convicted in 2006 of throwing a match against Ken Doherty and banned for eight years.

Nothing, though, could prepare the snooker world for what would happen on 2 May 2010. On the final day of the World Championship, a hydrogen bomb of unprecedented magnitude was about to detonate. The match-fixing guillotine was about to drop on one of the game's all-time greats.

Popularly known as the 'Fake Sheikh', Mazher Mahmood had already gathered plenty of experience as an undercover journalist. His speciality was in sting operations – posing as a businessman, secretly recording high-profile figures and aiming to expose corruption. Previous eminent victims had included David Mellor, Princess Michael of Kent, the Duchess of York, John Fashanu and Sven-Göran Eriksson. On 30 April, Mahmood and an associate met John Higgins and his agent Pat Mooney in a Kiev hotel room. Higgins – who had become world champion for the third time the previous year – had just been knocked out at the Crucible. After some prefatory business chat and light joshing, the meeting took a spicier turn as Mahmood outlined the plan of Higgins throwing some frames for money.

A hidden camera had been fixed on the coffee table, pointing at Higgins and Mooney, recording everything. Here are some extracts of the transcript as published by *The Guardian*:

John Higgins [laughing]:	There is no cameras is there? Oh yeah. Frame three I'm going to lose. Yes, yes. [There's] no risk, because you can miss. If you start leaving, leaving and leaving chances people are saying, What's happening here? But against other players it's no problem.
Undercover reporter:	I don't know the sport that well, but what I'm saying is that you can miss one, but you can't keep missing them?
Higgins:	You can. Yeah, yeah, you can.
Undercover reporter:	We agreed four frames during year one, right? We are agreeing the figure now. What is the figure we are agreeing?
Pat Mooney:	Three hundred . . . agreed.
Higgins:	But then I am thinking to myself, How do I swallow 200,000 or 300,000 pounds or euros coming into my account?
[to Mooney]:	I have got a property in Spain, I'm thinking to myself. Is there any way, if

	you got a small mortgage on the property or something and you can pay it off . . . would they look me out if you paid it off in a lump sum?
Undercover reporter:	So, four frames, one per?
Higgins:	Yep.

The video culminates with Higgins, Mooney and the 'businessmen' rising to their feet for a celebratory toast of vodka; there is a recital of '*Za váshe zdoróvye*' ('To your health' in Russian), a clinking of shot glasses, and the footage ends. The *News of the World* unleashed the scoop. HIGGINS BET ON HIMSELF TO LOSE, claimed the front-page headline. Snooker was plunged into meltdown.

It is customary for snooker to be painfully under-represented in the national newspapers. This story, though, was an exception. 'John Higgins "fix" allegations leaves snooker in turmoil,' said the *Daily Mail,* 'as three-times world champion is suspended.' 'John Higgins suspended in snooker match-fixing probe,' said the *Mirror.* 'Snooker is in crisis after new world No. 1 John Higgins was suspended,' declared the *Express.* A vicious frenzy had ambushed the snooker world. WPBSA chairman Barry Hearn said:

I don't see any place in sport, in any sport, for anyone who affects the credibility or the integrity of any sport . . . I'm not going to make knee-jerk reactions on this . . . It's come as a huge shock and obviously an enormous blow to the integrity of the sport which is vital for the expansion plans we have. It's really been a shattering experience and one which will be immediately looked into by our disciplinary people under the WPBSA rules.

Snooker had a dagger in its breast. How it could ever recover was unclear. The wound looked catastrophic, fatal. Hearn admitted that he was considering his position. 'This particular story,' he explained, 'has the potential to affect the integrity of the entire sport.'

'Integrity', the word repeated by Hearn, is a charged word, a vital word, derived from the Latin *'integritas'*, meaning 'intact', 'unbroken'. To have integrity is to remain complete – free from damage, corrosion, vice. In one stroke, snooker had been devastatingly emptied of this quality. The trauma within the snooker fraternity was acute.

'It's the darkest day I've ever experienced in snooker,' said Steve Davis. 'Everybody is in shock. Everyone's walking around in bits . . . There are other alleged incidents under investigation and no smoke without fire is bad enough but this has taken it to another level. The severity, the profile is just shocking. I think the integrity of the game has effectively evaporated overnight. It's the lowest ebb it's ever been. What a terrible wake-up call. It's just too awful to contemplate.'

Once again, the word 'integrity' sits at the heart of Davis' comments. This was not just a controversy for John Higgins as an individual. It was an injury to snooker's soul. Everyone involved in the game – everyone who followed the game – felt something of the same hurt. If the integrity of snooker had gone, what of any value remained? Higgins – who had been immediately suspended in the wake of the allegations – released a statement: 'I have built my reputation on honesty and integrity. Sadly, others have now damaged that reputation and it is now left to me to clear my name. I have never been involved in any form of snooker match-fixing.'

The investigation took four months, culminating in a two-day tribunal. Several nuggets of new information emerged in court.

One was that Mooney had met Mahmood to discuss the prospect of frame-throwing on several occasions prior to the Kiev hotel date. Higgins, in contrast, had only been told that the topic might crop up minutes before the meeting itself. The judge was broadly 'unimpressed by Mooney as a witness', finding 'much of his account highly implausible'. In short, Mooney was pinned as the villain.

'I think it was made clear,' said Hearn, 'who the culprit is.'

Mooney was banned from snooker for life. Higgins, though, was cleared of the most serious charges. He had been led on by his agent; in the hotel room – intimidated by what appeared to be an approach by the Russian mafia – he had played along with the idea of throwing frames, but had never harboured any real intention of doing so. His punishment was a £75,000 fine and a six-month ban, for 'giving the impression' he might break betting rules, and for failing to report the approach.

The manner in which Higgins had been ensnared by the *News of the World* quickly became an object of scrutiny. The motives and the methods of the paper – and in particular of Mahmood – were called into question. The day after the tribunal concluded, journalist Roy Greenslade raged in the *Guardian* that Higgins 'had been tricked into the meeting by his partner's duplicity, which itself was the direct result of the paper's subterfuge'. The whole affair 'was testament only to grubby journalism. Yet again, the paper has brought journalism into disrepute.' What had initially looked like a noble, if hard-nosed, journalistic revelation now looked more like a cynical publicity stunt. A few years after this whole episode, Mahmood's career came crashing down in spectacular fashion. A *Panorama* investigation, entitled *The Fake Sheikh Exposed*, alleged that Mahmood had deployed criminal methods to obtain evidence against the singer Tulisa Contostavlos. Suggestions emerged that he had lied in court. He was charged with perverting the course of justice. In 2016, he was sentenced to fifteen months in prison.

The exculpation of John Higgins brought about a conflicted legacy of relief and unease. The great legend of snooker was not a match-fixer. He was innocent. Clearly this was good news. But what was the moral of the story, exactly? What, if anything, should be made of a shattering scandal that had itself originated out of a swamp of dishonour? In the end, things had taken a distinctly postmodern turn. Truth had not been shining any light into the forest of falsehood. In reality, falsehood had simply been staring at itself; falsehood stood grimly on both sides of the mirror, with truth nowhere to be found. Lies had been layered upon lies. 'All societies end up wearing masks,' wrote Jean Baudrillard in *America*. Perhaps truth was simply too much to expect.

At least Barry Hearn was still at the helm. He had promised to crack down on corruption – setting up an Integrity Unit for precisely this purpose. 'This is a question of zero tolerance,' he had affirmed. 'We will be making it clear to players it is totally against the rules for anyone to have any financial gain whatso-ever from any betting activity within the sport . . . It is a total, complete blanket on any form of gambling. Anyone who breaks these rules will have an instant lifetime ban.' Yes, times had been tough. But the worst, at least, was over. Snooker had lived through its darkest nightmare. It would never have to suffer such an ordeal again . . .

By the time of the Higgins affair, Stephen Lee had been a top player for well over a decade. A precocious talent, he was renowned for the smoothness of his cue action – a 'Rolls-Royce' action, as Dennis Taylor would routinely purr in commentary. He had been a fixture in the top sixteen since the late 90s

– winning every now and again, rather than regularly, but always threatening, often going deep.

Around 2008, though, his form had dipped significantly. He had dropped out of the top sixteen – a big potential problem in a player's career. In those days, a top-sixteen ranking provided automatic entry into tournaments. Outside it lay the prospect of qualifying rounds, and potential penury if you were unable to make it through. At the very moment that the John Higgins scandal erupted, Stephen Lee was being investigated for suspicious betting patterns around one of his matches at the 2009 UK Championship. It took over two years for the WBPSA to confirm that no further action would be taken. Just another instance, it seemed, of smoke without fire. No more to be said. All was well.

Except: all was not well. A week later the levee broke. In an October 2012 Premier League match against John Higgins, Lee had squandered such an extravagant array of chances in the course of his 4–2 defeat that Judd Trump immediately posted a series of tweets – later deleted – questioning the result's integrity ('stewards enquiry please,' Trump had written, 'something not right'). Suspicious betting patterns had once again surrounded the match. Lee was promptly suspended. The WPBSA's statement ran as follows:

> On 2 October 2012 the Crown Prosecution Service announced that there will be no criminal proceedings in the match-fixing allegations against Stephen Lee made in 2010. Following this decision by the CPS, the WPBSA started its own investigation into these allegations.
>
> On 5 October 2012 the WPBSA met with the Gambling Commission in order to review material collected by the Gambling Commission which may prove relevant to the WPBSA investigation . . .

On 12 October 2012 the WPBSA was informed of suspicious betting patterns relating to a game between Stephen Lee and John Higgins played on 11 October 2012 . . .

The WPBSA has carefully considered both the initial information from the Gambling Commission, which was reviewed on 5 October 2012, and the new information regarding suspicious betting patterns in relation to the match between Stephen Lee and John Higgins from 11 October 2012.

The WPBSA has concluded that it would not be appropriate for Stephen Lee to continue to compete on the World Snooker Tour whilst these investigations are undertaken and therefore WPBSA chairman Jason Ferguson has taken the decision to suspend Stephen from competition whilst this inquiry is ongoing.

Lee was reported to be 'absolutely devastated'. When it was confirmed that he would face a formal hearing, his lawyer released a statement affirming the player's innocence. 'Mr Lee is shocked by the suggestions made against him,' it read. 'He has been a professional snooker player for twenty years and has always sought to uphold the highest standards as required of such a player.'

The three-day hearing took place in September 2013, and the conclusions it reached were ugly. This, it transpired, had been no one-off error of judgement. Lee was construed to be a serial offender – a match-fixing career criminal. He was found guilty of influencing the outcome of a whole string of matches over the course of two years. The WPBSA dealt him a twelve-year ban.

Within days, Ronnie O'Sullivan was on Twitter, darkly suggesting that the Lee case was merely the tip of the iceberg. 'I've heard there's many more players who throw snooker matches,' he wrote. 'I suppose Steve lee [sic] was just caught out . . . They will prob fine me for talking about it. They don't like you doing that. Like to keep things under the carpet.'

His comments did not go down well with Ken Doherty: 'He has cast aspersions over the game and over the people who play it. It's not fair. It's not right. Too many people love the game and wouldn't do anything to hurt it . . . What Ronnie has said has damaged the dignity and the integrity of snooker.' Once again, the *integrity* of snooker – its wholeness, its heart – was at stake. Were Ronnie's remarks really doing the damage, or had that not already been amply done by Lee's nefarious actions? Either way, snooker's nightmare of match-fixing had darkened and deepened, swinging the game dismally away from respectability just when it needed it most.

The tale of Stephen Lee is a sad one, starting out as it did with such rare levels of promise and potential. The whole thing seemed to make no sense. This had not been a player down at the foot of the rankings, strapped for cash and going astray through desperation. Lee had already earned handsome sums from the game – and had clearly possessed the ability to earn much more, without snatching at the forbidden apple of corruption. 'Why would you want to do that?' wondered Doherty. 'Why would you throw that away? He had another five or six years of making that money. It's just ridiculous he did it. He's a very, very silly boy.'

And when sorrows come, as Claudius bemoaned to Gertrude, they come not single spies, but in battalions. The match-fixing saga was not the final woe for Stephen Lee. The following year, he was found guilty of fraud – he had sold his snooker cue to a fan, without actually handing over the cue. In 2018, he was arrested in Hong Kong on the charge of teaching snooker without a work permit – his passport was confiscated, and he narrowly avoided prison. The days of Lee enchanting fans with his Rolls-Royce cue action had become a very distant dream.

It is hard to find much that is positive in the grimy chronicles of match-fixing. One thing they have at least done, though, is sharpen the consequences for indiscretion. A good example was the one-year ban imposed on Jamie Jones in 2019. Jones hadn't been guilty of any match-fixing himself; he had simply known about a case regarding close friend David John and had failed to report it. In short, he was banned for not dobbing in his mate.

Such a no-tolerance philosophy was the necessary riposte to the menace of corruption. But the threat still looms, and always will do, so long as money is on the table and human weakness is at play. A troubling reminder of this came with the abrupt suspension of several players, on alleged match-fixing charges, in December 2022. This is, after all, a post-truth age. Or so they say. All that can be hoped for is that integrity survives its wounds and somehow wins. As George Eliot noted in *Adam Bede*, being truthful is harder than it seems: 'Falsehood is so easy, truth so difficult ... Examine your words well, and you will find that even when you have no motive to be false, it is a very hard thing to say the exact truth, even about your own immediate feelings – much harder than to say something fine about them which is *not* the exact truth.'

9

PERFECTION

Have no fear of perfection – you'll never reach it.
Salvador Dali, 1952

'Ronnie O'Sullivan is a seven-time champion of the world,' announced Daniel Harris in the *Guardian*, after the great man lifted the 2022 world title. 'He did so after playing a near-perfect tournament, and there's no reason to think he's done yet.' Phil Haigh used the same language in the *Metro* after Judd Trump's 2019 Crucible win – in which he 'hammered Higgins 18–9, making seven centuries in the process, in what was a near-perfect performance'. It is a compound, *near-perfect*, that manages to express adulation while also, at the same time, existing as a badge of fallibility. These great players, they were so brilliant, they were almost flawless – almost but, then again, not quite.

Perfection is a perfect example of a contradiction. It is the ultimate aim of any effort, and also the one thing that will always remain unobtainable. Salvador Dali's famous line expresses a philosophical acceptance of this fact. Samuel Johnson came to a similar conclusion. It is, he wrote, 'reasonable to have perfection in our eye, that we may always advance toward it, though we know it never can be reached'. There is a powerful paradox at work here: our ambitions pull us towards perfection, at the same time as it continually resists us. Perfection is a black hole beyond the horizon, always lurking beyond the observable human landscape of shortcomings and failures. Psychoanalyst Jacques Lacan conceived of the '*objet petit a*' – the unattainable object of desire, for which we are constantly striving but which we cannot, and must not, ever grasp.

With perfection an impossible dream, thinkers and artists have often turned to imperfection as the real lifeblood of happiness. In Japanese philosophy, the practice of *wabi-sabi* centres around the embracing of imperfection. George Orwell claimed that 'the essence of being human is that one does not seek perfection'; 'every book,' he said, 'is a failure.' Victorian writer John Ruskin went further, suggesting that it is only by welcoming imperfection that liberated, creative work becomes possible: 'To banish imperfection is to destroy expression, to check exertion, to paralyse vitality.' Perhaps, for creative purposes, perfection is not merely impossible – it is restrictive, or even harmful. 'A perfect poem is impossible,' argued Robert Graves. 'Once it had been written, the world would end.'

In sport, perfection is often irrelevant. At a statistical level, any achievement almost always gestures in ghostly fashion towards something even better. However many goals, points, or runs you score, you could have scored more; however fast you manage to run, you could have run faster.

Even the most apparently miraculous exploits are transient, beatable. In athletics, Michael Johnson's supremacy was such that fellow competitor Roger Black admitted, 'Let's face it, the rest of us are just running for second.' His 400m world record of 43.18 sec., set in 1999, looked beyond human reach for nearly two decades until Wayde van Niekerk eased past it in 2016. In the 1968 Mexico Olympics, Bob Beamon's long jump of 8.90

metres went so preposterously beyond what seemed possible that a fellow competitor told him he had 'destroyed' the event. Famously, officials had to resort to manual measuring tape, after discovering their electronic equipment didn't reach far enough. It was labelled the 'jump of the century', a sublime effort that could never be surpassed, until one night in Tokyo, twenty-three years later, when Mike Powell went five centimetres further.

In snooker, though, there *is* a statistic that appears to embody perfection. The balls on a snooker table add up to a maximum potential break of one hundred and forty-seven. Fifteen reds, all with blacks, followed by all six colours. A maximum: a '147'. The most sacred number in snooker. It sits atop the Mount Sinai of baize mythology: a deity in numerical form. Even the elegance and symmetry of the number itself – the even spacing of one, four, seven – seems to evoke the shining otherworldliness of its significance. There is nothing like it. A 147 possesses a unique, precious magic. As O'Sullivan puts it, 'The 147 is the ultimate, the greatest thing you can do in the game; snooker perfection.'

In snooker's early days, century breaks were a rare thing, never mind maximums. The highest break at the first ever World Snooker Championship, in 1927, was only sixty. It was not until 1955 that the first official maximum break was made. Fittingly, its author was Joe Davis – the original pioneer of snookering greatness. As Clive Everton recorded, it was 'an amazing achievement, snooker's equivalent of Sir Roger Bannister's epoch-making, sub-four-minute mile'.

Davis made the break in an exhibition match against Willie Smith; it would be over twenty years before a maximum was seen in tournament play. And that later break should have been televised, too. John Spencer's match against Cliff Thorburn at the 1979 Holsten Lager International started so late that most of the audience had left. With very few people watching, the promoter gave the TV crew a meal break before the evening session. It turned out to be a bad decision. In the second frame, Spencer made the first 147 ever seen in a professional tournament, but no one had been there to film it. 'We television folk were informed of this,' wrote Everton, 'as we emerged from the nearby McDonald's.'

The first maximum actually televised was in 1982. Somewhat inevitably, it was made by Steve Davis; somewhat ironically, John Spencer was the opponent.

It was the quarter finals of the Lada Classic. The score was two frames each. Spencer began the fifth frame with a loose break off, hitting the pack far too thick and leaving the white dangerously among the metropolis of reds. Davis potted the first few balls with customary calm. If anything, he appeared even more spectral than usual, his face the smoky grey of a raw oyster. He had just returned from a ten-day tour of Australia with Barry Hearn, and was suffering from jet lag: later, Davis would suggest his fatigue might have helped soothe his nerves towards the break's jittery business end. Most of the work on the reds was straightforward: two particular shots, though, indicated the rare confidence he possessed at this point in his career. First – on thirty-two – there was an audacious double into the middle pocket to rescue position. Later, on the last red, he left himself high up the table by the brown – a nine-foot pot, far from easy, but one that he knocked straight in. Fifteen reds; fifteen blacks. Phase one of the journey to perfection was complete.

With just the colours remaining – all on their spots – things should have been straightforward. The only thing that *could* cause a problem was pressure – and it duly did. From shot to shot, Davis' position deteriorated as he potted the baulk colours. Awkwardly straight on the brown, he had to slam it in to get close to the blue. But he hit the shot poorly; there may have been a bad contact, too, as the cue ball shuddered to a halt near the baulk line.

The blue, now, was nasty: much thinner than it should have been. Davis allowed himself a wry grin and a shake of the head – the vexed disappointment of someone whose train has just been delayed. He potted the blue cleanly, but had to send the white all the way round the table, a risky round-the-houses shot, to get on the pink. He was trusting to some luck that he did not get. The white finished in one of the worst possible places – right above the pink, requiring a thin cut with the rest.

'Well, come on, Steve,' said an audibly quivering David Taylor in commentary. 'Pull a fabulous shot out. I'm sure you can do it.' As he contemplated the mess he had made of things, Davis' grin widened. The shot required careful study. He needed to play it with deep screw to hold for the black. Very tough. A big test of technique and nerve. 'Come on, get in,' said Taylor, as Davis lined it up . . . and in it went.

The white, though, lost a bit of pace from all the screw, and finished low for the black. Not ideal. Not *difficult*, but certainly missable . . . a few years after this moment, Davis would learn a sharp lesson on how easy it can be to miss a crucial black ball under pressure. Before getting down for the shot, he blew on his hand. 'This was something I had seen the great Björn Borg do,' he later explained. 'I had never done it before and I don't think I ever did it again. But perhaps, subconsciously, it worked for me.' In the commentary box – suddenly possessed by some bizarre, fate-tempting demon – John Pulman started to say *I bet Steve at this moment can see the pocket closing up and closing up and getting smaller*, before Taylor rattily cut him off. Things were tense.

The crowd's silence thickened . . . but the black went in, and bedlam broke. Davis's face wore an expression of childlike disbelief. After shaking Spencer's hand, he took a moment to lean on the table, as if dizzy, shaking his head with folded arms. For the first time on television, snooker had witnessed the elegant perfection of a maximum break.

The World Championship would see its first maximum the following year. It happened early in Cliff Thorburn's epic clash against sloth nemesis Terry Griffiths. And it started, of all things, with a fluke; Thorburn missed a simple red, only to watch it rebound and knock a different red into the opposite corner. It was a nervy shot, in truth, giving no hint at what was to come. After this stroke of luck, though, Thorburn gradually got into his rhythm. It was a slow rhythm, it must be said – Thorburn arthritically descending into each shot like one of the bascules on Tower Bridge. But as reds and blacks began to disappear, it became clear that the balls were magnificently spread. Nothing on the table was safe. 'Every time we talk about these wonderful breaks,' said Jack Karnehm in commentary, 'they go and break down. So I'm going to let him finish this break. I'm a wee bit superstitious.'

With one red left, Thorburn took a breather in order to blow his nose on an oversized handkerchief. He had, in fact, been suffering from a heavy cold; perhaps, as with Davis, an element of fatigue was at some level calming his nerves. By the time Thorburn had reached the colours, play had been stopped on the opposite table. The expansive figure of Bill Werbeniuk could be spotted peeking round the partition like some festive genie or imp of destiny. In contrast to Davis, Thorburn's position on each colour remained flawless as yellow, green, brown, blue and pink all smoothly disappeared. As he settled down for the black, Karnehm whispered the immortal words, 'Oh, good luck, mate.'

But Thorburn didn't need the luck. After the black went in he sank to his knees, shaking his arms in triumph. Werbeniuk advanced to bury him in a giant bear hug. Griffiths joined it, and for a moment the three of them stood there, unsteadily swaying, arm in arm, like drunken revellers on a stag weekend. 'Just look at the pictures,' said Karnehm, as every member of the audience rose to their feet to applaud. Here was a golden moment for the treasure chest of snooker history. The Crucible, snooker's spiritual home, had witnessed snookering perfection for the very first time.

Maximum breaks remained a rare thing for many years to come. Some of them are firmly entrenched in the sport's folklore: Kirk Stevens' dashing, white-suited 1984 performance in the Masters; Jimmy White's 1992 maximum in front of an adoring Crucible crowd; Stephen Hendry's first maximum at the Crucible – inevitably made against White – in 1995.

Which, though, is the greatest of them all? Can there even be such a thing?

The concept of perfection should be one-dimensional – a flat plane. All perfect things must, it seems, be equally perfect. The alternative does not make any logical sense. A perfect thing cannot be *more* perfect than another perfect thing . . . or can it? If a maximum break really is snooker perfection, then do all maximum breaks involve an equal level of perfection? Or could it be possible that perfection is multi-layered, a house of many tiers, able to accommodate various distinct levels of a perfect phenomenon? Is there, in other words, a hierarchy of perfection to a 147 – and if so, is there a maximum break that stands as the most perfect one of all?

By 1997, Ronnie O'Sullivan had been professional for half a decade; at the age of twenty-one, he had already gathered something of a reputation as an impulsive under-achiever. After winning both the UK Championship and the Masters as a teen-ager, his potential for greatness could not have been clearer – but his results since had been up and down. In the first round at the Crucible that year, he was up against bespectacled journey-man and future maths teacher Mick Price. O'Sullivan had shown some good recent form, winning both the German Masters and the Asian Classic earlier in the season. And against Price, he was in control from the start, easing into an 8–5 lead. It looked a quiet match – playing itself out very much according to form. No drama seemed likely.

In the fourteenth frame, O'Sullivan was in with a middle-distance red after a shaky Price safety. Fifty seconds later, the first four reds and blacks had already disappeared. The figure smoothly speeding round the table was the peak rendition of the young O'Sullivan. In his early years, his wide-ranging personal difficul-ties had led to poor care of his physical body. 'By the time I was twenty,' he explained, 'I'd got myself up to fifteen and a half stone, a thirty-seven-and-a-half-inch waist, and I could have fitted two fifteen-year-old Ronnies in my playing pants. I'd become huge – a rhinoceros of a fella – and I wasn't even aware of it.' But he had recently, for the first time, discovered running, losing three stone as a result. The O'Sullivan of the 1997 World Championship was sleek and chiselled, a picture of youthful vitality, a slickly coiffured and spotlessly tailored desperado of slender waist and shaven jaw.

It is sometimes said, when a top player is mid-break, playing well, that they are making the game look easy. In this break, O'Sullivan was potting reds and blacks with such fluid simpli-city that snooker looked like a toy, a trivial child's game. There was a prize of £147,000 in place for a maximum, but O'Sullivan did not seem to be concerned. Every ball floated easily in; posi-tion on every shot seemed automatic; every little flick and cannon seemed to happen flawlessly, as if predestined.

After four minutes, he was already on the colours.

'Perfect,' hailed Dennis Taylor in commentary, as O'Sullivan landed just the right side of the blue.

'Yes, absolutely perfect,' John Virgo agreed.

And five minutes and eight seconds after he potted the first red, it was all over. The black was in; O'Sullivan had tossed his chalk into the crowd, giving someone somewhere a memento to cherish, a souvenir of virtuoso mastery. Snooker had seen a faultless frame. The purity of the maximum break had now appeared in its most divine form. Perfection had been perfected.

O'Sullivan's break is still frequently hailed as snooker's high-water mark – in terms of quality and brilliance, the best single frame in history. For many observers, nothing else has ever come close. And yet, bizarrely perhaps, it can still feel wrong to apply the term 'perfection', even to this most apparently perfect of frames. However implausible it might presently seem, someone, someday, will produce something faster; something more fluent, something better. History demonstrates that this will be so. Even the figure of 147 is not quite as impassable as it generally seems. A 147 *isn't*, actually, a maximum break . . . not really. Not technically. It is possible – at least in theory – to make a break even higher.

The 'free ball' rule is not a regular feature of professional snooker matches. In short, for the uninitiated, if a player commits a foul, but leaves their opponent snookered, that player can nominate a different ball as a substitute so that they are not disadvantaged. It most commonly happens towards the end of a frame, when snookers are required. But when it happens at the *beginning* of a frame, the player has a potential sixteen reds and blacks to play for, rather than the usual fifteen. In other words: a 155. This is the true maximum; the very highest break possible in snooker.

The set-up itself, never mind the break, requires such an outlandish set of circumstances that it has always been more of a theoretical concept than a visible phenomenon – the Higgs Boson, one might say, of snooker breaks. Across over a hundred years of professional snooker, a 155 break has *almost* never happened . . . but very, very rarely, it has been known. In 2005, Jamie Cope made a witnessed 155 break in practice. And in 2021, Thepchaiya Un-Nooh made a 155 in his local club that was captured by CCTV – the only footage of a 155 that has ever been recorded. Beyond the 'perfection' of a 147, then, another level of perfection does in fact exist – a highest possible performance, a hyper-maximum, reliant on such a wildly improbable set of prior conditions that it is very unlikely it will ever be seen in a tournament. But – as Eleanor Roosevelt once said – if life were predictable, it would cease to be life. You never quite know.

In the end, though, it is imperfection with which we will always be more at home. We cannot escape imperfection, however much we might try. Perfection, in truth, is a mirage. If you ever think you have encountered it, you are mistaken. This is a point made by Alexander Pope, in 'An Essay on Criticism':

Whoever thinks a faultless piece to see.
Thinks what ne'er was, nor is, nor e'er shall be.
In ev'ry work regard the writer's end,
Since none can compass more than they intend,
And if the means be just, the conduct true,
Applause, in spite of trivial faults, is due.

Not everyone, of course, is a perfectionist; some find it much easier than others to accept that, whatever they do, there will be flaws and failures involved. Ability, talent, brilliance – these often seem to be the problem. The greater the genius, the more the individual appears cursed by the demon of perfectionism. Here is O'Sullivan, snooker's premier genius, once again: 'I would much rather play the perfect match than win another world title . . . A perfect game would be one where I didn't make a single mistake, or only one that was forced by an excellent safety shot from an opponent. And then when you get a chance, just clear up. A hundred break, 130, 140 or a 147. That's how I think it should be played – and if it isn't, then it's substandard. The problem is that I know it's not possible to play to that level all the time, but in my head I know I'm capable of it.'

For the very greatest, only perfection is good enough; even if it be a delusion, an unattainable dream, still it is the necessary goal. Nothing else will do.

10

LUCK

You know what luck is? Luck is believing you're lucky.
Tennessee Williams, A *Streetcar Named Desire*, 1947

In *Casino Royale*, Ian Fleming details James Bond's fondness for gambling:

> Bond had always been a gambler. He loved the dry riffle of the cards and the constant unemphatic drama of the quiet figures around the green tables. He liked the solid, studied comfort of card-rooms and casinos, the well-padded arms of the chairs, the glass of champagne or whisky at the elbow, the quiet unhurried attention of good servants. He was amused by the impartiality of the roulette ball and of the playing cards – and their eternal bias. He liked being an actor and a spectator and from his chair to take part in other men's dramas and decisions, until it came to his own turn to say that vital 'Yes' or 'No', generally on a fifty-fifty chance. Above all, he liked it that everything was one's own fault. There was only oneself to praise or blame. Luck was a servant and not a master.

The love here is, in part, for the atmosphere of the casino – the fever and the luxury. But it is also luck itself that Bond values. Much of the time, luck is characterised as something beyond our control. But here, Bond offers up a more interesting philosophy; in his eyes, you are answerable to your own luck. If you decide to gamble, you might lose. But you choose the numbers on the roulette wheel; you choose whether to stick or to twist; you, in the end, make the call. If you lose, the bad luck is on you.

'When it comes to luck, you make your own,' Bruce Springsteen sang in 'Lucky Town'. Is it really true, that we make our own luck? It is a comforting thought, in some ways – to think that, if we do the right things, then maybe our luck will change. Goethe once said that superstition is the poetry of life. The world is full of perils, troubles and fickle fortunes. Since the beginning of civilisation, people have sought reassurance in the thought that the right rituals might fend off the demons of destiny. That rabbit's foot will bring you luck; make sure you don't break that mirror. Philosopher David Hume was disdainful about this need for superstition: 'The mind of man,' he wrote, 'is subject to certain unaccountable terrors and apprehensions ... As these enemies are entirely invisible and unknown, the methods taken to appease them are equally unaccountable, and consist in cere-monies, observances, mortifications, sacrifices, presents or in any practice, however absurd or frivolous, which either folly or knav-ery recommends to a blind and terrified credulity.'

However absurd or frivolous it might really be, though, super-stition is everywhere. Some hotels are still built without a thir-teenth floor (our fear of thirteen, the hub of many theories, is often blamed on Judas, the thirteenth guest at the Last Supper). And writers, too, could be very superstitious types. Charles Dickens never began to write unless the ornaments on his desk were arranged in a particular order. John Cheever liked to write his stories in his underpants.

In the world of sport, superstition is of course commonplace. English cricketers live in fear of Nelson, a score of 111, believed to resemble a set of stumps without the bails; in Australia there exists a parallel fear of eighty-seven, thirteen short of a century. In golf, Tiger Woods always wears a red shirt on the final day of a tournament. Before a match, tennis legend Rafael Nadal always places two water bottles to the left of his chair, one neatly behind the other, aimed diagonally towards the court. 'Some call it superstition, but it's not,' he once claimed. 'If it were superstition, why would I keep doing the same thing over and over whether I win or lose?' A cogent question, maybe – but it is just possible that Nadal is missing the point, slightly, about superstition. We know, deep down, that it's all ridiculous, absurd, and that superstitions don't actually work; the point is that we follow them anyway.

Snooker is by no means a stranger to the forces of superstition. Steve Davis embraced a whole range of them. He developed a fixation with a set of cellar doors, outside the Brown Bear pub in Sheffield, just down the street from the Crucible. In 1980 he had walked over them on his way to his victory over Terry Griffiths – clearly, they were a good-luck sign. The following year, he made sure he walked over them every day, and he ended up as world champion. After his shock 1982 first-round defeat against Tony Knowles, it was obvious where to put the blame. 'The weather was very bad,' he complained after the match. 'We had to get a taxi round to the venue and didn't actually tread on this lucky piece of board that we trod on last year. I think that's really where we went wrong. So I must apologise to the pub owner and I'll be back next year.' It was hard to tell how seriously he meant it. 'You might as well laugh,' he unlaughingly added.

In more recent times, superstitious rituals have remained widespread. Referee Paul Collier always uses the same coin to conduct his pre-match toss-up. Over the lockdowns of 2020, Neil Robertson developed a tangled, wig-like mop of curly locks; but after finding himself playing well with the new look, he worried that a haircut might lead to a Samson-like loss of powers. 'If I get my hair cut and get beat,' he said, 'then everyone will blame it on the haircut.' For several seasons, Chinese player Fan Zhengyi harboured an unusual superstitious habit of *refusing* to make century breaks; once the frame was won, if on a break of 80 or 90, he would deliberately miss. And most famously of all, there is the Crucible curse, dictating that no first-time winner will ever successfully defend their title; after nearly half a century, its spell remains unbroken.

We are never far from the folkloric myths of our elders – on the lookout for our own four-leaf clovers, wishbones or stones of jade. Luck, though, is a deity of cruel authority: it will not be appeased with gestures. Every sport has an element of luck. So much can hang not on the big calls, but on the little flicks and nudges, uncontrollable slips, bounces, near misses, bumps and flutters of fortune. In snooker, luck is everywhere: it is written into the essence of the game. Every time a player takes a shot, a roulette wheel of sorts spins somewhere, a hand of cards is dealt.

For certain shots, luck becomes almost the main factor. Whenever a player has to screw into the pack of reds – usually off the blue or off the black – the gods of luck are watching. Such shots are hard to perfect; huge amounts of skill are required to make the correct cannons, split the reds nicely, control the cue ball. But it is impossible to predict every element of the outcome. Skill only goes so far. 'That is so *unlucky*,' has become a jaded cliché of the commentary box. Balls can end up covering each other, blocking the path to the next pot. The white can stick to a red or be knocked unhappily towards the cushion. If the gods are especially upset, a red might even implausibly slide off into a pocket, resulting in a foul shot and a grief-stricken look to the heavens.

Nothing, though, quite rivals the savage jeopardy of the 'kick'. These are the true snookering *Nazgûl*, tenebrous demons of the game. To this day, they remain a mystery. They lurk like invisible landmines, impossible to predict; no one is quite sure why they happen. But happen they do, and they can wreck a player's plans, cutting them off in full flow; even a player in the most supreme form can suffer a kick and miss something simple, through no fault of their own.

What is the kick? In essence, there are occasions when, without any warning, the cue ball does not strike the object ball as it should. Instead, a bad contact occurs; at such moments the cue ball, and perhaps the object ball too, will be seen visibly to jump or kick. This almost always leads to deviation from the ball's expected angle of travel – sometimes dramatically so, the object ball slanting weirdly off target, as if beguiled by some sinister, unseen force. The curse of the kick has struck and the ball is missed.

Back in the eighties and nineties, kicks were relatively rare. But as the years went on they became more common, and the urgency of the problem escalated. 'There was a crisis point,' explained 2019 Indian Open champion Matthew Selt, 'when you'd be nervous playing certain shots.' Countless studies have been conducted. Theories have proliferated. Bits of chalk, dust particles and imperfections in the cloth of the table have all been blamed at one time or another. A consensus formed that, in truth, *all* of these can potentially cause the problem. Snooker's solution has been multi-pronged. A new kind of chalk was developed which leaves less residue on the balls. Table manufacturers developed a pioneering 'anti-kick' cloth, made with small amounts of carbon fibre. The results were rapid; in recent years, the frequency of kicks has plummeted. Still, though, they have not disappeared. Occasionally a kick will rear its head and cause some damage. The beast sleeps, but it is not yet killed.

One reason why kicks are so brutal is that they seem not to conform to James Bond's philosophy of the casino. A kick is not at all the player's fault; it appears, instead, to be a pure distillation of bad luck, with no hint of culpability involved. But luck is a reactive element. Like lithium or like radium, it is not usually found in its pure form. Much more common is a more complicated relationship between the forces of destiny and blame. Springsteen might not be entirely right – you don't *always* make your own luck – but often, to some extent, you do.

In 2006, Stephen Hendry was playing Bond in the first round at the Crucible – not James Bond, this, but Nigel Bond, a former world finalist who had once been as high as number five in the world, but whose ranking was now fixed in the ancillary ranks. Hendry's career had been in slow decline for a few years, but he was still expected to dispense with his veteran opponent. The match, though, went right down to the wire. Hendry recovered a 7–3 deficit to lead 9–8, but he could not find the fatal blow.

The deciding frame was a nerve-shredder. Everything fell to the final three balls. After Hendry missed a tough blue, Bond had his chance: he potted the blue magnificently into the middle pocket and sliced an ultra-thin pink into the corner. These were inspired, Olympian shots, more suggestive of a strutting World Champion than a wily journeyman well past his prime. Bond studied the table. He had the look of an office clerk, examining a broken photocopier. Seven points ahead, he was, with the black over the pocket. A shock victory over the god of the Crucible was right there, there for the taking.

'This is it,' observed Clive Everton in commentary. The black was no more than six inches from the top corner pocket – pretty much unmissable, even for a club player. The white was parallel, just past the middle pocket. The *only* thing Bond needed to watch was a possible in-off into the opposite middle. But Bond was an experienced campaigner. There was no way he would fall victim to something so careless. And in any case, at such an angle, only the most outlandish slice of bad luck could land him in trouble. He potted the black safely; but he'd hit it much harder than he needed to, and the white was spinning off towards the middle . . .

Hendry, who had already dismantled his cue, watched the white flop into the pocket with a baffled frown. The crowd noise was bestial, like something from a boxing match. As he sat back in his chair, Bond's face wore an amnesiac blank of shock. The scores were now level. The spectacle of a re-spotted black awaited. The odds, now, seemed heavily to favour Hendry; Bond was in such a state that, for his next couple of shots, he was hardly able to hit the ball. But he somehow managed to survive, scrambling the balls towards safe positions. In fact, it was Hendry – perhaps he had switched off mentally, presuming he was beaten – who was struggling, underhitting the ball badly. After several consecutive bungled safeties, he left Bond a clear chance of the black into the middle. 'Maybe this,' said Everton, as dozens in the crowd called out, *Go on, Nige.*

The black did not go in cleanly – it wiped its feet, as they say – but it dropped. After one of the most extraordinary fusions of carelessness and bad luck ever seen at the Crucible, Bond had gone and won the match anyway. Afterwards, he was understandably jubilant, basking in his revenge for a few 'pastings' from Hendry over the years. 'I was shaking when I potted the black the first time,' he said of the in-off. 'As soon as I hit the shot I knew the white was going in.' His opponent's post-match interview was a more laconic affair; Hendry barely managed a sentence. When asked where the defeat sat alongside others in his career, he offered an impeccably Hendrian riposte: 'Along with all the rest,' he said, before walking off.

'Life is to be lived, not controlled,' wrote Ralph Ellison in his 1952 novel *Invisible Man*. Even Shakespeare offered conflicting images of our level of control over fate. On the one hand, there is Romeo, fearing the pull of 'some consequence yet hanging in the stars'; he and Juliet are rendered as 'star-crossed lovers', apparently doomed by destiny to meet their tragic end. In contrast, Cassius in *Julius Caesar* affirms that he and Brutus have only themselves to blame for their lack of power: 'The fault, dear Brutus, is not in our stars,/But in ourselves, that we are underlings.' Had Bond's in-off been an extraordinary stroke of bad luck, or was it simply bad snooker – an error of judgement he should have been careful enough to avoid?

His narrow escape meant he did not have to spend the rest of his life brooding over the question. But the answer, in the end, is both. Luck and agency were both involved, as they so often are, in a cryptic mixture. This is the reason we are so often told that players get the 'run of the ball' when they are playing well. The cause is not some malign fiend of the baize, punishing victims at random with bad-luck thunderbolts. The run of the ball favours those whose play is better, whose touch is more precise; all the little flicks and nudges where a bit of luck is involved are more likely to go their way.

Perhaps Heraclitus was right, that our character is our fate. After all, despite the gripes from players over the years about bad karma, bad fortune, bad luck, the game's greatest player is sceptical about the significance of such things. 'I don't believe in fate,' says Ronnie O'Sullivan. 'I believe you make your own luck and your own destiny.' One feels that Ronnie and agent 007 would have got on nicely.

11

Music

Without music, life would be a mistake.
Friedrich Nietzsche, *Twilight of the Idols*, 1888

A reverence for music is a constant across all cultures. There is evidence that it predates speech itself. The bonds between language and music are rich and deep; poetry is intimately connected to song. In ancient Greece, the *aoidoi* would ritually sing lines of epic poetry. William Blake was known to sing his work to friends. Modernist kingpin Ezra Pound proposed that music was a guiding light for poetry, crucial to its life: 'Poetry begins to atrophy,' he wrote, in his *ABC of Reading*, 'when it gets too far from music.' Philosopher Arthur Schopenhauer attempted to explain music's matchless power by arguing that, uniquely, it does not point towards anything outside of itself. 'The effect of music is so very much more powerful and penetrating than is that of the other arts,' he wrote, 'for these others speak only of the shadow, but music of the essence.'

As Schopenhauer attested, music does not describe anything; other art forms might mimic truths about the world, but music embodies them. Music is purity, an acoustic manifestation of transcendence: it is the sound of the beyond. And we cannot live without it. 'Without music,' wrote poet and playwright Edna St Vincent Millay, 'I should wish to die.'

Perhaps for obvious reasons, music seems to fit poorly with snooker. In important ways, snooker is a game of silence. Players float wordlessly round the table. They do not shout; they do not call out; they do not speak to each other. In this respect, they are like dumb-show artists, silent-movie actors or dancers. In the slow snookering air, there is only the click of ball against ball, the dull thud of ball into pocket; the sound of a snooker game is soft and subdued, composed mostly of no sounds at all.

And the audience, too, sit largely in silence, huddled intently like the audience at a Shakespeare play. Anyone who does call out will be quickly silenced by the referee and perhaps even removed from the arena for improper conduct: such things as noise are for other sports, not for the baize. In the same way that snooker seemingly pushes against time, it also seems, perhaps, to push against sound; in a noise-saturated world, snooker is a quiet room, a monastery of wordless contemplation. The tension of a snooker match is the tension not of the bellowed chant or the frenzied scream, but a deeper, more primal tension – the tension of silence itself.

As we have seen, though, there was no such thing as a barrier in the mind of Barry Hearn. It was the spring of 1986; the World Championship was approaching. The previous year had seen dreamscapes unfold at the Crucible. The whole nation remembered the marvel of the black ball drama; about a third of them had stayed up to watch it. For millions, the final between Davis and Taylor had brought a tear to the eye. For Barry Hearn, it had brought the elegant, upright curves of pound signs.

He had already been developing his promotion company, Matchroom Sport, for a few years. To start with he had two players signed up. The first, of course, was Steve Davis: the crown jewel and the main attraction, the world's number one player and, by the mid-eighties, comfortably the highest-earning sportsperson in Britain. The other, more surprisingly perhaps, was Tony Meo – an old mucker and schoolmate of Jimmy White, talented for sure, but not a player who had found consistent success. He had been recruited, in part, to give Hearn's team a touch of spice, a bit of edge. 'Meo is the young crazy guy,' Hearn once explained – the perfect foil for Davis, the 'sophistique, man-about-town, aspirational sportsman'.

By early 1986, Terry Griffiths, Dennis Taylor and Willie Thorne had also joined Matchroom. It was a halcyon era for snooker – the very peak of the iridescent snooker boom. The '85 Crucible final had elevated an already popular sport into a form of British national obsession. Steve Davis, it was said, appeared on TV more than any other person besides newscasters. Since 1983, he had even been presenting A Frame with Davis, a bizarre snooker-cum-comedy-cum-chat show in which two celebrities would play a frame of snooker against each other while Davis coached them and quizzed them about their careers (eminent guests had included Norman Wisdom, Jimmy Greaves, Willie Carson and Bobby Davro). Hearn was doing all he could to ride the wave. There had been tours of the Far East, TV interviews, commercials, even a Matchroom aftershave. And now an ambitious new horizon had opened up in his mind – a fresh possible landscape for high-profile exposure and commercial success. Snooker, he thought, could venture into *pop music*.

The idea of Hearn's snooker stars up on a stage, singing some pop hits, erred on the outlandish. Snooker players, though they performed to audiences, were introspective beings. Raised in the murk of subterranean halls, speaking little to others, they appear more closely to resemble Morlocks or Calibans than pop stars. Their comfort zone is the lit, green rectangle of the table; the outside world is not their element. They are not natural stage acts. They do not, in general, enjoy the chiselled looks of boy band members or catalogue models. But as he did so often, Hearn had sensed something in the air – some possibility of seizing the moment, to channel the effervescent popularity of snooker into a surprising and profitable new direction.

Pop music in the 1980s was, among other things, a place where gaudiness, tackiness and comedy found a comfortable home. Novelty songs prospered, often making it into the upper reaches of the charts. Kids' TV show *TISWAS* spawned The Four Bucketeers, a band comprised of presenters from the show; their single, 'Bucket of Water Song,' made the Top 30 in the summer of 1980. Comedy icon Kenny Everett stormed into the Top 10 with 'Snot Rap'. The Evasions took the unlikely material of Alan Whicker's nasal narratives as the basis for their single, 'Wikka Rap'. As an accompaniment to his film *To Be or Not to Be*, Mel Brooks released 'The Hitler Rap,' a typically Brooksian masterpiece of bad-taste burlesque. Another kids' TV show, *Swap Shop*, led to the founding of Brown Sauce – a power trio of Keith Chegwin, Noel Edmonds and Maggie Philbin – whose hit single, 'I Wanna be a Winner', even included the line 'Don't wanna join Claire Francis in the riggings, pot the black with Hurricane Higgins'.

There was plenty of precedent, it turned out, for unlikely pop acts finding chart success through a novelty angle. All Hearn needed was the right musicians to help him. And it did not take him long to make the perfect choice. Chas Hodges and Dave Peacock had been on the musical scene for many years. Throughout the sixties, they had worked separately as session musicians, playing with a host of acts from Bill Haley to Jerry Lee Lewis. By the early seventies, though, Hodges had become impatient with the expectation that he follow the trend and sing in an American accent. He wanted to do something more inno-vative, risky and authentic – he wanted to sing songs in his own voice, the voice of north London where he grew up.

He and Peacock began to collaborate – initially under the name Oily Rags (rhyming slang for 'fags' – cigarettes), but then, more simply, as Chas & Dave. Across the late seventies and early eighties they had a string of hit singles. What had caught Hearn's attention, though, were the songs they had composed for Tottenham Hotspur – 'Ossie's Dream', for their FA Cup final bid in 1981, and 'Tottenham, Tottenham' the following year. Both songs made the UK Top 20; after Spurs won the FA Cup, 'Ossie's Dream' reached as high as No. 5. With their working-class roots, tongue-in-check humour and history of making successful music with non-musicians, there was no doubt – these were the right men to take snooker into the world of pop.

Hearn called; deals were done; a song began to sketch itself out. Hodges explained:

> I asked Barry to give me a rundown on each of their personalities so as to provide fuel to fire up the song. I wanted each one to have their own verse . . . Armed with all of that we set about composing a song. I'd already thought of the title which Dave liked. 'Snooker Loopy'. Now it needed their personalities put in the verses, a chorus that begins and ends with 'Snooker Loopy' and a tempo and a tune for the whole thing.

Once a demo was ready, Hearn called up Steve Davis to give him the news that they were going to make a record. 'I slumped further into my seat,' Davis recalled. 'I didn't say anything for a second. And then I announced, "Barry, I'm not doing it."' But Barry, as usual, managed to talk him round. The 'Matchroom

Mob' – Steve Davis, Tony Meo, Dennis Taylor, Terry Griffiths and Willie Thorne – were heading into the recording studio.

'Snooker Loopy' is a swaggering, rockney knees-up that might not appear in many all-time greatest song lists, but had enough catchy earworm potential to give it a chance at the charts. The words of the chorus – 'Snooker loopy nuts are we, me and him and them and me' – amiably captured the game's spectacular popularity. Chas & Dave also gave fans and followers an immortal mnemonic for the order of the colours: 'Pot the reds then screw back, for the yellow, green, brown, blue, pink and black.' And in the verses, they playfully took aim at each Matchroom Mob member, mocking their idiosyncrasies and reputations – sending them up as larger-than life caricatures, mythical heroes of the eighties cultural zeitgeist.

In the video, the Mob appeared in the studio, bobbing awkwardly in a drab assortment of granddad cardigans and woolly jumpers, mouthing the chorus with Chas at the piano and Dave on the bass. In a nod to snooker's popularity, a crowd of photographers and cameramen were assembled to capture the spectacle, filming and clicking away. In the middle of these, Hearn himself could be seen, leather-jacketed, beaming a billionaire grin.

Each verse took a mob member as its *topos*. In honour of his 'Eye-talian roots', Meo modelled a series of flash suits before appearing at a table, sucking up a strand of spaghetti. Dennis Taylor was cast in more homely fashion, eating a bowl of cornflakes in his pyjamas. Griffiths appeared in a miner's helmet. Thorne's baldness was lampooned, with the other mob members swarming round him in comedy bald wigs. Davis was forced to revisit the missed black ball of the previous year. A decision had been made, hazardously, to have the players sing the last line of the verse in which they featured, leading to some of the less tuneful moments in music history. "Cause I wear these gohhh-ggles,' Taylor croaked, wiggling his glasses at the camera. 'Perhaps I ought to chalk it,' squeaked Thorne, feigning to rub a cube of chalk on his head.

'Snooker Loopy' entered the charts at an unpromising number ninety-eight in April 1986. But then the World Championship started and it began to climb. A slot was secured on *Top of the Pops* – with Chas & Dave appearing live, but, perhaps mercifully, without the players themselves. In the middle of the 1980s, a *Top of the Pops* appearance was a very big deal indeed; the show regularly attracted well over ten million viewers. The effects were swift. 'Snooker Loopy' shot up to number eleven, and then, the next week, it was in the Top 10. Chas, Dave and the Matchroom Mob had made it to No. 6. 'I am not sure what Madonna, George Michael or Whitney Houston made of us as we climbed above them in the charts,' Davis later mused.

One of the less well-chronicled aspects of snooker's foray into pop is that there was, technically at least, a rival snooker record out there too. A snookering battle of the bands was at play, though it was not one that many people noticed. Howard Kruger – known to most as 'H' – was a promoter and agent who harboured ambitions to match the profile of Hearn's Matchroom stable. He had just signed Alex Higgins to his company, Framework. Kruger's team – a decidedly more roguish outfit of Higgins, Jimmy White, Tony Knowles and Kirk Stevens – were forged into a baize-maverick supergroup christened Four Away. Kruger sent them into the studio to record a version of 'The Wanderer'.

The iconic song has been covered countless times by a host of celebrated artists, including Bruce Springsteen, Status Quo, Bad Company and The Beach Boys; the version by Four Away is not one of the more distinguished in its history. 'We don't profess to be singers,' explained Higgins at an accompanying press conference, 'but equally, "The Wanderer" is a song that everybody knows. We've changed the words slightly, to suit our own purposes and, er, go out and buy it, that's all I can say.' Stevens chimed in with a promise that 'a world tour is planned for some time in July; and Alex wants us to go back into the studio to finish the album'. Such dreams, though, did not materialise; upon its release, 'The Wanderer' failed to chart.

In stark contrast, for Barry Hearn and Matchroom, the dramatic success of 'Snooker Loopy' had brought with it a new challenge – a follow-up single. With one Top 10 hit in the bag, another song seemed like it must be a good idea. It turned out not to be. 'Snooker Loopy' had been a solid tune – perhaps not Chas & Dave at their blasting best, but fun and a creditable piece of work. In contrast, its sequel – 'The Romford Rap' – was a disaster, an eardrum-melting nightmare of moog farts, ersatz rap, sax belches, and shudder-inducing lyrics that, despite their admirable ethos of inclusivity, have not withstood the passage of time: 'Whether you're a paddy or a taff or a jock or a jap . . . Whether you're yellow, green, brown, blue, pink or black . . . From Brixton, Bow or north of the Watford Gap . . . You can do the Romford rap.'

The video, though, was much worse – an eyeball-scorching, soul-withering horror show. The players were each made to dress in the colour of snooker balls and dance backwards and forwards, Bez-from-Happy-Mondays-style, surrounded by women in *Playboy* Bunny outfits on a mock-up of a giant snooker table. By this time, Neal Foulds and Jimmy White had joined the Matchroom crew, a decision that White was now more or less instantly regretting. The video was filmed in The Hippodrome, one of White's regular nightclub haunts, giving his experience a bleakly disorientating, bad-dream feel: 'Suddenly, there I was, in the same place in the middle of the afternoon, far too sober and far too clean. "Have we really got to do this?" I asked Barry, but he wasn't having any of it.' About a minute in, there is a close-up of White, his face a picture of misery, skin somehow even whiter than the all-white suit he had been forced to wear; you could almost see the street credibility evaporating out of him like steam from a coffee cup.

'The Romford Rap' peaked at number ninety-one in the charts, sinking, to absolutely no one's disappointment, without a trace.

Snooker's unlikely flirtation with the pop world nevertheless shows how fashionable the game really was in its 1980s heyday. A game of quiet concentration – a game, one might say, that is singularly hostile to sound – had ventured into music, and succeeded. It is also, perhaps, a reminder that things are rarely simple. Perhaps the apparent antithesis between snooker players and musical performers is not so absolute as it might at first seem. Author Gordon Burn pointed out, 'There has always been a strain of vaudeville running through snooker.' In its early days, professionals developed slick routines of trick shots and wise-cracks that they could deliver to exhibition audiences, wowing onlookers with their skills. Throughout the nineties and noughties, the (now-discontinued) World Trickshot Championship gave top players the chance to show off their best witticisms and anecdotes – revealing often surprisingly strong repartee and stage presence.

Snooker players, after all, are performers of a sort. They are used to having an audience: a watching crowd is their bread and butter. And this fact might go some way towards explaining one of the most implausible post-retirement careers in the history of British popular culture: the rebirth of Steve Davis as a thriving club DJ and recording artist.

'What you can judge,' explained Davis of his new direction, 'is how much thrill it's giving you and how proud you are. And in that respect I'm more proud of what's happened recently, maybe because it's fresher. Winning snooker events became the norm. But this is all so unexpected, beyond belief – when the snooker, in the end, *was* expected.' Davis has long been an aficionado of avant-garde music, listing cult rockers Soft Machine, alien prog-rock insurgents Magma, and art-rock experimentalist Albert Marcoeur among his inspirations. A meeting in 2006 with composer Kavus Torabi – at a Magma gig – led to a friendship that soon became a series of musical collaborations. Davis started to perform as a DJ; in 2016, he played at Glastonbury. His underground music radio show, *The Interesting Alternative Show*, has run for several years on Phoenix FM. His band with Torabi – The Utopia Strong – has yielded an album and several live recordings. There has even been a book, *Medical Grade Music*, published in 2021. It is an incredible new calling for someone who had previously made his name for being 'the non-personality who became a personality'.

Especially interesting, in Davis' musical musings, is his proposition that his snooker and his music are more closely related than it might appear. The output of The Utopia Strong is not rehearsed – they are an improvisational band. And musical improvisation is, according to Davis, similar to snooker in important ways. 'Improvising music is more like sports than actual rehearsed music, because you're in the moment,' he observed. 'You don't know what's going to happen, so you're really on the seat of your pants. I have absolutely no knowledge of playing a rehearsed piece of music, I don't know what that would be like.' It is not an obvious connection, but it is a cogent one. A snooker player is, underneath it all, a form of improvisational performer – picking up on the unpredictabilities of the table and spontaneously generating a response, moment by moment, shot by shot. A snookering century break and a Frank Zappa guitar solo might be distant cousins, but cousins they nevertheless are.

Music, then, is not entirely the enemy of snooker. A look beneath the surface reveals that it does, in fact, occupy a non-trivial place in the world of the baize. It is not to be forgotten that Peter Ebdon, too, briefly voyaged into recording artist territory, releasing a daringly tedious cover of David Cassidy's 'I Am a Clown', back in 1996. After he won the World Championship in 2016, Mark Selby performed a half-decent karaoke rendition of 'Sweet Caroline' to a crowd of friends and fans.

And in recent years, the once-austere atmosphere of the match arena itself has been invaded by music every time a player enters. Players are now greeted not just with applause, but with a rousing theme song of their choice – much like boxers or wrestlers. The temptation is to see a player's choice of walk-on music as in some way reflective of their character. O'Sullivan tends to go for 'Rock 'n' Roll Star' by Oasis. Stephen Maguire prefers the strutting hair-metal power ballad of Whitesnake's 'Here I Go Again'. For David Gilbert, interestingly, the darkly brooding 'Insomnia' by Faithless; for Shaun Murphy, the hammy cheerfulness of 'Disco Inferno' by The Trammps. Music, now, is part of the game's identity – and perhaps, in more hidden ways, it always has been.

'Everyone has a special relationship with their record collection,' said Steve Davis, who amply deserves the last word. 'It's just that mine is bigger than most.'

Colour

Colour is the touch of the eye, music to the deaf, a word out of the darkness.

Orhan Pamuk, *My Name is Red*, 2001

Our understanding of colour is shrouded in mystery. Is colour part of the real, material world? Or is it, in fact, all a matter of perception – an activity of the mind?

For thinkers across the ages, firm conclusions have proved elusive. Galileo claimed colours are 'no more than mere names so far as the object in which we place them is concerned ... they reside only in consciousness. Hence, if the living creature were removed, all these qualities would be wiped away and annihilated.' Colour perception taps into peculiar uncertainties we all have, somewhere, about how we see the world – that vague, deep-rooted suspicion that, just maybe, other people see things differently.

It is a classic pub-table question: *do we all see colours in the same way?* Is the shiny pink ball that you see on a snooker table the same kind of pink that everyone else sees? Or is it a pink specially for you, unique to the perception frameworks of your own individual mind? 'Colour,' Henri Matisse boldly said, 'helps to express light – not the physical phenomenon, but the only light that really exists, that in the artist's brain.'

A snooker table is a patch of grass. This, at least, is the reason why it is green in colour. Snooker descends from billiards, a game that can be traced back many centuries in both England and France. In his satirical poem 'Mother Hubberd's Tale', published in 1591, Edmund Spenser refers in disparaging terms to 'all thriftless games that may be found;/ With mumming and with masking all around,/with dice, with cards, with billiards'. King Louis XI owned the very first indoor billiard table in the fifteenth century; the word 'billiards' is believed to stem from the French *bille*, meaning ball and perhaps also *billette*, meaning stick. Billiards, in its turn, derived from outdoor lawn sports such as skittles and croquet. The creation of indoor tables may well have been an effort to replicate the experience of outdoor games in more controllable, rainproof conditions; for billiards – and thus, by extension, for snooker – we may have the unpredictable weather of northern Europe to thank.

No other game places colour at the heart of things quite like snooker does. One could, with some confidence, call it the quintessential game of colour. Each ball on the table has its own place, its own status and role; the green backdrop, meanwhile, faintly summons a connection to folkloric origins, the grasses and gardens of the game's ancestry. But on a snooker table, everything is more regularised than nature; the set-up is scientific and angular.

The colour aesthetics of a snooker table are both bold and abstract. There are shades of Mondrian, to a certain extent, with his stark grids of red, black, white and yellow. But perhaps closer is Kandinsky and his canvases of abstract circles. In his 'Several Circles' (1926), he presents a scattering of circles across a black backdrop, like pastel planets against the void of space. 'Colour,' he once wrote, 'provokes a psychic vibration. Colour hides a power still unknown but real, which acts on every part of the human body.'

It would be misguided to ask which ball is the *most important* on a snooker table. Such a question fails to recognise the intricate complementarity of the balls and their relationships with each other. It is undeniably true, though, that snooker players cultivate a uniquely rich, uniquely intimate rapport with the white ball. It is the only ball they are allowed to strike with the cue; there is a sense of connection, even of ownership. The white ball is an ally, a confederate, a weapon – the conduit between the player and potential points. The only ball that does not, itself, have any scoring value, the neutrality of the white perhaps renders its colour appropriate.

White has long been associated with purity and innocence. But the white – the pale full moon of the snooker table – can bring sadness too; it cannot score you points, but if it drops into a pocket, it can lose you some. The pallor of white signals sickness and even death; one thinks of Keats' lovesick knight-at-arms, 'Alone and palely loitering' in 'La Belle Dame Sans Merci', or the dead soldiers in Wilfred Owen's 'Anthem for Doomed Youth': 'The pallor of girls' brows shall be their pall'.

Perhaps, in the end, there is a darker side to the white ball. It is faceless and blank: a colour that is not really a colour at all. And everything depends on it – in snooker, the white, and what you do with it, is your only hope. In *Moby-Dick*, Herman Melville reflects on white: 'For all these accumulated associations, with whatever is sweet, and honorable, and sublime, there yet lurks an elusive something in the innermost idea of this hue, which strikes more of panic to the soul than that redness which affrights in blood.'

And red, the colour of open wounds and fresh blood, is at snooker's very core; one could claim it is the game's most critical colour, as there is not just one but fifteen red balls, a whole army. The red balls are snooker's soldiers: heroic martyrs, constantly in the business of sacrificing themselves for a player's chances. The colour's sundry associations – with love, passion, anger, warfare, danger, blood and sex – express this boldness of spirit. It is a dynamic colour; a colour of vigour and life; the colour of fire. It can evoke beauty and joy, as in Robert Burns' famous lyric, 'My love is like a red red rose/That's newly sprung in June'.

But there is a darker side to red, too; a menacing, violent quality. 'Will all great Neptune's ocean wash this blood/Clean from my hand?' wonders Macbeth after murdering Duncan. 'No, this my hand will rather/The multitudinous seas incarnadine,/Making the green one red.' In *Dracula*, Bram Stoker describes the sinister, animalistic allure of female vampires, with their red lips and red tongues:

> All three had brilliant white teeth that shone like pearls against the ruby of their voluptuous lips. There was something about them that made me uneasy, some longing and at the same time some deadly fear. I felt in my heart a wicked, burning desire that they would kiss me with those red lips . . . The girl went on her knees, and bent over me, simply gloating. There was a deliberate voluptuousness which was both thrilling and repulsive, and as she arched her neck she actually licked her lips like an animal, till I could see in the moonlight the moisture shining on the scarlet lips and on the red tongue as it lapped the white sharp teeth.

The vitality of red is both generative and destructive. In the midst of the quiet of a snooker table, there sits a triangle of wild energy. The reds are the dispensable underclass – belittled as lowest in value, but more consistently crucial than any other ball. They are the life and soul of a snooker game – eschewing airs and graces, but at the heart of everything.

The baulk colours are bonded with a loose unity – the unity of the proletariat, the disinherited. The word 'baulk' originally meant a border, or ridge of land; its presence on a snooker table really stems from billiards, where a player must periodically play shots across this line to continue their break. In snooker, the function of the baulk is less conspicuous. It does, though, operate as a kind of state line, creating a clear district for the rank-and-file Orion's belt of yellow, green and brown. It could fairly be argued that the baulk area of the table is the most neglected in snooker. With so much break-building action taking place around the black spot, the baulk end tends to remain quiet, abandoned – a disused area of urban blight and derelict streets.

This, after all, is the cheap part of town – where the real estate is accessible and affordable. It is also often a key locale for safety play, with players trying to hide the white behind the shelter of a colour or nestle it against the cushion. The baulk end, in other words, is not the romantic lead; it is the unsexy support act, the place where honest work gets done. Sorely under-appreciated in chronicles of the baize, it harbours its own particular, quiet beauty.

The yellow ball is the weakling of the six colours – a snookering runt of the litter. The links between yellow and cowardice are fitting. One thinks, too, of Malvolio in *Twelfth Night*, and his embarrassing self-mortification in yellow stockings:

> I do not now fool myself, to let imagination jade me; for every reason excites to this, that my lady loves me. She did commend my yellow stockings of late, she did praise my leg being cross-gartered; and in this she manifests herself to my love, and with a kind of injunction drives me to these habits of her liking. I thank

my stars I am happy. I will be strange, stout, in yellow stockings, and cross-gartered, even with the swiftness of putting on. Jove and my stars be praised!

One of the most famous humiliations in literature, Malvolio's choice of clothing is not a strong advert for the colour. Yellow does not evoke strength and the yellow ball could not ever call itself strong; in general, a player will only choose the yellow after a red when there is no other option for good position. Nevertheless, there can be no denying its bright, cheerful, sunny connotations. The yellow – always the lacquered, vivid yellow of freshly cooked scrambled eggs – is a ball that seems happy enough with its humble status.

The green ball has its own unique mystery. The same colour as the table, it is like a ball in disguise. Sometimes, on old or cheap TV sets, it can be difficult to see. The connotations of green are mixed; 'Beware, my lord, of jealousy,' says Iago to Othello, 'it is the green-eyed monster that doth mock the meat it feeds on.' But alongside the negative links with envy, jealousy, and sickness, green can also signal the flourishing of nature and new life, as in Blake's poem 'The Ecchoing Green':

The sky-lark and thrush,
The birds of the bush.
Sing louder around,
To the bells chearful sound.
While our sports shall be seen
On the Ecchoing Green.

With a poetic eye, the green ball might be imagined as an incarnation of natural legends and fables, channelling the Green Man of European myth or the Wild Man of the Woods. Perhaps more plausibly, though, the greenness of the green ball on the green table gives it both an anonymous feel and also a kind of functional quality – appropriate, perhaps, to the middle-ranked ball of the baulk colours. The green, one might say, is the most unassuming ball in snooker: quiet, modest and ordinary.

The brown, captain of the baulk team, can count itself unlucky to be brown. It is not a colour with the most auspicious associations. Sitting as it does, though, in the very middle of the baulk line, it commands a certain amount of authority. Worth four points, its value is far from trivial; for this reason, it is the colour a player will most often select when forced to play a baulk colour. Beleaguered by fecal overtones, the brown is never likely to escape its scatological destiny as the butt of ignoble snookering jokes. But it is important to note that the brown also evokes earthiness and reliability. It is a serious colour, with serious connections. A 'brown study' – a phrase sadly fallen out of use – once signified a mood of deep, melancholy contemplation: 'I fell into a brown study as I walked on,' narrates Dickens' David Copperfield, 'and a voice at my side made me start.' The brown ball hovers ambiguously between the grave and the comical, an enigmatic ball of conflicting meanings.

In the very middle of a snooker table sits the blue. No other area of the table is so free or so open. It is the perfect place for the blue, with its accompanying connotations of vast oceans and expansive skies. Blue, after all, is the symbol of freedom, the *liberté* of the tricolour. And there is a friendly, benign feel to snooker's blue zone. It is often a helpful resort for a player who has lost position elsewhere. A straight or near-straight blue into either of the middle pockets is, probably, the easiest shot in snooker. This helps to create a feeling of ease and comfort in its neighbourhood; it is not the place where the sharpest difficulties, or biggest disasters, are likely to occur.

The air of optimism is fitting; in polls and surveys across the world, blue is consistently people's favourite colour. Artist Yves Klein, famed for his obsession with blue, eloquently offered the following explanation of its power: 'Blue has no dimensions, it is beyond dimensions, whereas the other colours are not . . . All colours arouse specific associative ideas, psychologically material or tangible, while blue suggests at most the sea and sky, and they, after all, are in actual, visible nature what is most abstract.' Blue thus sits prettily at the table's heart; pleasant, popular and welcoming. Its wintry associations with sadness and sorrow fade into the background; it is the sunny side of blue that snooker's blue ball seems to evoke, perched in the middle of things, the blue star around which all else revolves.

The pink ball is hot stuff: chic and sexy. It sits atop its pyramid of reds with the lush shine of a frothing strawberry milkshake. This is where the serious end of snooker begins, the zone of big breaks and proper, heavy scoring. The colour has long evoked sophistication and elegance; Degas' ballet dancers were often painted pink. It is a sensual colour – a colour of sugary sweets, of neon, glitz and pop. Warhol used it endlessly, producing a pink Marilyn Monroe, a pink Neil Armstrong, even a pink Mao Zedong.

'I believe in pink,' said Audrey Hepburn, connecting the colour to the fizz and the pleasure of life. 'I believe that laughing is the best calorie-burner. I believe in kissing, kissing a lot. I believe in being strong when everything seems to be going wrong. I believe that happy girls are the prettiest girls. I believe that tomorrow is another day and I believe in miracles.' The pink, in short, is fun – sparkly and alive, brimming with zesty allure.

But the king of snooker balls . . . this is a matter beyond doubt. While a hierarchy of importance might be wrong, there most certainly is a hierarchy of power and, at its summit, the black ball reigns supreme. The game's most valuable asset, worth a princely seven points, it is the powerhouse on which all the highest ambitions converge, the ball all players pursue as the central pillar of their breaks. The black brims with both triumph and tragedy. It has yielded some of the great moments of snooker joy, from Dennis Taylor's immortal late-night coup to the exalted honours board of maximum breaks; but it has also brought exquisite pain, from Davis' missed Crucible black, to Hendry's missed Masters black, to the missed blacks of Ken Doherty and Thepchaiya Un-Nooh on the precipice of 147s.

It can be the colour of emptiness – dark and threatening, like the black void yawning outside the windows of Edward Hopper's *Automat*. At the same time, it is also the colour of mystery and intrigue. It is the yin to the yang of the white ball, the two balls occupying opposing poles in the poised symphony of snooker. After all, for all its focus on colour, snooker is, at its core, an intricate waltz of black and white – the totality of light's full spectrum, balanced against light's absence; two shades of conflicting purity, beyond the end of colour itself. As Coco Chanel deftly put it, 'Women think of all colours except the absence of colour. I have said that black has it all. White, too. Their beauty is absolute. It is the perfect harmony.'

What, though, about the purple ball in snooker? And the orange ball, too? These questions are not quite as unhinged as they might sound.

In the 1950s, Joe Davis was growing frustrated with the increasing mastery of the game shown by top players. The game was in the doldrums – it needed an injection of new life. And so Davis came up with 'Snooker Plus' – a variant that brought two additional balls to the table. There was now an orange ball – worth eight points – between the blue and the pink; and there was a purple ball – worth ten points – between the blue and the brown. Part of the point was that, to make a maximum break, things were much more difficult – a player needed to navigate up and down from one end of the table to the other to pot the purple after every red. A maximum was now an eye-watering 210, if anyone could ever reach it . . . in the end, though, no one ever did. Snooker Plus did not catch on. In contrast to Davis' hopes that the game would be more challenging, in fact it was far too easy; with so many colour options on the table, it was near-impossible for a player to run out of position.

And, looking back now, there is something unpleasant, even grotesque about the look of a Snooker Plus table. The orange and purple simply do not belong. The table is too crowded; the aesthetic has been spoiled. The equilibrium of snooker must be left just how it is. Snooker is indeed the quintessential game of colour – and its canvas of colour is perfect, an immaculate masterpiece of red, yellow, green, brown, blue, pink and black, in a peaceful bath of green.

13

INTERNATIONALISM

National literature does not mean much these days; now is the age of world literature.

> Johann Wolfgang von Goethe, in *Conversations with Goethe*, Peter Eckermann, 1836

'It's all about social media and money. These days they all seem so lazy.'

This was the judgement of the 'Belgian Bullet', Luca Brecel, on the eve of the 2022 World Championship. He was responding to the fact that, for the first time ever, not a single British player under thirty was seeded at the Crucible as a top-sixteen player. According to Brecel, they only had themselves to blame. Their attitude was lousy. As a result, the young talent reaching the top was no longer coming from Britain, as evidenced by Brecel's own rise up the rankings.

Ronnie O'Sullivan chimed in with a similar sentiment. He criticised a lack of focus in younger British players. 'A lot of these kids are on their phone chatting and whatever, and I think that is not really the way to approach your work or your sport,' he said. 'That is time to switch the phone off, engage in what you are doing and focus for that period of time. You can't really do that if you're on your phone checking Instagram, Twitter, Facebook or wherever it is they do.'

The empire, perhaps, is crumbling. Such comments hint at the possibility of an international takeover. With the British grip on the game weakening and with vast new audiences having opened up across the world, maybe now is the time for the ascendancy of truly global snooker. It is an unexpected journey for a game that, for much of its history, was a peculiarly British pursuit.

Snooker was a creation of the British army in the clubhouses of the late Victorian Raj. Off-duty officers would routinely entertain themselves round the billiard table with a range of gambling games. There was 'life pool', there was 'black pool' and, notably, there was a game called 'pyramids', involving a familiar-sounding triangle of fifteen reds. According to Clive Everton, 'every time a player potted a red, all his opponents paid across the agreed stake money per ball'. But it was Colonel Sir Neville Chamberlain who, in the 1870s, developed these various games by adding other coloured balls to the mix. Initially, the yellow, green, pink and black were brought in; the brown and the blue came later. As a betting game, the new formula was immediately popular. All it needed was a name.

For some time, first-year cadets had been referred to as '*neux*'; for reasons that are not fully clear, this became corrupted to 'snooker' (though there is a traceable logic here – '*les neux*', phonetically pronounced, morphing over time to 'snooks' and then 'snooker'). Towards the end of his life, Chamberlain gave an interview in which he explained how 'snooker', once a teasing term for army newbies, ended up as the name for the game he had invented:

> The term was a new one to me but I soon had the opportunity of exploiting it when one of our party failed to hole a coloured ball which was close to a corner pocket. I called out to him, 'Why, you're a regular snooker.'

I had to explain to the company the definition of the word and to soothe the feelings of the culprit I added that we were all, so to speak, snookers at the game so it would be very appropriate to call the game 'snooker'. The suggestion was adopted with enthusiasm and the game has been called snooker ever since.

By the end of the century, the game had been brought back to England. The story of snooker had well and truly begun.

It remained, though, an obscure game for many more years – it was generally eclipsed by billiards, which was still seen as the more serious, more respectable choice. It was not until 1919 that the first set of official snooker rules were drawn up. In 1927, the inaugural Professional Championship of Snooker took place across scattered English venues, from London to Nottingham to Liverpool, with the final held in Camkin's Hall, Birmingham. This event is now recognised as the first ever World Championship. There was, though, not a single player involved outside the British Isles; the development of snooker as a global game had not yet gathered steam. And no one was able seriously to compete with Joe Davis, the four-time billiards-champion-turned-snookering-colossus, who consistently towered over everyone else in the game's early decades – winning the initial 1927 tournament and then triumphing another fourteen times, before retiring undefeated from World Championship snooker in 1946.

In these formative years of snooker, Britain emphatically remained the sport's hub. The majority of events were held in Britain; the World Championship was based in Britain (and would remain so until 1965); the majority of top players were British. But the game was steadily expanding elsewhere – especially in Commonwealth countries like Canada, South Africa, Australia and New Zealand.

There is, from this era, an oubliette of lost names, overseas players who have largely faded beyond memory but who deserve their own place in snooker history. There was New Zealander Murt O'Donoghue, for instance – the first player ever to clear the table from their opening shot and also the first to make a maximum break – though it was not officially recognised, as it was not on a standard table. Australia produced a formidable snooker force in the form of Horace Lindrum, who ran Joe Davis close in three world finals before triumphing himself in 1952. However, the integrity of his title is hotly contested, since most top players had broken off to play in a 'Professional Match-Play Championship' after a clash with the game's authorities. Technically – if not undisputedly – Lindrum was the first overseas world snooker champion.

The post-war period is justly famed as a doldrums era for snooker. Management of the game was chaotic. Only a small pool of professionals played – as few as six, by the early 1960s. Competition was so sparse that, for several years, the World Championship switched to a 'challenge' format between just two players. And yet the international dimension of the game somehow remained alive, with tours to South Africa and Australia. The first three World Amateur Championships took place in the exotic locales of Calcutta, Karachi and Sydney. And a pool of talent continued to develop outside Britain. In the 1965 challenge final, South African Fred van Rensburg faced up against the dominant force of the sixties, John Pulman, though it turned out to be a one-sided affair. And in 1968 – the last year of the challenge format – the losing finalist against Pulman was a doughty Australian by the name of Edward Francis Charlton.

'Steady' Eddie Charlton became, arguably, the original overseas player of snooker's golden age. An impressive sporting all-rounder in his youth – gifted at cricket, boxing, football, tennis, surfing, and speed roller-skating – he had begun his career in snooker's dark days. But as the glitzy, colour-TV, *Pot Black* era arrived, he remained a leading figure – part of the first generation of snooker players to become true household names.

Charlton, though, was hardly an obvious star. A creaking tortoise of mind-numbing deliberation and interminable safety, his brand of snooker was infamously defensive even in an era when safety was the norm. Every one of his movements appeared to be in slow motion – from the way he lined up his shots, to the way he chalked his cue, to the way he crept round the table – as if he had been jabbed with tranquillisers, or was running out of battery. This, though, became a curious part of his charm – his freakish caution gave him an odd anti-charisma, turning him into the sort of secretly loved cartoon villain that everyone pretended to hate. Three times a world finalist, Charlton was never a true great, but he remains an affectionately remembered, old-school combatant. For many years he was talked about as perhaps Australia's best-ever player, although this claim, in the end, turned out to have a limited shelf life.

As snooker boomed in the 1970s, the game continued to function at two contradictory levels – as a British sport, with its management and infrastructure based in Britain, and as an international game, with a significant degree of worldwide appeal. While the majority of top players continued to come from the British Isles, a handful of international players found some success. There was Perrie Mans from South Africa – famed for his brilliant potting and abject positional play, who won the 1979 Masters without making a fifty break. There was Warren Simpson from Australia, who made it to the final of the 1971 World Championship. But the overseas reach of snooker was best embodied in this era by a string of Canadians – Cliff

Thorburn, Bill Werbeniuk, Kirk Stevens and Jim Wych – who provided the sport with a healthily global aura, as well as plenty of character.

Canada had been a snookering seedbed for some years, with as many as 200,000 people playing the game across the country's 2,500 pool rooms. It was a shady scene, for sure, as Canadian novelist Mordecai Richler has explained – stuffed with hustler sleaze and sticky-fingered gangsters, 'thieving peddler[s]' and 'small-time pornographer[s]'. And the Canadians who joined the professional ranks reflected this colourful culture. There was Thorburn, the scarred streetfighter, whose resolve had been toughened by vicious hardship, uncertain days when he had to hustle and win just to afford a bed for the night. There was Werbeniuk, the larger than life, ale-swigging reveller. There was Stevens, the wild and unpredictable hedonist, with his Hollywood hair and all-white suits, his distinctive air of danger and caprice. And there was Wych, the support act and the straight man, a complementary figure of phlegmatic calm. Eyebrows were raised in 1980 when Thorburn, Stevens, and Wych all made the Crucible quarter finals, meaning that – together with Charlton – half the line-up was from overseas.

But it was Thorburn, the brooding baize strategist, who stood out from the others as Canada's finest player. His 1980 Crucible victory was a watershed moment in snooker's journey towards internationalism. And the difficulties he overcame, as a non-British player, are not to be underestimated. In his early experiences of UK tournaments, he struggled to adapt to the alien conditions: the tables played differently, the balls were a lot heavier and the pockets were tighter. On the eve of his first-ever world final in 1977, a friend from back home accidentally phoned him up at five in the morning after miscalculating the time difference. The constant transatlantic journeys were gruelling and exhausting; it took Thorburn a long time, and deep reserves of effort, to reach his goal of glory. But reach it he did. On 5 May 1980, the world title was his. And it is no surprise that, in the immediate wake of victory, he was quick to highlight the challenges he had faced.

'It's very difficult, to play in front of Alex Higgins' home crowd,' he explained, looking out at the audience with his sad, blue eyes, before offering a generous appraisal of his opponent. 'I just hope you stick with him, because he's the biggest draw in the game of snooker today.' As Thorburn smilingly posed with the lid of the Crucible trophy as a makeshift hat – a rare moment of flippancy – it seemed that snooker might be in the middle of a sea-change, on the cusp of a new, more vigorously global era. But this was something of a false dawn. Even back in Canada, Thorburn's victory failed to lift the game's profile in any dramatic way. Over there, snooker still endured an image problem, with 'neither the Canadian media nor the Canadian public regarding snooker as a bona fide sport'. The game continued to be stigmatised as socially suspect and disreputable.

As snooker swelled towards its mid-1980s peak, Britain very much remained its home town. A peculiar chemical reaction was being realised between snooker and British culture. The qualities snooker brought with it – of slow-paced, cosy, televisual comfort – blended with a jewel cabinet of long-held, much-cherished British rituals: the sacred consolations of tea and toast, living room, snug TV, rain outside, putting-the-kettle-on everydayness. The soothing routines of home were, if anything, made more vital by the sharp edges of Thatcherism and its double-edged brew of entrepreneurial enterprise and growing inequality. 'There was that huge communal experience in television,' producer John Lloyd has observed. 'In some ways, that was the hallmark of the decade.' Nineteen-eighties Britain was the perfect place for snooker to flourish. Across the living rooms of the nation, Britain was hooked.

The identity of snooker retained a kind of schizophrenic quality, somehow existing both as a British institution and as a game with some enduring international tentacles. Overall, British dominance continued – although it would, in fact, be more accurately described as British and Irish dominance. The issue was in some ways more about geography than nationhood, and the practicalities of surviving a professional calendar of tournaments based in one specific corner of the world. Ireland retained a thriving snooker culture, as amply demonstrated by Ken Doherty's 1997 World Championship victory – the first overseas champion since Thorburn, albeit another from the British Isles and so geographically proximate to the snookering mothership.

A scattering of international names came and went, some of them minor, some making a more significant mark. There was Bob Chaperon, also from Canada, who emerged from nowhere to win the 1990 British Open and who faded just as quickly back into obscurity. There was Dene O'Kane from New Zealand, a former magician, who used to practise meditation from the guru Maharishi between each frame. There was Alain Robidoux, the dour French Canadian, who became best known for a bitter Crucible encounter against Ronnie O'Sullivan, in which he claimed his opponent's left-handed play was disrespectful. There was Tony Drago of Malta, famed for his phenomenal speed, and still the author of the fastest-ever century in a professional match. And there were two players from south-east Asia, an area of the world where the game was just starting to catch fire – James Wattana from Thailand and Marco Fu from Hong Kong, both of whom became multiple ranking-event winners.

Still, though, no player from beyond the British Isles had been able to claim a position as the world's very best. Would the international revolution ever really emerge? Could snooker's centre of gravity ever truly shift?

Unemployed in Melbourne some time in early 2003 was a young snooker player by the name of Neil Robertson. At this point, his fledgling career was in ruins. He had recently dropped off the professional tour for a third time and he was witness to an ugly altercation:

> I was in the queue at the job centre. I had no other option. I didn't have any qualifications having left school at fifteen . . . I didn't really want to do anything and didn't know what I was going to do. I remember being in there, and there was this guy kicking off at the counter because they weren't going to pay him . . . He was kicking off, swearing, saying, 'Fuck this,' 'Fuck that.' I was like, 'Oh my God, is this my life ahead?'

The moment was a significant turning point not just in the life of Robertson, but in the history of twenty-first-century snooker. He simply could not accept the future he stared into – a grimly snookerless future. He promptly turned round and walked out. A few months later, he was holding aloft the World Under-Twenty-One Snooker Championship trophy, an accolade that came with an even more precious prize: a wildcard spot, back on the tour.

Robertson had grown up in a 1990s snooker culture that might seem surprisingly rich, given the few Australians who made it to the professional ranks. Cue sports were big. There was a strong amateur game. 'Snooker was really popular in Australia,' he explained. 'It was before the times of satellite television . . . the participation rate was really high.' Eddie Charlton remained a national icon: in 1993, he had been inducted into the Sport Australia Hall of Fame. And Robertson, whose father owned a Melbourne snooker club, quickly made a name for himself on the cue sports scene. He won the Australian Under-Eighteen snooker championship at the age of just fourteen. Just two years later he turned professional. But Australia was a very long way indeed from the sport's hub. In order to make it, it was clear what he had to do. He had to move to England.

Robertson's early experiences abroad are not exactly the best advert for life in Britain. 'I moved to Leicester in 2002, absolutely hated it and was convinced I didn't want to be any part of the game,' he has said. 'I just thought, I can't live in this country coming from Melbourne. No disrespect to Leicester, but it's not Melbourne.' It is pretty clear that, in these tough formative years, he did not exactly develop a love for his adopted country; England, he notes, is 'a very depressing kind of country if things aren't going well for you'. His candid descriptions of loneliness, isolation and displacement reveal just how difficult it is to forge a career on the other side of the world, thousands of miles from home. After he left the tour he was forced to return to Australia. 'As an overseas player – many have fallen victim to it before – with the homesickness, struggling to feel as though you're really making a life for yourself,' he explained. 'You have to restart everything. You have to find new friends.' In order to succeed, he would need to sacrifice everything. And so he did.

After his Damascene job-centre moment in 2003, Robertson did not look back. He burst into the world's top sixteen within two seasons. The trophies started to pile up: first the Grand Prix, then the Welsh Open, then the Bahrain Championship, then the Grand Prix again. In 2010, he made it all the way to the Crucible final, where his opponent was former champion and tough-as-leather scrap-merchant Graeme Dott. It was never going to be an easy match. But Robertson increasingly took control of it, building an overnight lead and eventually easing away to win 18–13.

The response in Australia was overwhelming. The story was plastered across the front pages. OUR BOY POTS BLACK ON CUE, ran the headline in the Adelaide *Advertiser*. ROBERTSON'S VICTORY PUTS A SPORT BACK IN THE FRAME, claimed the *Sydney Morning Herald*. He was soon all over Australian TV – appearing on *Cup Fever*, *Wide World of Sports* and even a talent show called *Red Faces* (where he was tentatively introduced as the winner of the 'world billiards championship'). In one stroke, he had become his country's new sporting superstar. Before July was out, he was back home in Melbourne, proudly parading the Crucible trophy around the MCG stadium in front of over 80,000 AFL fans.

Beyond any shadow of a doubt, Neil Robertson is the greatest overseas player in the history of snooker. He has now collected nearly two dozen ranking titles. In 2014, he became the first player to make a hundred centuries in a single season. He has won the UK championship three times and the Masters twice. In 2019, a trio of snooker pundits – Dave Hendon, Alan McManus and Hector Nunns – judged him to be the eighth greatest player of all time. But despite the dazzling success, there are still plenty of indications that life as an Antipodean snooker player is not exactly a picnic: he is, almost always, away from home. At their worst, the crowds treat him as such.

In February 2022, at the Players Championship, Robertson tweeted, 'While it's true it's tough support wise being an Aussie here playing snooker in the UK, tonight was utterly ridiculous. The same guy mouthing F off and sticking 2 fingers at me as I was breaking off at 9-5. He was absolutely smashed and not sure how they kept serving him.'

This kind of boorish idiocy does at least underline the true nature of Robertson's achievement. As an Australian in a British-based game, forging his career on the other side of the planet from his home, his friends and his family, there is a strong case to make that his is the most extraordinary career snooker has ever seen. Robertson takes his meals in a well-deserved seat at the topmost table of immortal snookering legends. His remarkable success has crucially progressed the internationalism of the game towards becoming a truly global, twenty-first-century sport.

It is not actually in Australia, though, that the game has really exploded. The international explosion has certainly happened – in a very big way. But it has happened somewhere else.

The Chinese snooker boom had been brewing for a long time. One might even trace its origins all the way back to the 1980s, when Barry Hearn organised his Matchroom tours of the Far East, where the appetite for snooker was already keen. In those early days, though, it was more about developing a fanbase for commercial gain than the discovery of new playing talent. The first-ever ranking tournament to be held in China, the 1990 Asian Open in Guangzhou, featured no Chinese players. There was one player from Hong Kong – Franky Chan – who performed creditably, making it through to the last sixteen. But for many years, the much-talked-about popularity of snooker in China did not really translate into the emergence of top professionals. Millions played it, millions watched it, but what China lacked was a snookering figurehead – someone they could believe in as a true potential champion.

Ding Junhui was a prodigy of once-in-a-generation brilliance. By his mid-teens, he was already dominating the game in Asia. In 2005, just two days after his eighteenth birthday, he lifted his first ranking trophy – the China Open – beating Stephen

Hendry in the final. Viewing figures in China had been in the region of 110 million. Right from the start, Ding was a radiant presence, thrilling to watch: a graceful poet of the baize. He was instantly talked about as a future world champion, destined to become a snookering great. His game was centred around a combination of sensational potting ability and a level of scientific positional precision that made his clearances of the table look not just easy, but inevitable – flawless in every detail, as if they had been carefully written out in advance.

'The best compliment I can give him,' Hendry once said, 'is that there are only two or three players in the world who – when you're sitting there – you consistently think you're not going to get back to the table.'

Ding swiftly established himself as one of the world's leading players, amassing an intimidating haul of trophies – in the 2013/14 campaign, he equalled Hendry's record of five ranking victories in one season, a streak that included three tournaments in a row. But carrying a whole nation's hopes on one's shoulders is a heavy burden; too much, perhaps, for anyone. Despite his success, a sense of fragility has always hovered over Ding. He has often seemed younger than his years, a precocious but vulnerable greenhorn in an unforgiving world.

The 2007 Masters final was especially hard to watch, with Ding reduced to tears as Ronnie O'Sullivan steadily dismantled him. It was not the snooker, though, that made it such a disturbing spectacle. The match was blighted with sinister intimations of racial abuse – a member of the crowd allegedly calling out, 'Go home to China,' between frames. After it was all over, O'Sullivan was seen putting an arm round Ding and whispering words of consolation, as someone was booted from the theatre to an ugly chorus of boos. Ding collapsed back into his chair, dabbing his eyes with a towel.

'If you're in another country, coming over here,' said Steve Davis euphemistically in the studio, 'it's always been a very vociferous crowd at Wembley.' It was a troubling scene, and a grim reminder of what overseas players sometimes have to face.

The career of Ding Junhui is not really one story, but two. On the one hand, it is a story of consistent top-flight success, involving fourteen ranking victories, over six hundred centuries, half a dozen maximum breaks and two brief periods as world number one – the story, in short, of the most successful player China has ever produced. At the same time, though, it is a story of unrealised dreams. Ding is a player of world champion class who has not yet managed to be world champion – whose worst performances have tended to happen at the Crucible, where he has only ever managed to reach one final. He still, of course, has a chance: but in 2022, he dropped out of the top sixteen for the first time in fifteen years, and time, increasingly, is against him. As things stand, he is Jimmy White's most formidable rival for one of the least coveted honours in snooker – that of the greatest player never to be world champion.

Perhaps Ding's time will come. In any case, whatever lies ahead, there is no doubt that his career has been momentous and transformational. Ding is a titanic pioneer of Chinese snooker. When he won his first ranking tournament in 2005, there were only two Chinese players on the tour; now there are twenty-two. And not only that: the avalanche of Chinese snookering winners, long predicted by players and pundits, has begun to emerge as a reality.

A stream of talented Chinese players have followed in his wake: Xiao Guodong, Liang Wenbo, Cao Yupeng and Tian Pengfei. But the next Chinese player to threaten really consistent success took the unexpected shape of Yan Bingtao. In a time when snooker increasingly favours all-out attack, Yan is a fascinating throwback to a different age; his penchant for slow pace, extended safety and percentage play conjures the venerable ghosts of Thorburn, Griffiths and even Charlton. 'Yan is a brilliant player and he has an old head on young shoulders,' John Higgins has said. And Higgins should know: in January 2021, Yan overhauled him with spectacular maturity and composure to become Masters champion at the age of twenty. A youngster with all the craft and nous of a veteran, Bingtao is a real contender to become the first Chinese world champion.

In 2021, though, a serious rival abruptly appeared. Zhao Xintong had been talked about for some time as a precocious talent, without making much of an impact. But in the early rounds of the 2021 UK championship, O'Sullivan made some bold claims about his potential: 'I think he's amazing,' he said. 'I think he's our Federer. I've never seen a more talented snooker player.' These were strong words to use about someone who had only ever made it to one ranking semi-final. But the comment operated like a Delphic prophecy, as if O'Sullivan, the godlike snooker sage, had somehow mystically known what would unfold in the days to come. Zhao breezed past Jack Lisowski in the quarters, then Barry Hawkins in the semis and – in an all-overseas final – against Luca Brecel, he strolled to the title in apparently effortless fashion. In the space of a few days, Zhao had gone from fringe player to bright new star of the sport.

And there was one particular player that Zhao reminded everyone of, with his eye-catching left-handed technique, his willowy speed round the table, the elegant simplicity of his cue action and his all-for-nothing attacking play; it was just like watching a young Jimmy White. Any comparison with such a snookering icon is a serious business. But the resemblances were striking, even spooky. Even White himself agreed: 'He is like me as a young lad. He has the same mannerisms: he sees a pot, goes for a pot. He is a little bit dangerous, but that is the way he wants to play.' Zhao proved his UK victory was no fluke by winning the German Masters a few months later; and in many people's eyes, he is now the favourite to be the first Chinese world champion.

O'Sullivan certainly thought so. 'I rate that Xintong better than all of them,' he has said. 'He's unbelievably talented but he just don't know the game. I spent a bit of time on the practice table. He's clearing the colours up, pots the brown and he's not even near the blue, he's near the cushion. I said, "That's not acceptable, mate, you should be getting whips." I tried to explain to him to try and get near to the ball. Just better positional play. He's a quick learner and he got it; it's just little things like that he needs to improve. But I rate him. Very, very good.'

The twentieth century was widely heralded as the American century; and in its turn, the twenty-first century has increasingly been mooted as the Chinese century. A 2020 report from the Centre for Economics and Business Research predicted the Chinese economy will overtake that of the United States before the end of the 2020s. And, alongside the Chinese economic boom, a magisterial Chinese snooker boom has taken place – one that has shaken the game into inconceivable new territory. The 2016 World Snooker Championship was watched by a Chinese audience of 210 million people. A brave new world is upon us. As David Bowie once said, tomorrow belongs to those who can hear it coming.

And the Chinese boom has itself helped to expand snooker's international reach. Recent estimates of worldwide TV audiences are in the region of no less than 400 million. Such numbers are staggering, unimaginable. The sport has been changed beyond recognition – the days of old-school Anglophone snooker, as the province of smoke-steeped,

INTERNATIONALISM

booze-drenched billiard halls, have been bluntly cast into the wastebasket of history. Snooker has leapt headlong into the twenty-first century: the present moment is, without any doubt, the most vibrant era that the game has seen. The future stretching ahead is one in which snooker will no longer be seen simply as a British game with international elements; instead, it will take its rightful place alongside the other great global sports.

And there is little doubt that China will be at the heart of this journey. The identity of the first Chinese world snooker champion remains, at present, unknown. But they will come: and not just one, but many. The future lies ahead, and it is a future of exhilarating internationalism – a snooker without boundaries.

14

WOMEN

But I hate to hear you talking so, like a fine gentleman, and as if women were all fine ladies, instead of rational creatures. We none of us expect to be in smooth water all our days.

Jane Austen, *Persuasion*, 1817

In 1871, twelve years after *On the Origin of Species*, Charles Darwin developed his revolutionary ideas in *The Descent of Man, and Selection in Relation to Sex*. Here, his focus was more comprehensively on human beings, and on the role of sexual selection in our evolution. In chapter nineteen – 'Sexual Secondary Characters of Man' – he attempted to sketch out some key differences between the sexes. 'Man,' he claimed, 'is more courageous, pugnacious and energetic than woman, and has a more inventive genius.' And he did not stop there:

The chief distinction in the intellectual powers of the two sexes is shewn by man's attaining to a higher eminence, in whatever he takes up, than can woman – whether requiring deep thought, reason, or imagination or merely the use of the senses and hands. If two lists were made of the most eminent men and women in poetry, painting, sculpture, music (inclusive both of composition and performance), history, science, and philosophy, with half a dozen names under each subject, the two lists would not bear comparison … if men are capable of a decided pre-eminence over women in many subjects, the average of mental power in man must be above that of woman.

It was not the only moment in Darwin's career when his views on gender were of the sort that would today raise an eyebrow. Earlier in his life, he had made a series of notebook entries on the pros and cons of marriage: 'Home, & someone to take care of house— Charms of music & female chit-chat.— These things good for one's health.— but terrible loss of time.' A wife, he noted, was an 'object to be beloved and played with. Better than a dog anyhow.'

With a generous eye, one might say that Darwin's views are unsurprisingly – even inevitably – characteristic of a Victorian male perspective. For all his revolutionary thinking, his views on gender – the attribution of a 'higher eminence' to men; the belief that artistic achievement should be ascribed not to opportunity, but natural capability – were resolutely nineteenth-century.

Man … has a more inventive genius. There is exquisite irony in the fact that, in the same year Darwin published these words, George Eliot published the opening instalment of *Middlemarch*. A towering masterpiece, the novel is now widely recognised as a supreme high-water mark in the history of English literature. 'It is possible to argue,' noted A. S. Byatt, 'that *Middlemarch* is the greatest English novel.' Eliot even satirised male intellectual arrogance in the character of Sir James Chettam, who haughtily ruminates on the superiority of the male mind: 'Man's mind – what there is of it – has always the advantage of being masculine – as the smallest birch tree is of a higher kind than the most soaring palm and even his ignorance is of a sounder quality.'

The world of sport in Victorian England was a hostile place for women. Plenty of stories from the era make this abundantly clear. Around the very time that Colonel Neville Chamberlain was laying the foundations for the game of snooker, some brave women were trying their best to pioneer English ladies' football.

It did not go smoothly. Matches could hardly begin before a misogynistic mob turned up to protest. Even the reporting press seemed far from convinced that women's football was a good idea. In June 1881, the *Manchester Guardian* reported:

> The score or so of young women who do not hesitate to gratify vulgar curiosity by taking part in what is termed a 'ladies' football match appeared last evening for the second time this week on the ground of the Cheetham Football Club, Tetlow Fold, Great Cheetham Street. The Club, however, had nothing to do with the affair . . . The players, attired in a costume which is neither grace- ful nor very becoming, were driven to the ground in a wagon- ette . . . Play – if kicking the ball about the field can be so described – was commenced pretty punctually.

The implications here – of the whole enterprise being *wrong*, of football being fundamentally inappropriate for women – are clear enough.

The match, in any case, did not last the distance. After about an hour, an angry mob invaded the field:

> At length, a great rush was made by those occupying the higher land, and the football ground was speedily taken possession of by the mob. Apprehending a repetition of the rough treatment they have met with in other parts of the country, the women no sooner heard the clamour which accompanied the rush than they also

took to their heels and ran to where the wagonette was standing. This they reached before the crowd could overtake them and amid the jeers of the multitude and much disorder they were immediately driven away.

Reports like this provide an ominously sharp insight into the Victorian sporting climate. Ladies' football, it seemed, simply could not happen without a riot taking place. As a result of such incidents, women's football disappeared from England for over a decade.

From the beginning, in other words, women's sport has faced significant struggles for its very existence. And snooker culture has not, traditionally, been especially female-friendly. Encoded in the customs of cigarettes-and-alcohol bar-room badinage is a sense that the snooker table is not a place for women. The working men's clubs, snooker's real cultural hub before the TV boom, often did not allow women as members – although they were usually allowed in as 'associates'. Lynette Horsburgh has written vividly about what it was like as a woman in the amateur game during the early nineties. In one match, at Fleetwood Conservative club, the start time was arranged at the crack of dawn so that it could take place before the committee members arrived. 'The club,' she explained, 'had a line across the room separating the bar from the tables and women usually weren't allowed to cross it, let alone play.'

But it got worse. On other occasions, she faced the sort of open hostility that recalled the ghosts of Victorian-era sexism:

Talbot Conservatives might have allowed me to compete but it was a different story with about six clubs in the first division of the Fylde League, which adamantly refused to let me play. I remember my team captain had been assured I would be able to play in our game at Cleveleys Working Men's Club. But when I arrived for the match, cue in hand, I faced a load of men shouting in disgust, 'It's a woman!' Shortly after, I was led out and told I could come back on New Year's Eve if I wanted to play there.

Any woman attempting a career in snooker clearly had their work cut out. 'There are not many women in top-flight snooker,' wryly observed Gordon Burn in the mid-1980s. And it is perhaps not difficult to understand why.

Nevertheless, the story of women's snooker is a story of survival against the odds, often in the most inhospitable of climes. The earliest competition – the Women's Professional Snooker Championship – ran from 1934 through to 1950. Ruth Harrison was the supreme force, winning every single one of the first eight tournaments. Daughter of a County Durham coal miner, it is not easy to find details about her life, which in itself tells us something. There are some surviving images of her at the table, leaning over her cue with vivid, intense eyes – a technically sharp, forward-leaning stance, reminiscent of Neil Robertson. Her career – undefeated as world champion over a span of fourteen years – expresses a level of dominance comparable to that of Joe Davis. But while Davis has long been in the loftiest heights of snookering immortality, Harrison has faded into obscurity. This fact alone highlights the scale of her achievement. The story of women's snooker begins with Ruth Harrison's unjustly forgotten name.

In these early years, women's billiards still received rather more attention than women's snooker. There is some extraordinary 1930s footage of Thelma Carpenter – Harrison's great rival, and a superior billiards player – performing a series of trick shots in an evening gown, *The Great Gatsby*'s Daisy Buchanan transmuted into a baize prodigy, while a small audience watches on and claps every shot. It is quite clear, watching her deliver a range of complex flicks, pots and flashy doubles with an impeccable technique, just how good she was.

Another clip from the era shows Joyce Gardner, seven-time women's world billiards champion, fluidly composing a break with a series of delicate cannons. 'Consternation has spread in the ranks of the old brigade,' run the intertitles, 'a woman billiards champion has appeared – Miss Joyce Gardner! . . . Miss Gardner has exceeded the century on many occasions and would be a doughty opponent for most men.' A patronising conclusion swiftly follows, 'Not quite up to the Lindrum standard, but then, there's only one Lindrum.' Another film – titled 'GIRL PLAYER WIELDS AN EXPERT CUE' – has Thelma Carpenter presenting to the camera, cue in hand, offering an advertisement for the women's game. 'It has always been the general view,' she explains in a clipped voice, 'that billiards is a game only to be enjoyed by men. But now there are many lady enthusiasts discovering what a delightful pastime it can be.'

Delightful pastime, perhaps; but it would be a long time before baize sports would be anything more than this for female players. Women's snooker was always likely to struggle through the fifties and sixties, with the men's game at its nadir; during this period, there was no women's professional game at all to speak of, although the amateur game did remain active. But as the snooker boom of the seventies kicked in, women's snooker saw something of an upturn. The Women's World Open was held in 1976 – effectively a return of the World Championship, resurrected after more than a quarter of a century. Since then, the Women's World Championship has been held most years, with a few occasional gaps.

Money was a persistent challenge, although the rising levels of interest in the men's game meant that, for the first time, sponsors could be found. As the 1980s unfolded, though, what women's snooker really lacked was a star. There was a need for a Steve Davis-style luminary – a dominant champion, a figure-head, someone to spread the word and to lift the game's profile. And in the end, this is precisely what emerged, in the form of Allison Fisher.

There can be little doubt that Allison Fisher is the greatest female snooker player of the twentieth century. She won seven World Championships, plus several women's and mixed World Doubles titles. But entering an early-eighties, male-dominated world, life was not easy. Contempt was all around her – in addition to, or perhaps because of, fearful insecurities about losing to a woman. She was signed up by Barry Hearn – not a main attraction, of course, but as 'a warm-up act' for his Matchroom players. And when she did play against any of Hearn's team, things could be tense. 'The ones I did beat didn't take it too well,' she said. 'They were not happy, not happy at all. They have big egos and a lot of the guys couldn't cope with losing to a female.' It seems, interestingly, like it was the very best, most assured male players who treated her with greatest respect. 'I paired up with Steve Davis and won three world doubles titles. John Parrott and Stephen Hendry played me like a player, not like a girl. Jimmy White was always wonderful.'

From the mid-eighties onwards, Fisher ruled the women's game. But despite her dominance and the big money flowing through men's snooker, the women's game was poorly looked after. Winnings were minimal; administration was often a sham-bles. The final straw for Fisher was the 1994 World Championship, held in India. 'We got there,' she explained, 'and it was just a concrete room with the air conditioning hanging out of the door and a red curtain on the wall.' She won the final comfortably – her seventh and, as it turned out, last World Championship title.

Her prize money as champion was £7,500; Stephen Hendry's prize money in the same year was £180,000.

Fisher had had enough. In 1995, she made the jump across to pool – where the money was far better and the gender inequality far less acute. It would be an understatement to say it was a successful move. She established herself as one of the all-time legends of pool, topping the world rankings for ten of the next twelve years and winning over fifty professional tournaments, including four world nine-ball titles. In 2005, she was the highest-earning pool player of either sex. She is regularly cited as the greatest female pool player in history. Allison Fisher, the 'Duchess of Doom', deserves properly to be recognised for what she is: one of the very finest sportspeople that Britain has ever produced.

Meanwhile, women's snooker continued to struggle. In the mid-nineties, the World Championship final shifted to the Crucible theatre – a move that seemed, on the surface, to be an upgrade, offering a more secure foundation for the women's game. But this was not the case. In 2003, the finalists – Kelly Fisher and Lisa Quick – arrived for their match to discover that the balls had been locked away in a cupboard and no one was able to find the key. An ominous warning sign, to say the least, that all was not well. Later that year, it was announced that the game's governing body, World Snooker Enterprises, was withdrawing their funding for women's snooker.

'I don't understand why they think it's OK to ditch the women,' said Fisher. 'It seems that as long as the men's competition is OK that's what matters to the governing body.' Within a year, she had left snooker behind, following her namesake Allison into the world of pool.

The opening decades of the twenty-first century have seen a greater focus on the issue of gender inequality in sport. All the way back in the early seventies, Billie Jean King had led a successful campaign for equal pay at the US Open; but it was not until 2007 that equal prize money was adopted across all four tennis grand slams. Opponents to equal pay have tended to argue along the lines that men's sport is simply more popular, more lucrative and more worthy of reward. This certainly seemed to be the opinion of Novak Djokovic, who claimed in 2016, 'Our men's tennis world, ATP world, should fight for more because the stats are showing that we have much more spectators on the men's tennis matches.'

Raymond Moore – former pro and CEO of the Indian Wells Masters tournament – was even less diplomatic. 'If I was a lady player,' he said, 'I'd go down every night on my knees and thank God that Roger Federer and Rafa Nadal were born because they have carried this sport. They really have.' It prompted a withering response from Serena Williams: 'There's only one way to interpret that,' she said. '*Get on your knees* . . . and thank a man . . . we as women have come a long way and we shouldn't have to drop to our knees at any point.' Two days later, Moore resigned.

Others have observed how equal pay, although significant, does not itself provide a full solution to the problem. Golfer Anya Alvarez has persuasively suggested that pay must be one thread in a deeper structure of promotion and support:

> Sure, equal pay is a hot topic, but in women's sports it's irrelevant until we start looking at the hurdles set in place to keep women from ever crossing the finish line.
>
> The truth is, women's sports will not achieve parity if the barriers that keep them in the trenches remain. We can talk about equal pay all we want, but it doesn't matter until we start investing equally in how we market and promote these athletes.

Some advances have been made, but parity is still a long way off. In her recent book *Game On: The Unstoppable Rise of Women's Sport*, Sue Anstiss argues that – although 'the landscape from women's sport is finally beginning to shift' – significant problems still endure: 'Female athletes still don't get equal funding or opportunities – even though they train as hard and make the same sacrifices as their male counterparts. In many sports, women receive less prize money, get fewer professional contracts, less sponsorship and a tiny fraction of the media coverage.'

And what about gender equality in snooker? A 2014 BBC study found snooker to be one of the worst offenders in all sport. The winner of the men's World Championship that year received £300,000. The women's prize, meanwhile, was £1,500. This was a paltry 20 per cent of the amount Allison Fisher had received a whole two decades earlier. Snooker, it seemed, was travelling fast in the wrong direction. In an era when gender equality in sport was slowly but steadily improving, for snooker things actually appeared to be getting worse. What exactly had gone wrong?

The recipient of the miserly 2014 prize pot was Reanne Evans. It had been her tenth world title – not only that, but her tenth in a row. Two more were to follow. Evans has been the pre-eminent women's snooker player of the twenty-first century – an all-conquering giant, reaching a level of dominance beyond even that of Allison Fisher two decades earlier. In total, she has won nearly seventy women's professional tournaments; at one stage she won sixty-one women's matches in a row. It is a level of success that, in most other contexts, would have brought tidal waves of wealth and fame. Steve Davis once hailed her as 'perhaps the best woman player I've ever seen', describing her as 'like the Jimmy White or the Ronnie O'Sullivan of the women's game. She has the feel for the game, she's at one with the table.'

To many observers, Reanne Evans has the strongest claim to be the greatest women's snooker player of all time.

From early on in her career, though, Evans has been open about the struggles facing her and all women players. 'Things started to go downhill when tobacco sponsorship was banned in 2003,' she once said. 'The men gave a small percentage of Embassy money to the ladies. Not a lot, but even that stopped.' The tobacco ban was a non-trivial setback for men's snooker; for the women's game, though, it was a grave, almost terminal injury. In 2005 – Evans' first year as World Champion – her prize money was a Lilliputian four hundred and fifty pounds. 'The hotel cost me more than that,' she observed. By 2019, things had improved, but only slightly; as World Champion that year, she received six thousand pounds. Progress has continued to be slow, stuttering, unreliable. In 2022, the prize money was still stuck at the same amount.

Evans' performances did earn her a reward beyond the cramped confines of the women's game – a chance at the men's tour. In 2019, she became the first female ever to compete in the Champion of Champions tournament. Writing for the *Metro*, Phil Haigh pointed out that, if she won her first-round match against Shaun Murphy, she would earn more than her takings as World Champion. It was a sad indictment of the available rewards for female players. But at the same time, Evans' presence on the men's tour also opened up a vivid new prospect; that of women playing against men, on an equal footing. There is, in theory, no reason why snooker should not become an entirely gender-neutral sport. After all, snooker does not require athleticism or muscularity, as the diverse range of male snooker-ing physiques amply testifies.

In 2019, Fallon Sherrock caused a sensation in the darts world when she made it through to the third round of the PDC

World Championship. Here was evidence that, given a chance, women could not only compete against men – they could win. 'The next step to it all,' Sherrock said afterwards, 'would be – oh, it's not just a woman beating a man. It's two great players playing against each other and the winner, yes it might happen to be a woman but it's not seen as "a woman", it's seen as a really good player.'

One person who agreed with this was Barry Hearn. 'There is no earthly reason,' he said, 'why we don't uncover – perhaps we already have – a superstar that can beat men on a regular basis and win the World [Darts] Championship . . . I think we're approaching the dawn of a new era.' Snooker shares with darts an equal playing field of physical accessibility; there is, in short, no biological barrier to a radically genderless future.

In that 2019 Champion of Champions match, Evans ended up narrowly losing to Shaun Murphy, 4–3. She had been 3–0 down, but came back to force a decider. After the match, Murphy defended her in strong terms: 'This woman here, she's a twelve-time champion of the world completely disregarded by the general British sporting public at large. People are throwing MBEs and awards out at people left, right and centre – she's got twelve world titles to her name and nothing after her name. It's a disgrace.'

Evans continued on the tour, threatening more with each season. In the 2021 Championship League, she drew two of her matches against Simon Lichtenberg and Tom Ford. In February 2022, another top female player – Ng On-yee – completed her first ever win on the men's tour, against the Chinese teenager Wu Yize. The more chances women are given to compete against top men, the more they learn, the more they sharpen their skills. The gap is not yet closing fast – but it is closing.

Snooker may not have the best track record regarding gender equality. But there is the possibility of something momentous in the years ahead. Given the right backing, snooker could pioneer a true transcendence of gender boundaries – bringing about a world where gender is no longer of relevance to the skill and the competence of the players.

'A gender-equal society,' Gloria Steinem once hopefully imagined, 'would be one where the word "gender" does not exist: where everyone can be themselves.' Perhaps gendered snooker is on its way out. Perhaps the future will no longer involve segregated snookering sexes; perhaps, instead of men's snooker and women's snooker, there will merely be one thing, snooker itself – universal, open to all, and anyone's game to win.

15

CLASS

I never preached anarchy. It was just a novelty in a song. I always thought anarchy was just a mind game for the middle class.

John Lydon, interview, 2014

In *Jude the Obscure*, Thomas Hardy's ill-fated protagonist moves to Christminster (Hardy's pseudonym for Oxford) to work as a stonemason. An impoverished young man with aspirations to be a scholar, Jude wanders past the ancient colleges plagued with yearning for the life of study he so craves:

For many days he haunted the cloisters and quadrangles of the colleges at odd minutes in passing them, surprised by impish echoes of his own footsteps, smart as the blows of a mallet. The Christminster 'sentiment,' as it had been called, ate further and further into him; till he probably knew more about those buildings materially, artistically, and historically, than any one of their inmates.

It was not till now, when he found himself actually on the spot of his enthusiasm, that Jude perceived how far away from the object of that enthusiasm he really was. Only a wall divided him from those happy young contemporaries of his with whom he shared a common mental life; men who had nothing to do from morning till night but to read, mark, learn, and inwardly digest. Only a wall—but what a wall!

The students are only yards away from him, but at the same time, they are living on a distant plane. The wall Jude faces is the wall of class divide: on its far side, there lies a world of privilege and freedom he will never be able to enter.

In sport, as everywhere else, complex codes surround matters of class. Pursuing a sport seriously requires money; sometimes a serious amount of money. But the circumstances vary tremendously, depending on where you look. At one end, there are certain sports that exist more or less exclusively as the province of independent school culture. In the case of Eton Fives, for instance, the court itself has a buttress sticking out from one of the side walls – a replication of the foot of Eton College's chapel stairs, where the game was invented. Real tennis – a game with historic royal links, favoured by Henry VIII – remains inveterately associated with the well-heeled. Several of its hard-to-find courts are at private schools like Canford, Radley and Wellington College; the oldest surviving court is in the grounds of Hampton Court palace. The game's leaders do their best to stretch its social scope. 'Because of outreach projects and new courts popping up we have a greater range of people playing,' said Ben Ronaldson, head of real tennis at The Queen's Club, in 2017. 'It is growing for sure, just quite slowly.'

But the spectres of class and money do not just loom over niche territory. More mainstream sports like rugby and cricket have become increasingly dominated by middle-class players from privately educated backgrounds. A 2014 survey found that over 60 per cent of top-level professional rugby union players paid for at least some of their education. In 2019, a wide-ranging report into elitism in the UK found that nearly half of men's county cricketers attended fee-paying schools – up by 10 per cent over the preceding five years. Andrew Flintoff made no secret of his anger about the direction of travel. 'I made it to the highest level of cricket attending state schools on an estate in Preston,' he said, 'but I can't see many doing that now ... Cricket is more elitist per head than rugby, rowing and the House of Lords. We've got to do something to get young, working-class people playing our national summer sport.'

Snooker, though, is quite different. It belongs with an alternative range of sports – not only football, but also boxing and darts – that are resolutely working-class. In some ways, on the surface at least, this is something of a surprise. Snooker looks like a game that should only be accessible to the wealthy. After all, a full-size snooker table is likely to set you back over ten thousand pounds. Not only that, you need somewhere to put it. Yet snooker culture has never revolved around the games rooms of the rich. The snooker halls and social clubs out of which the game emerged from obscurity were places of neither money nor privilege. For decades before the boom, snooker lived and breathed in mining towns, industrial estates, the tough ends of British cities; elitism might be a threat to some sports, but it has never been a threat to snooker. Snooker is a game of the streets: it is a game of the people.

This is in dramatic contrast to the game's earliest ancestry. The game of billiards was, to begin with, a game for the English and French nobility. Mary Queen of Scots was an avid player. She even had a table in her prison cell; according to legend, her executioners wrapped her body up in its cloth. An engraving exists of Louis XIV playing billiards with an assortment of coiffured courtiers – the Duke of Chartres, the Count of Toulouse, the Duke of Vendôme. The king appears in the pleated long coat of the age, with feathered tricorne, cravat, and a wig of dangling curls; using a mace – precursor of the cue – to strike the ball, he poses with his eyes turned to the viewer, playing the ball nonchalantly, without looking, as if competing in some patrician trick-shot championship.

As time went on, the game steadily spread beyond its aristocratic origins. Clive Everton noted, 'By 1727, billiards was played in almost every Paris café.' Public tables were the key to this change. As these became more available in taverns, inns and coffee houses, the game of billiards found a more socially catholic audience. No longer did you need your own table to play – you just needed to nip down to the tavern for a game and a tankard of ale. Here, perhaps, is the genesis of the intimate relationship between beer and the baize, the deep-set affiliation between the click of the billiard ball and the fizz of intoxication. By the beginning of the nineteenth century, across the lands where billiards was played, it had become a game for players from all walks of life, as Everton recorded: 'By 1800 there were enough public tables in French cafes, English ale houses and everywhere in America from private houses to the toughest frontier outposts to justify the claim that it was now a game for all classes.'

As snooker out-muscled billiards in the early twentieth century, the game found new homes a long way from the officer clubhouses of the Raj. The working men's clubs of Britain's industrial towns – in the north of England, in Scotland, in the Welsh Valleys – played host to local games, money matches and amateur tournaments in which local players honed their skills. The billiard halls all over Britain became repurposed, their tables used less for billiards. As the years went on, though, these halls steadily developed a particular kind of reputation for being less than salubrious hangouts for suspect characters engaged in shady dealings.

Perhaps it was the location of the halls. Perhaps it was the fact they were so dark – places of shadow and secret things. Perhaps it was something about the game itself, something to do with how quiet it can be, quiet enough so that mid-game talks can be had around the tables. Whatever the truth, by the middle of the century, snooker halls had become a little bit dangerous. The Kray twins bought the Regal Billiard Club in Mile End in 1954, making it the operational base for their protection racket. It became one of Ronnie Kray's favourite places. 'There were often evenings at the billiard hall,' writes their biographer John Pearson, 'when he'd just sit, brooding and menacing, sunk in silence.' But it was also a scene of violence. In a famous story, a rival Maltese gang turned up at the Regal and made the mistake of demanding some money. The Krays were unimpressed. Ronnie charged at them with a cutlass and chased them out onto the street.

It was at Zan's snooker club in Tooting that Jimmy White spent much of his formative years. He was there so often, and at school so little, that his headmaster cut him a deal: if he came to school in the mornings, he could go off to play snooker in the afternoons. White has vividly detailed what it was about Zan's that he found so captivating:

> It looked warm and inviting, dark and mysterious as a cave . . . The floor was awash with cigarette ash and stubs and there was a kind of dusty, musty, beery, smoky, almost soot-like smell. Men's voices were low, trousered legs and scuffed shoes shuffled by. I heard the click of balls and then a clunk and a faint rumble like thunder as a ball dropped into the pocket and ran along the channel just inches away from my face. If, like Alice, I had fallen down a rabbit hole and dropped into Wonderland, it would have been like this . . . This was real cowboy territory – full of villains and good gossip.

It was not the game, but the place itself that first drew him in; White was hanging around at Zan's for some time before he ever played snooker. There were some nights when he would climb out of his window and head to Zan's because 'it was somewhere to go – and far better than trying to sleep. Someone would take pity on me and buy me a cup of tea and I'd sit on the sidelines and watch, just taking it all in.' Before he had picked up a cue, White had become hooked on the aura of the snooker hall, the thrill of the threat and the mystery.

White's story is not exactly routine in its levels of delinquency and mischief. But for many players, the choice between education and snooker is an urgent one. One could go further, and say it is an either/or decision: there simply is not room for both. A poorly appreciated point arises, one that is partly about class, partly about channels of educational opportunity: in stark contrast to games like cricket and rugby, the infrastructure in schools and universities is just not there for snooker players to combine their education with the prospect of an elite level, professional future. In order to be good enough – in order to succeed – you have to do nothing but play snooker. Total commitment is the only choice.

Peter Ebdon has recounted the moment he gave up school for the game he loved. It was a precarious step: academically, he had been doing well. 'I left school before I sat my exams,' he says, 'and I think I broke my dad's heart. I was studying Latin and ancient Greek. The teachers were devastated when I said I was leaving for snooker. I know it was a ridiculous decision and I would be mortified if any of my children were to do anything like that.'

Steve Davis has vividly explained how, as a teenager, snooker swallowed up his time and focus, pushing everything else out of view:

I passed O-levels in English literature, maths, physics and French that summer, but snooker dominated my studies. Every Monday morning my French teacher would ask me what I'd done at the weekend and I would always reply in French that I had been playing snooker all weekend! *J'ai joué au snooker*, was my standard reply.

This is the accepted narrative for players who went on to achieve real success. School has to go. Only snooker can stand.

'School is finished,' remembered Stephen Hendry. 'I'm meant to be sitting four O-levels, but I don't turn up for two and the other two I fail. So that's the end of that. There is no real choice other than to play snooker for a living.'

Extra pressure stems from the fact that turning professional is not, by itself, enough to guarantee a good income. Michael Holt has reflected candidly on his own career – one which, he feels, has been defined by under-achievement. 'I should have gone to university and could have still played snooker afterwards,' he said. 'It wouldn't have been the end of my life if I had done that. If you turn professional in tennis or golf they tend to do it after their college education. They are still young at the age of twenty-one.' But snooker is unlike these other sports in that, in its lower reaches, players struggle to get by, as Holt observed: 'It's less of a gamble in golf and tennis because you could be a solid journey-man, like I have been, but in golf, I'd be rich.'

Neil Robertson has made the very same point: 'I was telling [footballer] John Terry what some snooker players are earning, and he couldn't believe it. He just said: "Wow." I said to him, "It is either top ten or top twenty or else don't bother." You only [need to] see what people around thirty or forty in the world are earning to see the problems. If you are a single guy, you can scrape by. But if you have got a family, snooker is not really a viable career choice.'

Snooker is a tough road; brutal, poorly lit and hard to follow. And the need for young cueists to sacrifice their lives to it has serious socio-political resonances. It exposes fissures in society – cataclysmic inequalities between the social profile of different sports, and the support structures they offer. Instead of ready solutions, though, what one more often finds is the ugly spectacle of class snobbery. SNOOKER STARS ARE 'THICKEST', ran a 2006 headline in the *Mirror*. The article was responding to a study of education levels across a dozen different sports; snooker, it turned out, was squarely at the bottom of the list. One might, perhaps, have hoped that a national newspaper could discriminate between qualifications and intelligence. But no matter: the sneering snobbery is instructive.

The qualification ranking produced by the 2006 study appears to offer a clear-cut ladder of class division. The top five sports, in order, are cycling, golf, rowing, athletics and cricket. The bottom five, also in order, are rugby league, boxing, horse racing, football . . . and in the very lowest circle, of course, sits snooker.

It is a predictable hierarchy. A young athlete or cricketer will have no problem completing their school and university education before turning professional; not only that, it is the standard narrative. The administration, support and competition are all in place to make such a path not just viable, but pretty good training – maybe even the best training – for a professional career. Nothing of the sort exists for snooker. And there is little attention to the social cost of such discrepancies. Instead, we get imbecilities like the *Mirror* article, claiming that snooker players who sacrificed their education for their career are somehow thick as a result. The rot is complex, insidious and difficult to cure.

16

Fashion

Vain trifles as they seem, clothes have, they say, more important offices than merely to keep us warm. They change our view of the world and the world's view of us.

Virginia Woolf, *Orlando: A Biography*, 1928

'The apparel oft proclaims the man': so claims Polonius, in Act I of *Hamlet*. He is speaking to his son Laertes – advising him to ensure, on his travels to France, that he maintains good taste in his choice of clothing. Polonius is recycling an ancient notion – that you can tell a lot about a person from what they choose to wear.

Virginia Woolf's line expresses something similar, investing clothes with a significance beyond either their physical properties or their practical use. *They change our view of the world and the world's view of us* . . . from this standpoint, clothes become part of the self – acquiring a form of ontological significance, shaping our experience of the world, and the way we are experienced by that world.

Coco Chanel also felt that the meaning of fashion went much deeper than clothes. For her, it was an emblem of social reality – expressing important truths about the texture of culture at a particular moment in time:

Fashion does not exist only in dresses; fashion is in the air, it is borne on the wind, you can sense it, you can breathe it, it's in the sky and on the highway, it's everywhere, it has to do with ideas, with social mores, with events . . . Fashion should express the place, the moment.

Chanel's philosophy identifies fashion as being a far from superficial phenomenon. Quite the opposite, in fact – as an embodiment of the cultural moment, it could not be more important. Despite such arguments, though, fashion has never been able to escape associations with vanity and narcissism. Any individual too interested in clothes is vulnerable to accusations of being shallow, perhaps even ridiculous. After all, our clothing is our surface appearance: anyone obsessed with it is a performer, a show-off and, thus, not to be trusted. 'Believe this of me,' says Lafeu about the deceitful Paroles in *All's Well That Ends Well*, 'there can be no kernel in this light nut. The soul of this man is his clothes. Trust him not in matter of heavy consequence.'

The dress of a snooker player is an extraordinary thing. Clothing in sport is generally sleek, streamlined, minimal – carefully designed to allow for optimal physical performance. Even in slower, more low-intensity pursuits, such as darts and bowls, participants invariably appear in the straightforward practical ease of a short-sleeved polo shirt. Snooker, though, is a different story. Players are expected to adorn themselves in the bizarre black-tie formality of the traditional English gentleman. There is nothing like it elsewhere in sport. It provides snooker with a strange, dreamlike feel. In terms of the outfits, watching a professional snooker match feels like watching a matchup between a pair of Victorian aristocrats.

Where does it come from, this snookering thirst for formal dress? Writer Patrick West has argued that its origins lie in the aspirational mindset of working-class practitioners of the game. 'The bowler hat,' he writes, 'was employed as a sign of social respectability for the lower-middle classes. Likewise, working-class Londoners from the 1930s began to wear bow ties and dinner suits when playing snooker because they sought to be perceived as respectable.' But this is frankly not supported by the evidence. Photos of early twentieth-century cueists, from well before the thirties, reliably present the subject in a formal tie and waistcoat.

There is a 1905 *Vanity Fair* print of H. W. Stevenson, one of the era's billiard greats, rigidly posed in full formal black tie, moustache ends curled in the imperial style. One can go back even further: an 1870 engraving of the Professional Billiards Championship shows The Guildhall in London packed to the rafters, with well over a thousand spectators. In it, both of the players are dressed in bow ties and waistcoats; the seated player even wears a bowler hat as he impassively watches on. Journalist and author Donald Trelford argued that it was John Roberts, pre-eminent billiards force of the late nineteenth century, who 'set the sartorial standards for the game, wearing a dinner jacket and high collar in the evening'. The formality of snooker dress, in short, is inherited directly from billiards – a tradition that goes back well over 150 years, to the Victorian origins of black tie itself.

For a long time, formal wear was the unchallenged norm for snooker. As soon as TV made the game famous, though, fashion creativity emerged: it no longer just mattered how you played, it also mattered how you looked. In the seventies and eighties, the boom years, certain players caught the public imagination for the flair of their dress. No player was quite as stylistically unforgettable as Kirk Stevens, whose flowing locks and dashing white suits became synonymous with the spicy side of snooker. There is, after all, a political dimension to fashion: what you wear can signify either conformity or rebellion. The suits of Stevens marked him out as a buccaneer and a rebel: a player who was not interested in playing by the rules. It caused scandal – 'You should have heard the gasps,' he once said, 'when I walked into the room' – but it certainly helped to stir and to freshen the theatre of the game.

Stevens was not the only player to use fashion as a marker of rebellious intent. Alex Higgins cannily harnessed the power of clothes – not only to affirm identity, but also to win the crowds. Over the years, he rotated his way through a kaleidoscopic range of waistcoats. In a rebuff to white-shirted traditionalism, his legendary clearance against Jimmy White in 1982 was made while wearing a shirt of bold sapphire blue. For the final, Higgins switched to a shirt of shamrock green with a bright red collar. Often, at the start of matches, he would skip into the arena wearing a fedora hat – lifting it up to the crowd and winking as they cheered him on, sending a clear message to his opponent that this was very much his crowd, his match, his sport.

But the most controversial aspect of the Hurricane's approach to dress was not something he wore – it was something he didn't wear. To the consternation of the management, he refused to wear a tie. He claimed that it was for medical reasons: he had a doctor's note. But it did not go down well, to say the least, with the traditionalists of the game. One voice of disapproval was eminent commentator 'Whispering' Ted Lowe. 'Part of their job is to entertain the public,' he raged, 'and to do that they should dress the part.' Players, he felt, should aim to be more like Steve Davis – a figure who 'always dresses impeccably, acts correctly,' and thus sets the right kind of standard.

For Lowe, this was far from a cosmetic problem. He saw the sartorial sins of Higgins et al as emblematic of nothing less than the decline of civilisation itself. The new generation of 1980s rebel player – 'walking around in jeans, dirty shirts, not turning up on time' – were a sinister threat to the order of things. It was a disturbing sign of the times, and a problem that went well beyond snooker:

> Perhaps that's today's world. You look at these chat shows and see the state of some of these stars who come on. Open shirts showing all their bellies. Necklaces. Medallions. *Plimsolls*, for Christ's sake. Can you imagine walking into a boardroom and facing your chairman dressed like that? I think it's disgraceful. No wonder the youngsters of today are so undisciplined.

Lowe's self-appointed role as angry keeper of tradition could not be clearer. One dreads to think what he would have made of *Love Island*, *Ex on the Beach* and *Naked Attraction*.

Higgins' anti-tie ethics were, for the most part, grumpily tolerated. But they sometimes landed him in trouble. In the 1983 Tolly Cobbold Classic, he began the match with his tie on – halfway through, though, he asked the referee if he could take it off. The television lights, he said, were too hot. The referee gave him permission: but his opponent, Dennis Taylor, was not impressed, and complained that this was all in breach of the rules. After losing the match, Higgins sniped in his press conference that he didn't mind losing, as it was only 'a Mickey Mouse tournament' anyway. He was forced to offer a public apology, and his prize money was donated to charity. The press reacted to the story with a combination of outrage and amusement. A cartoon appeared in the *Sun* depicting Higgins leaning across the table, entirely naked except for a tie. 'WARNING: HOT SNOOKER PLAYERS MUST NOT REMOVE THEIR TIES' reads the sign on the wall; 'What can I do? He's still wearing his tie,' moans the referee.

As the years passed, a tension remained at work in the dress code of the game: a kind of quiet, ongoing battle between the forces of formal constraint and self-expression. Most players continued to observe the conventional butler-style black-and-white format. Occasional dissidents, though, made a push to be more inventive – perhaps to test boundaries, perhaps to carve a public image that might live in the memory. A young Peter Ebdon caused shockwaves in the mid-nineties with his flowing ponytail and penchant for exotic waistcoats. In just his second visit to the Crucible, his waistcoat front was an elegant burgundy pageant of floral prints; in 1996, it was a marbled veneer of lapis lazuli blue; three years later, it was a bright crowd of golden stars. This flamboyance helped to create an enigmatic undertone to his image – a sense that his developing infamy for dour slowness was maybe not quite his whole story.

In spite of the seemingly stifling restrictions, snookering fashion has in fact managed to embrace all sorts of territory – from the elegantly classical to the queasily avant-garde. There has always been a place for eccentricity in snooker dress. Dominic Dale has styled himself at the experimental end of the spectrum, his brash wardrobe incorporating red shirts, cream waistcoats and black-and-white stripy shoes – his hair at different times dyed black, white or yellow. Elsewhere, fashion choices have been made not so much for aesthetic value and more for sentiment. Alan McManus raised eyebrows and Scottish hearts with the tartan trousers he wore at the Crucible in 2014; 'Maybe the tartan trousers are bringing me a little bit of luck?' he wondered, as he made it to his first quarter final in nine years. Barry Pinches likes to wear a waistcoat in the yellow and green of his beloved Norwich football club.

In the end, the game's authorities realised that it would be in their interests to harness style, rather than just to police it. With the right approach, the power of fashion could be used to raise the game's profile. In 2001, a few top players were targeted and asked to soup up their image. Ronnie O'Sullivan was one of them. He soon started to appear with highlights in his hair, his barnet assuming the cultivated boy-band disorder of David Beckham in this era. Beckham, in fact, was evidently a key exemplar for snooker fashionistas. In 2004, he grew his hair long and so Ronnie did too, holding his shoulder-length black mane in place with an alice band. The late Paul Hunter also followed suit, his blonde locks and good looks even earning him a nickname as the 'Beckham of the baize'. This was a new breed of snooker player: dapper, chic, shifting with the style of the times.

And the power of the fashion statement has continued in recent years. Shoes have proven to be a popular choice for experiments, with Christian Louboutin the typical designer of choice. Judd Trump set the tone at the 2013 Masters with a pair of his 'Rollerboy Spikes' worth close to a thousand pounds – although they turned out to be less than practical. 'I was all right in the practice room,' he said, 'but as soon as I went out there I just started sliding around.' After three frames, he ditched them for a standard pair. Not to be deterred, a few years later Shaun Murphy wore a pair of two-tone, black-and-white, Chicago-gangster Laboutins to the Crucible. Luca Brecel, a fashion forward leader in snookering style, has been seen in an assortment of blingy Louboutins, including one pair encrusted with a galaxy of sparkling crystals.

Snooker is now in a transitional moment, fashion-wise. The expectation that players accept the old-style, black tie formality has come under unprecedented threat. Judd Trump recently complained that snooker is 'stuck in a rut' with its insistence on formal dress. It is a fusty, antiquated look, one that does the game no favours with a younger audience. It has run its course:

it has to go. 'People don't want to go around dressed in waist-coats nowadays,' he explained. 'They did forty years ago but snooker is falling behind, stuck in their own ways and other sports have moved on.' Mark Allen chimed in with the very same point – snooker needs to wake up to the fact that change is long overdue. 'You look at every other sport. Young people look at TV and go, "I want to have what they're wearing." And unfortunately snooker's not like that.'

The authorities promptly responded: for the 2021 Champion of Champions tournament, personalised polo shirts were trialled. Trump, for one, was pleased. 'It is about time,' he said. 'It's nice to see them trying out new ideas and bringing snooker into the twenty-first century . . . The shirts are smart and I feel they will appeal to younger fans and viewers.'

Is it the end for snookering formality? Are the bow tie and waistcoat destined to meet their doom, as dead relics of a bygone era? It is hard to deny that there is something absurd about the game's traditional dress code. It is impractical and hopelessly uncool. It makes professional sportspeople look like prancing viscounts. And yet there is an argument – *maybe* there is an argument – to say it lends an elegance to the game, an air of sophistication that is worth something. There is an integrity to dressing smart: it brings seriousness, distinction. One might even say it carries a philosophical depth. 'A well-tied tie,' claims Lord Illingworth in Oscar Wilde's *A Woman of No Importance*, 'is the first serious step in life.'

Judd Trump is clearly one player who does not see it that way. The 2022 Masters saw a reversion to formal wear – and for the afternoon sessions, the dress code was the one thing, in Trump's eyes, even worse than a bow tie. A *neck* tie. 'I don't know who comes up with the idea to wear a tie in this day and age, but it's a stupid idea,' he spat. 'Don't get me started, the tie is so bad!

I've had my mum taking the lining out of my tie today because the lining is too thick ... It's mind-boggling how anyone can come up with this kind of dress code. The bow tie is bad enough but to have a tie in the way is ridiculous.' A sense remains that the traditional dress of snooker is menaced, vulnerable and ripe for ousting. What lies ahead, in the wardrobe of future players, is veiled in uncertainty. From somewhere, the ghost of Ted Lowe watches on with an anxious eye.

17

Naming

The Naming of Cats is a difficult matter,
It isn't just one of your holiday games;
You may think at first I'm as mad as a hatter
When I tell you, a cat must have THREE DIFFERENT NAMES.
T. S. Eliot, 'The Naming of Cats', 1939

'What's in a name?' complains Juliet at her window. 'That which we call a rose/By any other word would smell as sweet'. If only Romeo were not a Montague; if his name were different, he would still be just the same. Do our names really matter? Instinctively, we are likely to rebel against such a notion. We do not choose our names: they do not define us. The apparently arbitrary set of syllables by which we happen to be known can, surely, have no bearing on our true inner selves.

And yet there is evidence – unsettling perhaps – to show that the connection is more real than we might like to admit, as *New Yorker* author and poker player Maria Konnikova darkly explains:

Some recent research suggests that names can influence choice of profession, where we live, whom we marry, the grades we earn, the stocks we invest in, whether we're accepted to a school or are hired for a particular job and the quality of our work in a group setting. Our names can even determine whether we give money to disaster victims: if we share an initial with the name of a hurricane, according to one study, we are far more likely to donate to relief funds after it hits.

It is a bizarre idea – that with a different name, we might have had a different life. In unseen, unknowable, sinister ways, our name might shape and steer us, whether we want it to or not.

A *nickname*, though, is a different matter. We might not personally choose our own nicknames – but someone does. A nickname has been selected, somewhere, as suitable for us. It is thus reasonable to assume it says something about who we are. The word stems from the Middle English '*eke*', a word for 'also'. A nickname, then, is an also-name, a second name alongside your official one, signifying *you* while also hinting at the presence of an alter-ego, a second self. Since it has been chosen specially, there is even a case to say it says more about you than the more haphazard nature of your birth name. If so, it is a serious business. 'Nicknames, for the most part, govern the world,' claimed essayist William Hazlitt. 'A nickname is the heaviest stone that the devil can throw at a man.'

Perhaps no writer in history has been blessed with such a genius for naming as Charles Dickens. The names of Dickens – 'Seth Pecksniff', 'Uriah Heep', 'Smike', 'Bumble', 'Dick Swiveller' – are unforgettable masterpieces of nominative determinism, luridly conjuring the essence of his characters and helping to hint at their fate. In the process of running away to London, Oliver Twist meets 'a snub-nosed, flat-browed, common-faced boy' by the name of Jack Dawkins. He is not, though, generally known as Jack Dawkins. Oliver soon discovers that the boy 'had a rather flightly and dissolute mode of conversing, and furthermore avowed that among his intimate friends he was better known by the sobriquet of "The Artful Dodger".' The self-inflicted tag is often shortened to the 'Dodger', or sometimes simply 'Artful'.

It is a name that expresses, in one stroke, everything about him that is shady, mischievous, conniving, clever, slippery, delinquent, and shrewd – the perfect nickname, in other words, for 'as roistering and swaggering a young gentleman as ever stood four-feet-six, or something less, in the blushers.' The name of 'Jack Dawkins' does little to express his assets; it is only his nickname – deservedly immortal – that offers such insight.

Not all sports specialise in nicknames. Where they do emerge, though, they occupy different potential categories. The first is a name designed to evoke some attribute for which the player is known. West Indies fast bowler Michael Holding, for instance, ran up to bowl with such noiseless fluidity and speed that he became known as 'Whispering Death'. A young Mike Tyson ripped through his opponents with sufficient brutal ferocity that he was soon dubbed 'Iron' Mike. Quite often, though, nicknames are more like happy outcomes of word resemblances – manifestations of punning and phonic play that are disconnected from any sporting-related substance. These still, though, can leave an indelible mark. In this category, we could list eminent nicknames such as Martin 'Chariots' Offiah; Steve 'Tugga' Waugh; Phil 'What's-a-packet-a' Sigsworth.

Snooker is a space in which nicknames thrive. One might even say that a nickname is something of a prerequisite for a player. Faced with the prospect of a match against fellow novelist Julian Barnes, Martin Amis recognised this expectation, waggishly affirming his own snookering nickname philosophy as follows:

By analogy with 'Whirlwind' White and 'Hurricane' Higgins, I am known, in the snooker world, as 'Earthquake' Amis. A *flair* player, one who relies on *natural ability*, his only academy the pool halls and borstal rec-rooms of a *misspent youth*: inconsistent, foul-tempered, over-ambitious, graceless alike in victory and defeat, and capable of missing *anything*. On the other hand, I do hit the ball tremendously hard and with various violent spins.

Amis saw his opponent – 'persistent, deliberate, gentlemanly and unpitying' – as of contrasting temperament, a Davis-like figure of austere control. He christened him 'Barometer' Barnes: 'not a force of nature so much as a medium of measurement or response'.

The prevalence of nicknames in snooker tells us something about the game. It hints at something droll and thespian, some half-buried link with comedy and the music-hall stage. Nicknames, after all, are stubbornly unserious: their purpose is to tease, to mock or playfully to exalt. In the boom years, all the top players had a nickname. Higgins' alias, as the 'Hurricane', felt preordained, perfectly evoking both the speed of his play and the turbulence of his temperament; it became, arguably, the name by which he was best known. Ray Reardon's impish menace, widow's peak and oil-black helmet of hair spawned the moniker of 'Dracula'. Cliff Thorburn played slowly: he became the 'Grinder'. For related reasons, Eddie Charlton became 'Steady' Eddie. And the very greatest were granted not one nickname, but several. While *Spitting Image* helped to immortalise him as 'Interesting', Steve Davis was also, at various different times, known as the 'Nugget', the 'Ginger Magician', 'Ginger Mushroom', the 'Romford Robot', even 'Romford Slim'.

The nicknaming of players was part of the hypervivid techni-colour wonder of snooker at its cultural peak. The more dynamic and charismatic the player, the more precious their nickname seemed to become – part of their brand, part of their over-the-top identity. Jimmy White's label as the 'Whirlwind' also seemed touched by the hand of destiny – capturing not just the speed and tumult he had taken from the Hurricane, but also the brotherly bond that the two developed. Ronnie O'Sullivan was another player to secure a whole string of nicknames. There was his own preferred sobriquet, the 'Essex Exocet' – but over the years, this was increasingly sidelined in favour of the plainer, simpler 'Rocket' Ronnie. These three – Hurricane Higgins, Whirlwind White and Rocket Ronnie – will always remain linked in snooker history, the resemblance between their alliterative alter-egos evoking the kinship between them in a baize family tree of errant geniuses.

Elsewhere, some nicknames have signposted aspects of the game in which a player might excel. Alan McManus was a consistent player throughout the nineties, without ever quite achieving true greatness. One area where he really was exceptional, though, was in getting out of snookers – he seemed to possess an eerie omniscience regarding direction and pace, judging the complexities of spin and cushion slide so impeccably that trapping him in a snooker was almost a waste of time. And he became 'Angles' McManus to many – nonpareil in the art of snooker escapes. There were some, though, who thought Ken Doherty, the 1997 World Champion, was even better. 'Angles' McManus had a rival in 'Dimensions' Doherty.

As the years rolled on, their pre-eminence was threatened by arguably the greatest escapist from snookers that snooker had ever seen. Mark Selby – master strategist, unyielding adversary, austere sage of the angles – became 'Sat-Nav' Selby. It is one of a trio of nicknames that Selby has gathered across his career. His initial sobriquet of the 'Jester from Leicester', based on a penchant for banter with the crowd, had always seemed out of kilter with his reputation for merciless match play. But it was Ronnie O'Sullivan who devised the most delightfully melodramatic name for the player who became his nemesis: 'We nickname him the "Torturer",' he revealed.

Some players, for whatever reason, seem resistant to nicknames. And there are others – not always the game's most renowned figures – who seem to be nickname magnets. Anthony Hamilton is a fascinating figure in the story of snooker. A player whose cultured break-building drips with class, he has made over three hundred century breaks in a career spanning more than three decades. But he is one of the most notable underachievers the game has seen – lurking outside the barricades of the top sixteen for many years, and failing to win a single ranking tournament until he improbably picked up the German Masters at the age of forty-five. He has long been known as a snooker player's snooker player – esteemed by the cognoscenti, a real connoisseur's choice.

Maybe it is something to do with this mix of distinction and disappointment. Maybe it is something to do with his striking look – his curly locks and sculpted, Van Dyke beard giving him the refined air of an off-duty musketeer. Hailing as Hamilton does from Nottingham, he became widely known by two competing monikers – the 'Sheriff of Pottingham' and, rather more clumsily, the 'Robin Hood of Snooker'. His vague resemblance to the prominent nineties eco-activist brought him the discourteous epithet of 'Swampy'. And his winsome, self-deprecating wit in post-match interviews even occasionally led to a fourth nickname, that of 'Affable' Anthony Hamilton. In the end, he may go down in history as a gifted nearly man who could have been a contender – but in terms of nicknames, Anthony Hamilton is one of the giants.

The theatre of nicknaming is helped by the efforts of the match MCs who set a feelgood mood and summon the players into the battle zone. For some years, the best-known MC has been Rob Walker, whose manic energy makes him perfect for the job. He openly explained that MC introductions are not the place for subtlety. 'I am there to jazz it up a little bit,' he has said, 'and, yeah, of course sometimes it is a little bit cheesy. But by and large the players come out with a smile on their face when I'm introducing them, I want them to feel special, I want them to feel important and as long as the players are happy with what I am doing then I am happy with that.'

Walker has been personally responsible for several player nicknames. To begin with, Neil Robertson went by the rather pedestrian nickname of the 'Melbourne Potting Machine'; Walker replaced it with a vastly superior title, the 'Thunder from Down Under'. Liang Wenbo became a cult figure at the Crucible in 2008, after entering the arena too early, scuttling out again and re-entering to a surge of cheers. Since that moment, he was invariably introduced with 'Should he stay or should he go? Liang Wenbo.' The fact that this rhyme mangles Wenbo's name (actually pronounced 'Wen-*bwoar*') never seemed to present a problem.

'How lovely are the wiles of words,' wrote the poet Emily Dickinson. At the 2010 World Championship, Rob Walker was in the process of introducing Steve Davis, who had made it to the quarter finals for the first time in five years. 'Ladies and gentlemen,' roared Walker, 'he's a legend ... he's Dennis Taylor!' As Walker's face morphed into a mask of horror, it was obvious this was not a deliberate joke – maybe the occasion had got to him, but somehow, he had called out the wrong name. Without missing a beat, Davis sprang into the arena, grabbed a pair of glasses from someone in the audience, and put them on upside down. Nicknames, in the end, are wordplay – they are merriment, they are mischief and they are fun. They are a reminder that, alongside all its other qualities, snooker has never lacked a sense of humour.

18

AUTHORITY

Nothing strengthens authority so much as silence.
Leonardo da Vinci, 1452–1519

In the opening session of the 2022 Crucible final, Ronnie O'Sullivan – already 5–2 ahead – had a chance to clear the table. But in an effort to get on the final yellow, he messed up his position, snookering himself behind the blue. After missing the escape – and leaving things on for Trump – something happened. Or nothing happened. It was hard to tell.

The referee, Olivier Marteel, followed Ronnie to his seat to have a word. '*I saw it,*' he whispered. What he was referring to was unclear – nothing had been captured by the cameras.

And O'Sullivan was not happy at all about the accusation. 'Tell me, what did you see?' he gruffly demanded. 'You saw nothing.' As Marteel backed away, holding up his hands in what could have been either apology or self-defence, Ronnie pointed an angry finger. '*Don't start,*' he snapped.

Human beings have a complex relationship with power. There is plenty of evidence to suggest that we are hard-wired to crave it. But at the same time, our response to those in positions of authority is often one of suspicion – even, at times, outright hostility. In the hands of fallible humans, power brings with it the possibility of corruption and cruelty. In George Orwell's *Nineteen Eighty-Four*, O'Brien – in the middle of torturing Winston Smith – takes a break to explain his vision of power's irresistible grip:

> But always – do not forget this, Winston – always there will be the intoxication of power, constantly increasing and constantly growing subtler. Always, at every moment, there will be the thrill of victory, the sensation of trampling on an enemy who is helpless. If you want a picture of the future, imagine a boot stamping on a human face – for ever.

The prospect of power never fades; it will only get stronger – and as it does so, those who gain it will forever be seduced by the capacity for violence it brings. Fundamentally, it is not power itself that is the problem: people are the problem.

In sport, power sits with the referee or umpire. It can be a brutal job – tough, thankless, even dangerous. As the authority figure in the heat of battle, referees can cop an awful lot of stick. In football, referee abuse – from both players and fans – is commonplace. Referee numbers have plummeted by as much as a third in recent years, with many living in fear of verbal and physical attacks; a staggering 93 per cent of English football refs reported that they had been the target of abuse. In tennis, too, the umpire – although perched in apparent safety in their high chair – can find themselves in surprisingly grave peril. In February 2022, Alexander Zverev was kicked out of the Mexican Open after whacking his racket back and forth against the umpire's chair – inches from their feet – while belching out a frenzy of splenetic verbal slurs. Authority, it seems, comes at a price: if your judgements go down badly, you need to prepare yourself for grief.

Snooker, though, does seem to be different. For the most part, snooker referees are treated with quiet but acute respect. There is a ghostly quality to their presence; being as invisible as possible is a key part of the job. The referee must be still, hidden, a watcher in the shadows – out of the players' eyeline, silent and unnoticed, so that shots can be played without distraction, as if there was no referee at all. Referees are the solemn spectres of snooker. The scores they call out are the utterances of some disembodied voice, a sonorous deity of the baize. A snooker referee is simultaneously godlike and criminally undervalued – the unseen presence without whom no game could ever function.

But there is also something curiously deferential, even servile, about the role of the snooker referee. They pick the colours out of the pockets and re-spot them; the players do not have to. When asked, they will dutifully clean the cue ball or any object ball. If a player requires any equipment, such as the rest or the spider, the referee will extract it from its under-the-table lair. In the early days of billiards, all these more obsequious tasks were completed by a lowlier figure, the marker, while the referee looked on from the comfort of a chair, occupied with the more exalted task of ensuring that the rules were being followed.

In the 1930s, J. B. Priestley was in attendance at Thurston's billiard hall in London for a match between Joe Davis and Tom Newman. His write-up of the encounter contains what must surely be the most memorable description of a green baize referee ever put to paper:

> He was an essential part of the afternoon, not merely because he kept the score and called it out, but because he created an atmosphere. He was a young man, whose profile was rather like that of the Mad Hatter; his face was all nose, teeth and glittering eye; and

he had an ecclesiastical dignity and gravity of manner. He handed over the rest of the half-butt like one serving at an altar. To see him place the red on the spot was to realise at once the greatness of the occasion. Best of all was to watch him removing, with his white-gloved hands, specks of dust or films of moisture from a ball. The voice in which he called out the scores was the most impersonal I have ever heard. It was a voice that belonged to solemn ritual and it did as much as the four walls and the thickly drawn curtained windows to withdraw us from ordinary life and Leicester Square.

Priestley perfectly captures here the compelling gravitas of the referee's presence. Discreet they may be, but referees are also essential – a core component of spectacle and ambience.

It has been heartening to observe the respect given to snooker referees over the years – but there has, inevitably, been the odd ugly exception. In 1994, Alex Higgins was playing in the World Championship first round against Ken Doherty, in what would turn out to be Higgins' very last match at the Crucible. Overseeing it was John Williams – a fierce disciplinarian, the very strictest of the refereeing fraternity. Many believed he was specially selected for matches involving Higgins, as he was one of the few referees not daunted by the prospect.

Early on, he was on the Hurricane's side – warning and then removing an audience member in the front row who had been spouting abuse. Later on, though, the Williams-Higgins dynamic turned sour. Higgins had been persistently asking Williams to move to a different position, out of his eyeline. 'No, I'm staying here,' Williams brusquely replied. 'I've stayed here all day. Don't try to tell me how to referee, Alex. You play.' Higgins stared at the table, his limp face tired and haunted, lined with a pain that seemed to have little to do with the match he was playing. 'I had to qualify,' he murmured to himself. 'I've been waiting for three years.'

The scene was typical of the bleak timbre of Higgins' late career. Later that same year, in the UK Championship, he found a surprising bit of form – beating both Nigel Bond and Drew Henry to make it to the last sixteen. Against Dave Harold, though, the wheels came off, and he was trounced 9–4. In the post-match press conference – after complaining about a change to the start time and the number of kicks he had suffered – he offered some choice words about referee Jon Street. 'If you've got a gut feeling that a referee probably wants you to get beat, it's soul-destroying for anyone,' he said. 'I would have accepted a man off the street to referee; I would have felt much more comfortable.' From that day on, Higgins would never again win a professional snooker match.

It would be wrong, though, to think that Higgins is the only player to have had scraps of this kind. As the 2022 world final showed, Ronnie O'Sullivan's relationship with referees has not always been smooth. In a 2010 Crucible encounter against Mark Selby, Leo Scullion called a touching ball after O'Sullivan had nestled onto a red. Ronnie was not happy – the touching ball made it easy for Selby to play the white away up the table and he was adamant that it was the wrong call.

'There's no way in a million years that is touching,' he said, as Scullion stuck with his decision. An incensed O'Sullivan seethed in his chair, scowling, muttering, shaking his head, as Selby played what was now a simple safety shot. But Ronnie wasn't finished. 'You need to get your eyes tested,' he barked as he got up to play. 'Absolute mile gap there, mate.'

O'Sullivan has had a whole string of run-ins with referee Terry Camilleri – stretching all the way back to the 2007 World Championships, when he accused Camilleri of getting in his way as he moved round the table. A fug of animosity has hung between them ever since. At the 2017 Masters, O'Sullivan repeatedly asked a photographer to keep still while he completed a break – and he clearly felt that Camilleri was not on top of the situation.

'The referee?' he complained to Eurosport afterwards. 'How is he refereeing in the semi-finals of a major tournament?' On his blog later, he continued in the same vein: 'I felt the referee, Terry Camilleri, was not up to scratch during my semi-final match with Marco Fu at one of our sport's major events.'

The authorities were not impressed, and O'Sullivan may not have helped his case by also describing the photographer as a 'fucking nightmare'. He received a disciplinary letter.

In general, snooker referees do not chase the limelight. So when they do give insights about their own craft, they can be priceless. Jan Verhaas has been on the circuit since the early 1990s; a character so laid-back as to be almost horizontal, his serene temperament emerging as a key asset in the high-voltage setting of major tournaments. He is also six foot six, affording a commanding air of authority. When asked about the concentration required to do his job, his response was straightforward. 'Comes pretty natural with me,' he explained. 'I suppose I have the discipline to do that. Because I also know that if I lost my concentration, it's a lonely world out there.'

At a disciplinary level, he said, snooker refereeing is an easy job – in stark contrast to football, snooker referees only 'very rarely' get abuse; 'I mean, we are a gentleman's game.' It is only with the occasional character – he predictably cited Alex Higgins – that things can get tricky. 'All of a sudden, you couldn't do your job as a snooker referee,' he remembered. Instead, you had to be 'a bit of a schoolteacher, a policeman'. When needs dictate, it appears not to be a difficult role for Verhaas to assume.

As snooker's first high-profile female referee, Michaela Tabb was a barrier-busting pioneer. She was the first woman ever to officiate in a professional ranking tournament – and then, in 2009, the first to referee a World Championship final. But she did not find it an easy road. 'Even after two years,' she said, 'I still didn't believe in myself because I was just constantly having to work so hard . . . It stood out if I did something that was wrong because I was the only woman.' She had been fast-tracked, bypassing the standard, five-year apprenticeship route. It caused bad blood in places. 'As you can imagine, it didn't go down well with a number of referees,' she explained. 'In the beginning, the aggression from some of my fellow refs was really quite nasty . . . It really was hard and I had to toughen up very quickly.'

Tabb's courage, though, paved the way for dramatic cultural change – there are now plenty of female referees on the circuit. 'If I'm being honest, it's fabulous for me,' she said with under-standable pride. 'I know that my legacy is that all these young ladies that I can see on the television are doing that job because I did it.'

'Perhaps the meaning of all human activity,' wrote the great film director Andrei Tarkovsky, 'lies in artistic consciousness, in the pointless and selfless creative act.' It is in our nature to vener-ate generous, unselfish deeds, recognising them as embodying our noblest instincts. There is a deep selflessness to the role of the snooker referee – combining, as it does, an ethos of invisibil-ity with the aim of facilitating the smooth completion of a game for both players and fans. It is the creative act out of which the secure splendour of a snooker match materialises. Referees are subtle shades, the veiled celebrants guarding the game against chaos and anarchy. They are the unsung heroes of snooker.

19

Sex

Sex appeal is fifty per cent what you've got and fifty per cent what people think you've got.

Sophia Loren, 1957

Music, movies, bars, city nights, alcohol, drugs, money, danger, figs and chocolate . . . there are certain aspects of reality that, for good or bad, have long been linked to sex. At the same time, there are others that seem a long way from sex, harbouring a libido-crushing, anti-erotic power: sickness, for instance; tax returns; taking the bins out. It is perhaps not clear in which camp philosophy belongs. From different angles, philosophical thinking might look either appealingly profound or tediously dry. And the sex lives of the great philosophers were, it must be said, a ferociously mixed bag, ranging from the puritanical to the libertine.

Some philosophers were very wary of sex – one might even say, afraid of it. Immanuel Kant was certainly in this camp, offering a series of troubled warnings about what might happen to people if they allow their sexual instincts to take control. 'In loving from sexual inclination, they make the person into an object of their appetite,' he argued. 'As soon as the person is possessed and the appetite sated, they are thrown away, as one throws away a lemon after sucking the juice from it.' In stark contrast, Sigmund Freud stressed the centrality of sex to human drives, proposing that its influence can be found in all facets of human experience. 'The behaviour of a human being in sexual matters,' he wrote in *Sexuality and the Psychology of Love*, 'is often a prototype for the whole of his other modes of reaction to life.'

On the surface, snooker seems to position itself a very long way from sex. A game of quiet absorption and bow-tied tradition-alism, birthed in a fog of billiard-hall tobacco and the yeasty guff of warm lager, it appears not to offer the sexiest of settings. The players themselves are products of many years of subterranean living, their focus long turned away from the temptations of the outside world, their eyes only on the table. In an interview for *Woman* magazine in the eighties, Steve Davis made it very clear where his priorities lay. 'If I had to choose between sex and snooker, I'd choose snooker,' he explained. 'Snooker is my justi-fication, my fulfilment.'

There is, though, evidence to suggest that sex has been more significant in snooker history than one might expect. As the game enthralled the living rooms of the seventies and eighties, it was spotted that many of the most avid followers of the men's game were, in fact, women. 'You were always going to have women watching snooker in the eighties,' journalist Julie Welch has said, 'because you were watching men in captivity . . . there are these very elegant blokes, beautifully dressed, strolling round the table, leaning over the table. You'll see their bums, tight trousers . . . there was something quite *physical* about snooker; almost, dare I say it, sexual. You know, getting on to the table, fiddling around with that cue.'

Such comments cast a different light on snooker, investing it with a surprisingly sensual allure. Images of grizzled, fag-in-mouth, pot-bellied booze hounds give way to fantasies of dashing paramours, suave suits, writhing buttocks, outstretched legs. Is there something beyond the trivial in the notion of the snooker cue as a phallic symbol? What precise undertones of sexual possibility reside in the act of striking balls with long, hard sticks? Whatever the truth, it is certainly the case that snooker's female audience became a key market in the boom years. Certain players were even elevated to sex-symbol status.

Tony Knowles, born and bred in Bolton, emerged in the early eighties as one of the leading young talents in the game. He had burst onto the scene in thrilling fashion with his shock 10–1 demolition of Steve Davis at the Crucible in 1982. But it was his Italianate good looks that caught the eye of many female fans. Tall, dark, vaguely reminiscent of a young Harrison Ford, Knowles knew how to carry a suit and tie. 'They used to call him the melter,' John Virgo recalled. He arrived like a debonair prince of the baize, oozing movie-star charisma – destined, it seemed, for stardom and success.

But this is not quite how things turned out. Just as the 1984 World Championships were starting, the *Sun* launched a lurid three-part exposé. WHY GIRLS CALL ME THE HOTTEST POT IN SNOOKER ran the story: 'They climb through windows, bribe officials, shower him with presents and pretend to be his sister – just to get close to the twenty-eight-year-old, six-foot, two-inch sure shot.' The piece was stuffed with Knowles' boasts about his sexual exploits: 'I don't rate girls out of ten. I rate them out of two: those who say "Yes," and those who say, "No." I don't meet many who say, "No."' There was a picture of a sharp-suited Knowles lying on top of a snooker table, arms round a blonde girl who was *au naturel* beyond stockings and heels. 'They set the pictures up with a couple of page-three girls,' he later explained. 'Obviously, they had no clothes on. Very nice girls as well.'

He was paid twenty-five thousand pounds for the scoop but, in the end, it was unclear whether it had been worth the money. Barry Hearn certainly didn't think so. 'For him, it was a disaster,' Hearn claimed. 'I mean, we fined him five thousand quid for bringing the game into disrepute and a lot of people on the board were in favour of slinging him out. There was high feeling.'

Bruised by the scandal and the ill will it had spawned, Knowles soldiered on – only to find himself in a second scandal the following year. His ex-girlfriend had revealed to the *Sun* that, in the bedroom, Knowles fostered a predilection for wearing women's underwear. 'Tony was a turn-on in ladies' undies!' the paper gleefully declared. It was divulged that he had once turned up in a negligée to a 'vicars and tarts' fancy dress party. KNICKERS! pronounced both the *Sun* and the *Star*. Knowles was forced to give a press conference at which he sought to defend himself from accusations of depravity. 'I have not at any time sought sexual pleasure,' he glumly explained, 'from wearing women's underwear . . . This party was a one-off, and I have not attended anything similar since. The party was not in any way perverted or kinky.'

The stern response to these stories was symptomatic of snooker's image at the time. The game traded on a reputation for gentlemanly behaviour and civilised respectability. The debauchery of Knowles – which actually generated plenty of useful media attention – was not understood to be commercially beneficial. Instead, such behaviour was seen as damaging to the essence of why people liked and followed snooker. Disapproval reigned. For a time, there was a flurry of interest in T-shirts and badges proclaiming 'I said "No" to Tony Knowles'. Despite his status as one of the game's leading players, he was passed over for management opportunities. Barry Hearn did not touch him: he was damaged goods.

'He could've been used by the big boys,' Hearn explained. 'Someone could've got behind him and done something. And then he sold that story an' it just . . . It *definitely* would've cost him quarter of a million in lost earnings. It cost him his reputation.'

Knowles has always been adamant that these scandals wrecked his play and prevented him from reaching the level of success many had seen as his destiny. The statistics seem to confirm it – he never won another tournament after the end of the 1984/5 season. But the publicity was not quite all negative; on the back of the notoriety, he did at least receive a string of TV opportunities. Not all of them were wholly distinguished. As Clive Everton recorded, he was invited onto *That's Life* – one of the top-rated shows of the era – but their goal was not an in-depth interview: '*That's Life*'s idea was for Tony to play a few shots, bringing the ball not off the cushion but the redoubtable bottom of Mollie Sugden, doyenne of the sitcom *Are You Being Served?*' Knowles declined the offer.

For all the attention he received, Knowles was far from the only player to promote a sexy side to snooker in the 1980s. Jimmy White was given a full image overhaul by his manager, Harvey Lisberg: his wonky teeth were fixed, his suits were upgraded and he was equipped with a Leo Sayer perm of uncertain merit. 'For the sex point of view,' said Lisberg, 'the sex image for the women viewers, that's being dealt with. He's going to look better.' White's camaraderie with hedonistic dreamboat Kirk Stevens crackled with the unpredictability of two romping young rock stars. More conservative-minded hunters of snookering hunks, meanwhile, were likely to opt for the moustachioed sophistication of Cliff Thorburn or the bouffant-barneted charm of Terry Griffiths. This was a time when image was everything – snooker was sexy, and the sex of snooker was selling itself very nicely indeed.

As the twentieth century came to a close, though, there was one young player who took snookering sexiness to levels never before seen.

Star quality is not something seen in every snooker player – but Paul Hunter was a star. He was handsome, talented, humble and charismatic. His looks reminded people of David Beckham – there were some who thought he was a *better-looking* version of Beckham. He played the game with the kind of attacking flair that echoed Alex Higgins and, even more, his hero and good friend Jimmy White. And Hunter was happy with the attention he got: 'If people see me as a good-looking lad, successful in what he does, and I'm compared to someone like Beckham, it's got to be a compliment, hasn't it? It's better than being called ugly, I suppose. No, I love it, me.' His death from cancer in 2006, at the age of just twenty-seven, is one of the darkest tragedies ever to hit the game. Over sixteen years later, the snooker world remains in mourning – wondering what might have been, and what heights he might have reached.

As a player, Hunter is most famed for a trio of 10–9 victories at the Masters – wins that underlined both the excellence of his play and the toughness of his temperament. But the third of these Masters victories has also gone down in legend for different reasons. It was against Ronnie O'Sullivan – who was, at the time, very much at the peak of his extraordinary powers and would go on to win his second world title a few months later. The match began badly for Hunter. Ronnie stormed ahead with a blitz of seventy-plus breaks, taking a 6–2 lead at the end of the opening session. Hunter was in good form – he had won both his frames with centuries – but it looked like it would not be enough. O'Sullivan already had one hand on a second Masters crown.

Far from being crestfallen, though, Hunter decided to action what has now gone down in snookering folklore as 'Plan B'. He retired to the hotel room with girlfriend Lindsey. He needed to find a way to relax – something that might calm the nerves, ease the tension and restore the spirit. And so there was one thing on the menu. 'It was a quick session – around ten minutes or so – but I felt great afterwards,' he said. 'She jumped in the bath, I had a kip and then played like a dream.' He scored superbly throughout the evening, making three more centuries before overhauling O'Sullivan in the decider to win what was quickly hailed as 'one of the highest-quality matches witnessed in snooker'. Plan B had worked perfectly; as Hunter later explained, the 'B' 'is for bonk'.

O'Sullivan himself is not a stranger to sex scandals. In 2013 the *Mirror* ran an exposé on his night of passion with a fan. Emma Rowett had been given his number after a match, and they ended up back at his hotel. 'I couldn't believe I was having sex with Ronnie O'Sullivan,' Rowett revealed. 'He certainly lives up to his name the "Rocket" – he couldn't get enough.' On other occasions, his restive personality has got him into trouble; bored at a press conference in China, he was fined for making lewd comments, having suggested that his microphone might be a suitable locus for fellatio. For a time, he wondered if his addictive personality might include sex and signed himself up to Sex Addicts Anonymous. 'I thought I'd see what's around,' he explained in his autobiography; 'there might be a few nice birds there.'

There have also been scandals involving some more surprising names from the snooker world. Shaun Murphy's wholesome reputation took a knock in 2009 when his fling with a Bedford escort was revealed. And in perhaps the least likely of all snookering sexposés, even Steve Davis has been targeted. KINKY STEVE

WAS 'KING OF THE BEDROOM', ran a 2013 headline in the *Sun*. Beauty therapist Cheree Palla claimed that the two had enjoyed a passionate fling back in the nineties, when she was just nineteen. 'I was only young,' she revealed, 'and I don't think I really appreciated what an animal he was.' Davis, she said, was insatiable. They would be at it seven times a night. 'To this day not one man has even compared to Steve in the sack. I mean it – not even close.' It was not an allegation that Davis denied. 'I didn't lose much sleep over it in the end really. It's not like I had people all over the place,' he said. 'I think my street cred went up quite a lot actually.'

For those who seek to accuse snooker of being stuffy or dull, these stories offer a stark riposte. The game harbours pulsating, fleshly, carnal resonances. The sexual suggestiveness of the cue and balls iconography might seem facile, but it cannot easily be discounted. In early 2022, Madonna paraded round a pool table for what was billed as a 'billiard-themed photo shoot'. In ripped jeans, shades, and a cropped cardigan embossed with pearly dollar signs, she was shown potting a ball, reclining with her head fixed in the frame of the triangle, and lying down with the cue clenched between her teeth. 'Michigan-born Madge,' wrote Cassie Carpenter in the *Daily Mail*, 'certainly had phallic fun posing with the cue stick which she held between her legs.'

Subdued though it may seem, the green baize is a verdant space of erotic promise. It is perhaps worth noting, at this point, that along with green's links to nature come ancient associations with fertility and sex. There is an archaic English phrase, to 'give a woman a green gown', which signified the taking of her virginity. Robert Herrick uses the term in his 1648 seduction poem, 'Corinna's Going a-Maying', in which the speaker persuades his girl to go out and frolic in the fields: 'Many a green gown has been given;/Many a kiss, both odd and even.'

Since its origins, the green baize has been bathed in sexual possibility. In 'A Celebration of Charis', published in 1640, Ben Jonson presents a female lover detailing her vision of a perfect man:

> Young I'd have him too, and fair,
> Yet a man; with crispèd hair . . .
> Eye-brows bent, like Cupid's bow,
> Front, an ample field of snow;
> Even nose, and cheek (withal)
> Smooth as is the billiard ball

In these lines, the billiard ball is cast as an emblem of male physical perfection. The ball and sexual attractiveness are fused; in a single image, billiards and sex blend into one. It is a reminder that, between the materials of the green baize and the forces of physical attraction, there is a surprisingly deep, enigmatic bond.

20

ANGER

I was angry with my friend;
I told my wrath, my wrath did end.
I was angry with my foe:
I told it not, my wrath did grow.
William Blake, 'A Poison Tree', 1794

In the very opening of his *Meditations*, Marcus Aurelius expresses gratitude that he has inherited the ability to control his anger: 'Of my grandfather Verus I have learned to be gentle and meek and to refrain from all anger and passion.' Anger is a central enemy of Stoic philosophy – counterproductive and causing harm to all concerned.

Seneca the Younger, one of the most influential of the Stoics, wrote a lengthy work exclusively devoted to anger. In it, anger is pinned as a toxin, poisoning the perpetrator as well as enslaving them. 'Surely every man will want to restrain any impulse towards anger,' Seneca wrote, 'when he realises that it begins by inflicting harm, firstly, on himself! In the case of those who give full rein to anger and consider it a proof of strength . . . do you not, then, want me to point out to them that a man who is the prisoner of his own anger, so far from being powerful, cannot even be called free?'

Anger has oft been presented as the path of folly, or even madness. In the opening scene of *King Lear*, Kent attempts to caution the king, who has rashly disowned his daughter just moments earlier. But Lear's anger renders him deaf to advice: 'Come not between the dragon and his wrath,' he warns Kent. When Desdemona is faced with Othello's jealous rage, she experiences it as a menacing mystery – a passion detached from sense: 'I understand a fury in your words/But not the words.' Elsewhere, though, Shakespeare supplies anger with more of a moral purpose, as a force that can motivate individuals towards virtue, courage or revenge. 'Be this the whetstone of your sword,' says Malcolm to Macduff, after Macbeth has slaughtered Macduff's family. 'Let grief/Convert to anger: blunt not the heart, enrage it.'

Snooker is a game of many faces – one might fairly call it a game of contradictions. Its honouring of light and colour continually hints at the shadow of a surrounding dark. Its quiet, gradual narratives develop the potential for explosive drama. And alongside its genteel, civilised traits, there also sits something much more hot-blooded and primal. Anger is written into the story of snooker; over the years, there have been many occasions when it has besieged the apparent decorum of the snooker table.

There is no figure, though, who even begins to rival the febrile unpredictability of Alex Higgins. Whatever his mood at any particular moment, he was never, it seemed, far from something senseless, hostile, violent. His drinking certainly did not help. In a particularly infamous incident after a match at the 1986 UK Championship, he got himself into an ugly altercation with a group of officials; the snooker board's tournament director, Paul Hatherall, found himself grabbed by the throat and headbutted by Higgins just above the eye – after which, 'Higgins set about the business of trying to choke him with his own tie.' He was handed a twelve-thousand-pound fine and a five-tournament ban – a punishment criticised by Barry Hearn as 'ludicrously lenient'.

Four years later, with his career up the spout and dumped out of the Crucible in the first round, Higgins suffered another of his lowest moments – and once again, it involved violence against an official. Defeated and alone, with the lights lowered and the crowd long gone, he stayed in the arena for a long time after the match, hungrily gulping drink after drink. It was unclear what his eyes were focused on, as he sat there brooding – the now-covered table; the empty seats; the dim stage where, eight years earlier, he had pulled off his greatest triumph in front of a packed house of adoring fans, face damp with tears, baby girl clutched to his chest. Estimates vary about precisely how many vodka and oranges he went through. His biographer Bill Borrows suggested a total of twenty-seven shots. What followed, though, is clear: Higgins swayed through the back-stage area and calmly punched match official Colin Randle in the belly, before walking out to announce his retirement to the press.

His mind, in these moments, seemed overrun by an acid web of resentments. There he was, the player more than any other who had lifted the game from obscurity into prominence; and there he was, staring into the horrors of further debt, bankruptcy, even the threat of homelessness.

'Well, chaps, the current events over the last few weeks have not been very good, this way or the other,' he began in a sinister, mock-cheerful tone, 'so I would like to announce my retirement from professional snooker.' As he moved through a rambling monologue, his anger grew; the bile within him rose more and more clearly to the surface. At one point, a journalist tried to asked a question. *'I've not finished,'* Higgins snarled. 'I've had all sorts of shit thrown at me by the media for the past six or seven years,' he continued, now shakily up on his feet. Camera flashes bleached his face as he spoke. 'I was supposed to be a stalwart of the game, the guy who took all the brunt . . . I am not prepared to take it any longer . . . Let's see how you do without me, because I ain't playing no more.'

Throughout his career, Higgins had always been an outsider: it was one of the reasons he was so loved. He wasn't like other players. He was a maverick; he stood alone. It is certainly true that he did not enjoy much popularity among the professional ranks. Other players tended to give him a wide berth. He once turned up to a tournament sporting a black eye, claiming that he had been kicked by a horse; in truth, he had been punched by a fellow player, Paul Medati, during a private money match. The story is one of many suggesting friction between Higgins and other players. He had more than one violent face-off with Cliff Thorburn: on one occasion, Higgins threatened him with a bottle, leading to an ugly wrestling-match tussle. On another, after a drunken night of cards, Higgins made the mistake of calling him a 'Canadian cunt' – Thorburn responded by kicking him, as he put it, 'right in the nuts'.

Perhaps the most vicious dispute, though, was with fellow Northern Irishman Dennis Taylor. The two had been teammates in the 1990 British Car Rental World Cup. Taylor had been made team captain, a selection that had not pleased Higgins, who felt himself to be the better player. Northern Ireland made it to the final where they faced Canada. At a hastily convened mid-match team meeting – held in the ladies' toilets, so they would not be overheard – Higgins insulted Taylor's dead mother and warned him, 'The next time you're in Northern Ireland I'll have you shot.' Hours later, at a post-match press conference, he followed this up by saying Taylor 'puts money before country. He belongs back in Coalisland. He is not fit to wear this badge, the red hand of Ulster.'

There was a palpable strain of sectarianism in the jibes; while Taylor was a Catholic, Higgins was a product of the fiercely Protestant Shankill area of West Belfast. He issued a muted public apology which did not impress Taylor. It was with a sense of inevitability that the two were drawn against each other in the Benson & Hedges Irish Masters just a week later; the encounter remains one of the most notorious grudge matches in snooker history.

'I was determined I wasn't going to lose that match,' Taylor later recalled. '[I was] standing in the dressing room just looking in the mirror and . . . shouting to myself, "You can't lose, you can't lose."' In the end, it wasn't even close: Higgins went for far too many high-risk shots, and Taylor won it 5–2.

Higgins' story, though, involves plenty of even darker chasms; his anger was by no means confined to the snooker table. In his personal life, distressing episodes of domestic violence repeatedly surfaced. His marriage to Lynn Avison – immortalised in that picture of baby-hugging, family bliss at the Crucible, after his 1982 victory – became increasingly unstable as the years passed. Police were once called to his Cheshire mansion in the middle of the night; Higgins had smashed some windows with a golf club and thrown a TV out onto the lawn, having not taken kindly to suggestions that he was tinkering with the au pair. When the police turned up, he tried to grab a knife, declaring, 'That's it. There is only one way for Alex Higgins to end it.' He spent the night in jail. The marriage was over. 'I told him, "Alex, I'm never coming back,"' Lynn said. 'He just said, "Feck off!" But without me, he was lost.'

In subsequent relationships, a bleak pattern of flux and cruelty prevailed. In 1989, he attacked girlfriend Siobhan Kidd with a hairdryer, fracturing her cheekbone. Later, his relationship with Holly Haise was marked by mayhem. 'I loved him . . . I still do, but I don't want to be with him any more,' she once told the *People*. 'He's too frightening . . . he beat me up for the first two years of our relationship.' The violence reached a dark zenith in 1997 when – after being attacked by Higgins – Haise picked up a kitchen knife and stabbed him three times. Higgins lost a large amount of blood and the wounds to his arm and belly were far from trivial – but after being persuaded to go to hospital, he 'discharged himself, against medical advice and climbed into a taxi just as the pubs opened'.

Even in his later years, body ravaged by cancer, face fleshless and drawn, his whole body little more than bone, the threat of violence still remained. In 2007, at the age of fifty-eight, he was accused of punching a referee at an exhibition match with Jimmy White. The case was 'blown out of all proportion', Higgins claimed afterwards. And in some of the most bizarre footage from Higgins' final years, he was filmed on a night out with White and White's manager, Kevin Kelly; after a street dispute, the cause of which is unclear, Higgins can be seen punching Kelly and trying to kick him in the crotch, while White vomits against a nearby limousine.

Steve Davis was perpetually painted as the anti-Higgins, a player defined by calm control and moderation. There are not so many stories of raging and brawling in his career. But interestingly, even with Davis, there are one or two.

In the semi-final of the 1981 World Championship, his opponent was Cliff Thorburn. Towards the end of the penultimate session, *something* went down. There are conflicting accounts about precisely what happened. In his autobiography, Davis suggests that Thorburn had 'made a complaint about somebody in the audience whistling to put him off'. Gordon Burn, though, suggested the misdemeanour came from Davis himself – and that it was 'Davis claiming a frame as his own before his opponent had formally conceded' that riled Thorburn. There was a heated encounter backstage by the dressing rooms. By all accounts, it almost came to blows. Maybe Thorburn had overreacted; maybe his anger had been justified. Whatever the truth, it was a mistake. Davis' response was typical of the icy disposition that would see him rule the decade. 'When I closed my dressing-room door behind me,' he remembers, 'the main feeling I had was that I had broken him down.'

As Higgins faded from the game in the nineties, Ronnie O'Sullivan came to the fore as the most unpredictable presence in snooker. At the 1996 World Championships, he tried to enter the press room with his friend and one-time coach, Del Hill. But there was a problem: Hill was wearing jeans, in contravention of the dress code. This was pointed out by the press officer, Mike Ganley, who refused to let Hill in. In response, O'Sullivan punched Ganley in the groin and – in a grisly twist – bit into his lip. A disciplinary committee swiftly gathered – O'Sullivan was supposed to be playing his quarter final against John Higgins the following day. In the end, he was given a twenty-thousand-pound fine – but, to the surprise of some, he was allowed to continue in the tournament. Journalist Hugh McIlvanney felt the punishment was far too light, calling it a 'monumental abdication of responsibility'; Alex Higgins grumbled that it smacked of double standards.

On the table, O'Sullivan has always carried with him the spectre of disorderly turns: along with his brilliance comes the twitching background possibility that something violent might erupt. One of the most memorable skirmishes took place at the Crucible in 2018 against Ali Carter. After playing his shot, O'Sullivan deliberately refused to get out of Carter's way as he walked back to his chair. They bumped shoulders; Carter had to swerve to avoid a more hefty contact. From his seat, O'Sullivan loudly elaborated on the reason for his displeasure. 'Come on, you shoulder-barged me,' he declared, 'so I thought I'd give you one back.'

'Thank you very much,' said Carter. 'That's very nice of you.'

'Stop being angry then,' O'Sullivan replied.

The referee asked that they halt the verbals and carry on with the match.

'Yeah, I'm cool,' O'Sullivan unconvincingly assured him. 'I'm cool as a cucumber.' His face did not suggest so.

In the commentary box, Dennis Taylor could not believe what he was seeing: 'I've never ever seen that before, in forty years at the Crucible theatre.'

In truth, though, there was an element of handbags at dawn to the O'Sullivan–Carter incident. The reality is that, while things can get heated around a snooker table, it is rare for things to spill into actual violence. More often, there is a hammy, even vaguely comic feel to proceedings. This was certainly true in an undignified exchange between Quinten Hann and Andy Hicks at the 2004 World Championship. The whole match had been bad-tempered but things really kicked off at the end when, after winning, Hicks goaded Hann by pointing out that, in losing the match, he had now dropped out of the top sixteen. Hann responded with characteristic truculence, challenging Hicks to a fight; the referee had to step between them and jostle them out of the arena.

Afterwards, in one of the most peculiar twists that snooker has seen, fellow player Mark King jumped in to say that he needed the money and would happily fight Hann. A boxing match, soon christened 'Pot Whack', was arranged for June 2004, which Hann won on points.

These diverse tales of anger in snooker might surprise those who associate the game with slow quiet and fusty restraint. But a familiar binary emerges; there is a volatility within silence itself, something convulsive and unstable. Anger and silence are not antithetical; they can, and often do, coexist. William Blake's lines from 'A Poison Tree' – 'I was angry with my friend;/I told my wrath, my wrath did end./I was angry with my foe:/I told it not, my wrath did grow' – exist, among other things, as a warning about the toxicity of suppressed anger.

Snooker players insistently internalise; as they stalk the table, chalking their cue, brooding, pondering the state of the balls, they keep their thoughts and feelings to themselves. Inside that silence, there can be something of a much higher temperature, maybe even more ominous, than relaxed tranquillity. As the ancient Eastern proverb tells us, silence is the most powerful scream . . . in the quiet of snooker, anger has its own, unsteady place.

21

TELEVISION

Television knows no night. It is perpetual day. TV embodies our fear of the dark, of night, of the other side of things.
Jean Baudrillard, Cool Memories, 1990

Since the origins of civilisation itself, humans have assembled around the fireplace – not just for warmth, but for purposes of communal gathering, family bonding and storytelling. The Old English word '*heorðgeneatas*', appearing several times in *Beowulf*, is often translated as 'hearth-fellows' or 'hearth-companions'. Kinsmen or comrades are those who gather around the same fireplace as you to rest and to talk. The work of Dickens is stuffed with fireplaces; they appear as spaces of domestic cosiness as well as emblems of contemplation. Even Scrooge has a fire, albeit 'a very low fire indeed; nothing on such a bitter night. He was obliged to sit close to it and brood over it, before he could extract the least sensation of warmth from such a handful of fuel.'

Elsewhere, Dickensian fireplaces are expressive and vital. In a vivid passage from *The Old Curiosity Shop*, the fireplace is presented as a companion through time – its roar and crackle becoming a voice, its flames a picture house of the imagination: 'The fire? It has been alive as long as I have. We talk and think together all night long. It's like a book to me – the only book I ever learned to read; and many an old story it tells me. It's music, for I should know its voice among a thousand, and there are other voices in its roar. It has its pictures too. You don't know how many strange faces and different scenes I trace in the red-hot coals. It's my memory, that fire, and shows me all my life.'

The hearth endures through history and literature as a symbol for our sense of belonging – a source not just of physical, but also spiritual warmth. 'We do not lend the hearth quite the importance that our ancestors did, Greek or otherwise,' Stephen Fry has sagely observed. 'Yet, even for us, the word stands for something more than just a fireplace. We speak of "hearth and home". The word "hearth" shares its ancestry with "heart", just as the modern Greek for "hearth" is "*kardia*", which also means "heart".'

In January 1926, John Logie Baird gave the first public demonstration of a new technology that would take the place of the hearth in spectacular and unprecedented fashion. The machine through which Baird showcased a fuzzy image of his business partner's face was called a television. The images were warped and jagged, not exactly clear, but for the first time, moving pictures had been transmitted through the air. Later in his life, Baird remembered how he had felt after conducting his first successful tests with a ventriloquist's dummy: 'The image of the dummy's head formed itself on the screen with what appeared to me an almost unbelievable clarity. I had got it! I could scarcely believe my eyes and felt myself shaking with excitement.'

For all his delight, Baird could never have predicted quite how shattering the significance of his invention would be. In one stroke, the nature of home itself had changed. The living rooms of the world would now have a new hearth, a new heart. The TV would become the nucleus of the domestic space – a uniquely captivating phenomenon, addictive and all-pervading, the most influential technological development of the century. The world would be gripped, whether people liked it or not. In 1947, there were just under fifteen thousand households paying the licence fee in the UK. Two decades later, there were nearly fifteen million.

In the late 1960s, while snooker slept in a slough of obscurity, the BBC were looking for ways in which they might promote the new technology of colour television. The controller of BBC2, a certain David Attenborough, realised that snooker, with colour at its core, would be ideal for this purpose. There was little belief that this humble staple of working men's clubs would spark much national excitement – but it was a low-risk, low-budget option. The format would be simple – a single frame between two professionals, in a compact, half-hour slot. The first programme went out on 23 July 1969. It was the week of the moon landings; many at the BBC presumed that *Pot Black* would fade without a trace. Despite low expectations, though, the first episode fared quite well. Something was afoot. *Pot Black*, it seemed, might be something more than a gimmicky vehicle for colour TV – it might be a hit.

The show quickly shot to second place in the BBC2 ratings; over the coming years, it would remain one of the most popular on the channel. Snooker would be catapulted towards previously unimaginable levels of fame and esteem. *Pot Black* was a jewel, a flawlessly formed, pocket-sized TV treat. Every element of the show fitted together with mesmeric perfection. There was a catchy ragtime theme tune – George Botsford's 'Black and White Rag'. There were the players themselves, distinguished gents in ruched shirts, fat bow ties and waistcoats. And for the first time, the nation's TV screens were graced with the sleek green oblong of the table, an image that was to become one of the defining motifs of late-century British televisual culture. 'Snooker owes a lot to *Pot Black*,' remembers Steve Davis. 'It really was the breakthrough for the modern game.'

From the start, the show's commentator was a former billiard-hall manager by the name of Edwin 'Ted' Lowe. With his gravelly whisper, antiquated manner and malapropisms – 'The yellow is on the side cushion,' he once said, 'and, for those of you watching in black-and-white, it's just behind the blue' – he became as famous as the players themselves.

It would be no exaggeration, in fact, to say that Lowe is one of the most important figures in the history of snooker on television. His much-loved, much-mocked technique had been forged back in the fifties, when he was manager of the Leicester Square Hall; sitting in the audience to commentate on matches, but without a soundproof booth, he was forced to lower his voice so that the players could not hear him. His whisper became a quintessential part of the game's atmosphere; rich and dignified, somehow filled at every moment with both serenity and tension. Over fifty years after he first appeared on *Pot Black* – and over a decade after his death – 'Whispering' Ted Lowe remains a figure of snookering legend, the first and the greatest of the game's commentators; we shall never see his like again.

Commentary is a complex, under-appreciated art. The purpose of the commentator is never to take centre stage; rather like the referee, they must live on the periphery, working in the shadows, helping the action to blossom. It is not an easy business; commentators are rarely given much praise, but are regularly skewered for messing things up, being annoying or – in the eyes of a judgemental public – just doing a bad job. You have to be interesting, but not intrusive. You have to talk, but never too much. 'The moments of silence should be as precious as the moments when you are talking,' football's Clive Tyldesley has said, 'and used to determine what you want to say next . . . You are just a soundtrack to the movie. Very few people go to the cinema for the soundtrack.'

At its best, though, commentary can elevate a sporting moment – providing poetry, giving language to wordless drama. Mastery of the craft is key. In order to deliver technical information, deep knowledge of the game is also crucial. Even back when he was at his peak, Ted Lowe was unusual in not being a former professional. Most of his peers in the box – John Pulman, Jack Karnehm, Ray Edmonds, David Taylor, Jim Meadowcroft – had been players before picking up the microphone.

There is no doubt, though, that the most influential commentator to join the BBC ranks in the 1970s was Clive Everton. A university English graduate and former journalist, Everton had never been a great snooker player; his highest ranking was a modest forty-seven, and he had been more successful in billiards. But he brought a literary sensibility to snooker that it sorely needed. As the author of several histories of the game, and as the long-time editor of *Snooker Scene* magazine, Everton established a reputation as its pre-eminent chronicler. And as a commentator, he was stately and venerable – very much in the mould of Whispering Ted, specialising in decorous restraint and upright eloquence.

Over the years, the voices of BBC commentators have become part of the material of snooker history. The trio of John Virgo, Dennis Taylor and Willie Thorne established themselves alongside Everton as the crew beamed into the nation's homes at every major tournament; their familiar tones, dry jokes and even their most tired clichés all became fondly cherished, part of the charm of the game.

Commentary has always been crucial to the homeliness of snooker as a television experience. It makes the room warmer; it makes the tea or the beer taste better. 'When I'm sat in the commentary box,' Taylor once said, 'I always do it as if I'm sat in someone's lounge, telling them about what's going on. That's how I always go about it.' The commentator exists as a kind of bridge between the audience and the game – not just an instructor offering expertise, but a fellow viewer, a companion on the sofa, living every shot along with you.

As the years went by, a younger breed of commentators began to enter the fray. Steve Davis, John Parrott, Ken Doherty and Stephen Hendry were brought into the BBC mix; the microphone increasingly became a likely move for a top player in the twilight of their career – almost an ominous sign that retirement might be close.

More recently, Alan McManus entered the box and made an immediate impact with his resonant voice and penchant for baroque poeticisms – things like, 'The path that you hath travelled matters not,' and, 'A veritable compendium of power, preposterous potting and panache.' And as part of snooker's aim to sex things up and pull in the younger punters, even Judd Trump and Jack Lisowski have made some commentary appearances, despite their careers still running at full throttle. During the 2021 World Championships, the duo appeared during the interval in boldly casual combos – T-shirts, jackets and trainers – to flaunt a range of trick shots.

'We're going rogue this time, aren't we?' said Lisowski.

'Yeah, we're gonna freestyle this time,' replied Judd, before showcasing a light-speed banana shot off a long red.

But the magic of televised snooker is not only created by the commentators. The first and the last thing a viewer sees is the presenter. And a great presenter needs a whole range of qualities: they must be relaxed, engaging, articulate, clear and good-humoured. They must have an excellent rapport with players and pundits. They must be skilled interviewers, understanding what to ask, what not to ask. They must have excellent knowledge of the territory.

And for many years, there was one supreme force in the world of snooker presenting – David Vine. A versatile figure, he had amassed a wide array of experience including *Grandstand*, *Ski Sunday*, *A Question of Sport*, numerous Olympic Games – even, on one occasion, the Eurovision Song Contest. But over the course of more than twenty years, it was as the host of BBC snooker that he acquired cult hero status. His easy-going manner, tinted specs and liquid voice became synonymous with the game. 'Vine's deep tones,' wrote Peter Ferguson on his retirement, 'honed by years of dedication to filter tips, have introduced a galaxy of the game's stars into British households for a quarter of a century, with a late-night élan that links him forever to the green baize.'

Vine's reputation would have remained forever unrivalled if it had not been for Hazel Irvine, whose work as BBC host over the last two decades has been so masterful that she might – unthinkably – surpass Vine as the greatest snooker presenter in history. Affable, fastidious and knowledgeable, Irvine has very much worked in the Vine mould, mixing relaxed humour with rigorous professionalism. Once again, cultivating a sense of living-room intimacy has been crucial; 'There is definitely a family feel to it,' she once observed. The line-up of Irvine, Davis and Parrott in the studio, predicting, cogitating and reacting, has become an iconic part of twenty-first-century TV snooker. The three of them respond to events and share jokes much like family members gathered on the sofa – gathered, one might even say, round the television.

For a long time, snooker coverage was monopolised by the BBC, with the occasional foray undertaken by ITV: but these days it is a very different world. Snooker in the 2020s is a blazing multimedia experience, with online forums and social media constantly buzzing with stories, banter, predictions and opinions. ITV4 and Eurosport have become key providers of snooker coverage and their teams, at times, have a more adventurous feel; alongside stalwarts such as Neal Foulds, Jill Douglas and Colin Murray there have been experimentalist surprises, such as Radzi Chinyanganya from *Blue Peter*, and a more roguish attitude to punditry from Ronnie O'Sullivan and Jimmy White.

The home of World Snooker online, www.wst.tv, provides news, updates and video interviews, as well as live scoring throughout each tournament. The BBC website now offers an expansive cityscape of information. Access to snooker used to be controlled and limited; but now, at the touch of a button, everything is possible. The two-table set-up at the Crucible once meant that live coverage of one match would be sacrificed: but no longer. With two screens – and sufficient desire – it is perfectly possible to watch both matches *at the same time*.

'Snooker could have been invented for television,' Gordon Burn once rightly noted. 'In fact, it *was* largely re-invented to suit the medium that, in the space of a little over seven years, was to turn it from a marginal activity, capable of supporting no more than a handful of professionals, into part of the fabric of the national life.'

What is it, exactly, that is at the heart of this blissful marriage between television and snooker? Part of the answer is about colour and movement, the game's conspicuous celebration of the visual. A. S. Byatt has written of being captivated by televised snooker, vividly extolling the 'lines of force playing across a clear green screen, human dramas which were part of the lines of force, the suffering and exulting faces briefly picked out by the cameras, the subtleties of the unfolding stories picked out by the commentators.' The green backdrop may, as Donald Trelford has claimed, help to lend a soothing quality; perhaps it also, amid the cold and the rain of British days, brings the outdoors indoors, a delusion of green lawns in dark rooms.

The slow, soft, gradual development of a game of snooker is itself a kind of hearth, a breathing fire in the living rooms of the world. Its unhurried narratives mimic the bland beauty of the everyday, the manner in which quiet lives happen as moments of wonder separated by vast wildernesses of the uneventful and the humdrum. As historian Joe Moran has observed, 'The excitement of snooker had to be earned through the possibility of boredom.' Snooker, at this level, becomes a deep metaphor for the nature of our lives. Snooker is meaningful because it offers a simulacrum of one of the most significant locations of all, the location of home itself.

22

HOME

*How often have I lain beneath rain on a strange roof, thinking of
home.*

William Faulkner, As I Lay Dying, 1930

The haunting lyric 'Westron Wynde', little more than a frag-
ment, is of mysterious origin. It first appeared in the sixteenth
century, though some scholars think it might be as much as two
hundred years older. The four cryptic lines express a longing for
lost love, and for home:

> Westron wynde, when wyll thow blow
> The smalle rayne downe can rayne?
> Cryst yf my love were in my armys,
> And I yn my bed agayne.

The wind wished for here is the soft, western wind of spring
and, more surprisingly, more intriguingly, the speaker also
wishes for rain. The 'small rayne' suggests, perhaps, the fine rain
of England; some have wondered if the speaker is away in a
foreign land, maybe in the crusades. The final lines crave the
bliss of bed and a lover's arms. We do not know where, exactly,
the lover has gone: maybe they left; maybe they are waiting at

home for the speaker to return; maybe they are dead and it is a poem of mourning. However we read it, the ache for home is clear – but home, here, is not a place; or, at least, it is not only a place. It is something more profound, more internal – a state of happiness and inner peace. The 'bed' is where love lies, an emblem of emotional belonging.

This shard of yearning tells us something about home, how it is far more than just a location. 'Let's get one thing straight,' US author and journalist Meghan Daum has written, 'A house is not the same as a home. Home is an idea, a social construct, a story we tell ourselves about who we are and who and what we want closest in our midst. There is no place like home because home is not actually a place.' Our feelings about home might revolve around the building in which we live – but at heart, home is within us. It is a spirit, a soul – an imaginative as well as a material phenomenon, a treasure chest of all the things and the people to which we belong.

'The ache for home lives in all of us,' Maya Angelou poignantly wrote, 'the safe place where we can go as we are and not be questioned.'

People talk about the Crucible as the home of snooker. The vast majority of snooker is not played there; snooker is not even the main purpose of the venue, which, for most of the year, offers a menu of classic and contemporary plays. Moreover, in the eyes of some, the Crucible is hardly an ideal venue for snooker. It is cramped – especially in the two-table setup, in which there is only just enough room for the players to take their shots. The crowd capacity – less than a thousand – is staggeringly limited for the premium event in the calendar. And yet . . . and yet.

The Crucible will always be the home of snooker for reasons that are emotional, psychological and spiritual. It is a swirling cauldron of history, drama and memory. In this sense, the Crucible is not a place; it is, like the bed of 'Westron Wynde', an imaginative force, located not so much in Sheffield as in the heart of every snooker fan. It is where Alex cried into his baby's arms; where Dennis sank that final black; where Jimmy blew his chance; where Ronnie composed his perfect break. For snooker, the Crucible is where love lies. This is why calls for the World Championship to move provoke anger and fear. Barry Hearn's retorts to such threats have always been reassuringly robust: 'In my lifetime, however long that may be, there will be no changes. And after me, my son Edward will be here, with a little note in his dad's will which says "Crucible. We're staying".'

We look at the world once, in childhood . . . I remember being at home, curled on the carpet aged five, staring up into a sea of green . . . two figures taking their turns upon the stage, actors of divergent forms, one tall and thin, one short and plump, like a deliberately fashioned double act, some snookering Laurel and Hardy, in the process of composing snooker's greatest story. At that precise moment, everything was flawlessly cosy and safe. I was perfectly at home. All the elements of my reality made it so – the soft fuzz of brown carpet under me; the warm air; the amber glow of electric light; the familiar paintings on walls; the click, tap and whisper of the slow game on the screen. In many ways, the room now is less of a place than a feeling, a bubble of memory in which I was able to breathe freely, with all the weightless tranquillity of a dream.

As I sat watching the snooker, someone else was there – somewhere behind me in the shadows. I don't remember seeing them, exactly – they are not a direct part of this memory – but I know they were there. Perhaps they were watching along with me. Perhaps they were occupied with something else entirely – reading a book, taking a thick drag from a Marlboro Red, swigging a mug of tea. Perhaps they were not watching the tele-vision, but actually watching me, with a father's love for their child, watching from unseen shadows into which, many years later, they would return, the fags in the end doing their predict-able work to those big lungs, lungs that were strong and seasoned, but not strong enough.

We played snooker a handful of times. There was a snooker hall down the road. He could play a bit – it was a half-decent technique he had, awkward though it was, gurning over his cue like a gargoyle, glasses lopsided on his nose, head skewed a little to one side. Even as a boy I would beat him but, looking back now, those wins were a little too easy, too certain; maybe, just maybe, he did what fathers like to do, giving me a game and pretending to push but always making sure his son would win. 'The wonder of the world, the beauty and the power, the shapes of things, their colours, lights and shades; these I saw. Look ye also while life lasts.' The things I would trade for just one more frame, one more glance at that face.

For half a century, snooker has been beamed into people's homes like a mighty drug of clashing qualities, both stimulant and depressant, at once soporific and exhilarating. What is the real meaning of snooker? How deep, precisely, are those pockets?

The notion that sport has no meaning has never rung true. Sport reaches into us and becomes part of us, binding itself to the architecture of our lives. The Romans kept shrines to the Penates, gods of the household and the hearth – and snooker is just such a spirit, bathing living rooms in its sheltering green light. Green can be many things; it can be queasy, sinister, sad. But this is not the lonely green of Edward Hopper's *Nighthawks* diner, the green of sad night-time cities washed by artificial light. The green of the snooker table is a far more ancient green. It is the light of lawns, fields and forests, the light of nature, a green that Wordsworth understood to be both outside us and within us, a defining part of what makes us human:

And I have felt
A presence that disturbs me with the joy
Of elevated thoughts; a sense sublime
Of something far more deeply interfused,
Whose dwelling is the light of setting suns,
And the round ocean and the living air,
And the blue sky, and in the mind of man:
A motion and a spirit, that impels
All thinking things, all objects of all thought,
And rolls through all things. Therefore am I still
A lover of the meadows and the woods,
And mountains; and of all that we behold
From this green earth.

Acknowledgements

I want to begin by thanking Tim Bates, my agent at Peters Fraser + Dunlop, for believing in this project from the start and for being such a wise, reassuring presence. I also want to thank Andreas Campomar at Constable for all his encouragement and calm expertise. Thank you, too, to Holly Blood for her adroit guidance and her patience with my callow queries.

For their friendship and support through the long snooker match of life, I want to thank Benjamin Berlyn, Richard Fletcher, Will Griffith, Tim Inman, Neelu Kumar, James O'Brien, Annie Rigby, Timothy Smith, Richard Tacon, Ed Vainker, Duncan White and Sally Whitehill. A special thank you must go to Christian Dickman and Anthony Deane, for many years of the very finest snookering badinage. A trio of brilliant colleagues – Anna Camilleri, Nigel Mortimer and Hailz Osborne – have all, in different ways, inspired elements of this book.

David Jackson: this one's for you. I know that, somewhere, you're still smiling your kind and patient smile.

I am profoundly grateful to absolutely everyone who has ever been involved in the miraculous game of snooker. Make no mistake, you have helped to make the world a more beautiful place.

And to my mother, belated thanks for one of the greatest childhood gifts of all: the sublime grace of a six-foot snooker table.

My two daughters, Manon and Hermione, and my wife Nouska, are my sun, my moon and all my stars. I owe them everything. They are all the light and colour I could ever wish for.

BIBLIOGRAPHY

Amis, Martin, *Visiting Mrs Nabokov and Other Excursions* (London: Jonathan Cape, 1993)

Anstiss, Sue, *Game On: The Unstoppable Rise of Women's Sport* (London: Unbound, 2021)

Auden, W. H., *The English Auden*, ed. Edward Mendelson (London: Faber and Faber, 1977). Reprinted by permission of Curtis Brown, Ltd. All rights reserved.

Austen, Jane, *Persuasion* (London: Penguin, 1998)

Balzac, Honoré de, *The Wild Ass's Skin*, tr. Helen Constantine (Oxford: Oxford University Press, 2012)

Barnes, Julian, *A History of the World in 10½ Chapters* (London: Picador, 1990)

Baudrillard, Jean, *America*, tr. Chris Turner (London: Verso, 1988)

Baudrillard, Jean, *Cool Memories*, tr. Chris Turner (London: Verso, 1990)

Beauvoir, Simone de, *All Men Are Mortal*, tr. Leonard M. Friedman (New York; London: Norton, 1992)

Beckett, Samuel, *Worstward Ho* (London: John Calder, 1983)

Berryman, John, *Poems*, selected by Michael Hofmann (London: Faber and Faber, 2004)

Blake, William, *Songs of Innocence and of Experience*, ed. Robert Essick (San Marino: Huntingdon Library, 2008)

Bloom, Harold, *Shakespeare: The Invention of the Human* (London: Fourth Estate, 1998)

Borrows, Bill, *The Hurricane: The Turbulent Life & Times of Alex Higgins* (London: Atlantic Books, 2002)

Boru, Sean, *The Little Book of Snooker* (Stroud: The History Press, 2010)

Burn, Gordon, *Pocket Money: Britain's Boom-Time Snooker* (London: Faber and Faber, 1986)

Burns, Robert, *Selected Poems* (London: Penguin, 1996)

Byatt, A. S., 'I Was A Wembley Virgin,' *Observer*, 30 June 1996

Chaney, Lisa, *Chanel: An Intimate Life* (London: Penguin, 2011)

Chaucer, Geoffrey, *The Riverside Chaucer*, ed. Larry D. Benson (Oxford: Oxford University Press, 1987)

Coleridge, Samuel Taylor, *Complete Poetical Works* (Oxford: Oxford University Press, 1969)

Darwin, Charles, *The Descent of Man, and Selection in Relation to Sex* (London: John Murray, 1871)

Davis, Steve, *Interesting: My Autobiography* (London: Ebury Press, 2015)

Davis, Steve and Torabi, Kavus, *Medical Grade Music* (London: White Rabbit Books, 2021)

Dickens, Charles, *A Christmas Carol* (London: Vintage, 2009)

Dickens, Charles, *The Old Curiosity Shop* (London: Vintage, 2010)

Dickens, Charles, *The Pickwick Papers* (London: Vintage, 2009)

Eliot, George, *Adam Bede* (London: Penguin, 2008)

Eliot, George, *Middlemarch* (New York: Modern Library, 2000)

Eliot, T. S., *The Complete Poems and Plays* (London: Faber and Faber, 1969)

Ellison, Ralph, *Invisible Man* (London: Penguin, 2001)

Everton, Clive, *Black Farce and Cue Ball Wizards: The Inside Story of the Snooker World* (Edinburgh; London: Mainstream Publishing, 2007)

Everton, Clive, *The History of Snooker and Billiards* (Haywards Heath: Partridge Press, 1986)

Faulkner, William, *As I Lay Dying* (New York: Norton, 2010)

Faulkner, William, *The Sound and the Fury* (London: Vintage, 1995)

Fleming, Ian, *Casino Royale* (London: Vintage, 2012)

Fowler, Alastair, ed., *The New Oxford Book of Seventeenth-Century Verse* (Oxford; New York: Oxford University Press, 1991)

Freud, Sigmund, *Sexuality and the Psychology of Love* (New York: Simon & Schuster, 1963)

Fry, Stephen, *Mythos: The Greek Myths Retold* (London: Penguin, 2017)

Glück, Louise, *Poems 1962–2020* (London: Penguin Random House, 2021)

Graves, Robert, 'The Art of Poetry No. 11', *Paris Review* 47 (Summer 1969)

Greenblatt, Stephen, ed., *The Norton Shakespeare* (New York: Norton, 1997)

Greene, Brian, *The Elegant Universe: Superstrings, Hidden Dimensions and the Quest for the Ultimate Theory* (London: Random House, 1999)

Hardy, Thomas, *Jude the Obscure* (London: Penguin, 1994)

Hazlitt, William, 'On Nicknames', *The Works of William Hazlitt II: Sketches and Essays* (London: Oxford University Press, 1936)

Heidegger, Martin, *Being and Time*, tr. Joan Stambaugh (Albany, NY: State University of New York Press, 2010)

Hendry, Stephen, *Me and the Table: My Autobiography* (London: John Blake Publishing, 2018)

Hodges, Chas, *Chas & Dave: All About Us* (London: John Blake Publishing, 2013)

Hook, Philip, *Art of the Extreme 1905–1914: The European Art World 1905–1914* (London: Profile Books, 2021)

Hume, David, *Political Writings*, ed. Stuart D. Warner and Donald W. Livingston (Indianapolis; Cambridge: Hackett, 1994)

Huxley, Aldous, *Music at Night and Other Essays* (London: Chatto & Windus, 1931)

Johnson, Samuel, 'Study, Composition and Converse Equally Necessary to Intellectual Accomplishment', *The British Essayists; with Prefaces, Historical and Biographical Vol. XXIV*, ed. A. Chalmers (London: Nicols, Son, and Bentley, 1817)

Jones, Emrys, ed., *The New Oxford Book of Sixteenth-Century Verse* (Oxford; New York: Oxford University Press, 1991)

Jones, Owen, *Chavs: The Demonization of the Working Class* (London: Verso, 2012)

Jonson, Ben, *The Complete Poems* (London: Penguin, 1988)

Kant, Immanuel, *Lectures on Ethics*, tr. Peter Heath (Cambridge: Cambridge University Press, 1997)

Keats, John, *Selected Poems* (London: Penguin, 1996)

Keats, John, *The Letters of John Keats*, ed. H. Buxton Forman (London: Reeves & Turner, 1895)

Kundera, Milan, *Slowness*, tr. Linda Asher (London; Boston: Faber and Faber, 1996)

Larkin, Philip, *Collected Poems*, ed. Anthony Thwaite (London: Faber and Faber, 1988)

Locke, John, *The Works of John Locke*, vol. X (London: Thomas Davison, 1823)

Lowell, Robert, *Collected Poems*, ed. Frank Bidart and David Gewanter (London: Faber and Faber, 2003)

Malone, Aubrey, *Whirlwind: The Incredible Story of Jimmy White* (Studley: Know The Score Books, 2009)

Marcus Aurelius, *The Meditations of Marcus Aurelius* tr. Meric Casaubon (New York: Cosimo Classics, 2005)

McLuhan, Marshall, *The Gutenberg Galaxy* (Toronto: University of Toronto Press, 1962)

Melville, Herman, *Moby-Dick: or, the White Whale* (Ware: Wordsworth Editions, 1993)

Millay, Edna St Vincent, *Letters*, ed. Allan Ross Macdougall (Maine: Down East Books, 1982)

Milton, John, *Paradise Lost* (London: Penguin, 1989)

Moran, Joe, *Armchair Nation: An Intimate History of Britain in Front of the TV* (London: Profile, 2013)

Morrison, Ian, *The Hamlyn Encyclopedia of Snooker* (Twickenham: Hamlyn, 1985)

Nabokov, Vladimir, *Speak, Memory: An Autobiography Revisited* (London: Penguin, 2012)

Nietzsche, Friedrich, *The Will to Power* (London: Penguin, 2017)

Nietzsche, Friedrich, *Twilight of Idols and Anti-Christ* (London: Penguin, 1990)

Nunns, Hector, *The Crucible's Greatest Matches: Forty Years of Snooker's World Championship in Sheffield* (Worthing: Pitch Publishing, 2017)

Orwell, George, *In Front of Your Nose: 1945–1950* (Boston: David R. Godine, 2007)

Orwell, George, *Nineteen Eighty-Four* (London: Penguin, 1954)

O'Sullivan, Ronnie, *Running: The Autobiography* (London: Orion, 2013)

Owen, Wilfred, *The Collected Poems of Wilfred Owen*, ed. C. Day Lewis (London: Chatto & Windus, 1964)

Pamuk, Orhan, *My Name is Red*, tr. Erdağ M. Göknar (London: Faber and Faber, 2001)

Plath, Sylvia, *The Bell Jar* (London: Faber and Faber, 1966)

Plath, Sylvia, *The Journals of Sylvia Plath 1950–1962*, ed. Karen V. Kukil (London: Faber and Faber, 2000)

Plato, *Laws Vol. I*, tr. R. G. Bury (London: William Heineman, 1926)

Pope, Alexander, *The Rape of the Lock and Other Major Writings* (London: Penguin, 2011)

Pound, Ezra, *ABC of Reading* (New Haven: Yale University Press, 1934)

Priestley, J. B., *Self-Selected Essays* (London: Heinemann, 1932)

Rafferty, Jean, *The Cruel Game: The Inside Story of Snooker* (London: Elm Tree Books, 1983)

Richler, Mordecai, *On Snooker* (London: Yellow Jersey Press, 2001)

Roberts, Jonathan, *William Blake's Poetry* (London: Continuum International, 2007)

Ruskin, John, *The Stones of Venice Vol. II* (New York: John Wiley & Sons, 1887)

Seneca the Younger, *Dialogues and Essays*, tr. John Davie (Oxford; New York: Oxford University Press, 2007)

Shakespeare, William, *A Midsummer Night's Dream*, ed. Linda Buckle (Cambridge: Cambridge University Press, 1992)

Shriver, Lionel, *The Post-Birthday World* (London: Borough Press, 2015)

Stitt, Peter, 'The Art of Poetry: An Interview with John Berryman', *Paris Review* 53 (Winter 1972), pp. 177–207

Stoker, Bram, *Dracula*, ed. Roger Luckhurst (Oxford: Oxford University Press, 2011)

Tanner, Michael, *Schopenhauer: Metaphysics and Art* (London: Routledge, 1999)

Tarkovsky, Andrei, *Sculpting in Time*, tr. Kitty Hunter-Blair (Austin: University of Texas Press, 1986)

Tate, Tim, *Girls with Balls: The Secret History of Women's Football* (London: John Blake Publishing, 2013)

Trelford, Donald, *Snookered* (London: Faber and Faber, 1986)

Twain, Mark, *Notebooks & Journals Vol. I: 1855–1873* (Los Angeles; London: University of California Press, 1975)

Welch, Ian, *Greatest Moments of Snooker* (Swindon: Green Umbrella, 2007)

West, Michael, *Transcendental Wordplay: America's Romantic Punsters and the Search for the Language of Nature* (Athens: Ohio University Press, 2000)

Wharton, Edith, *The House of Mirth* (New York: Norton, 2018)

White, Jimmy, *Behind the White Ball* (London: Arrow, 1999)

White, Jimmy, *Second Wind – My Autobiography* (Liverpool: Sport Media, 2014)

Wilde, Oscar, *The Importance of Being Earnest and Other Plays* (Oxford: Oxford University Press, 2008)

Williams, Luke and Gadsby, Paul, *Masters of the Baize: Cue Legends, Bad Boys and Forgotten Men in Search of Snooker's Ultimate Prize* (Edinburgh; London: Mainstream Publishing, 2005)

Williams, Tennessee, *A Streetcar Named Desire* (London: Penguin, 2009)

Woolf, Virginia, *Orlando: A Biography* (London: Vintage, 2000)

Wordsworth, William, *Complete Poetical Works* (Oxford: Oxford University Press, 1936)

Online sources

en.espn.co.uk/snooker/sport/story/376747.html

news.bbc.co.uk/sport1/hi/funny_old_game/3797515.stm

news.bbc.co.uk/sport1/hi/other_sports/snooker/3056307.stm

news.bbc.co.uk/sport1/hi/other_sports/snooker/4486887.stm

news.bbc.co.uk/sport1/hi/other_sports/snooker/4921138.stm

www.chinadaily.com.cn/sports/2007-01/22/content_789116.htm

archive.nytimes.com/www.nytimes.com/books/99/06/13/specials/byatt-possessed.html?_r=1&scp=1&sq=possession%2520byatt%2520showing%2520off&st=cse

babel.hathitrust.org/cgi/pt?id=loc.ark:/13960/t24b35r41&view=1up&seq=101

chomsky.info/reader02/

inews.co.uk/sport/football/clive-tyldesley-commentator-england-amazon-prime-369242

kmhk.com/the-greatest-quotes-in-rock-history/

lithub.com/what-makes-a-house-a-home/

matchroom.com/news/snooker-final-tv-peak-close-six-million/

metro.co.uk/2019/08/28/michael-holt-gives-brutally-honest-take-snooker-career-dont-think-done-worse-10645009/

metro.co.uk/2020/04/29/barry-hearn-explains-problem-genius-ronnie-osullivan-warns-judd-trump-new-king-12628274/

metro.co.uk/2021/04/17/neil-robertson-reveals-superstition-behind-eye-catching-hair-at-world-snooker-championship-14425726/

metro.co.uk/2022/01/11/judd-trump-blasts-ridiculous-masters-dress-code-and-lack-of-wst-response-to-his-ideas-15898140/

metro.co.uk/2019/05/08/judd-trumps-best-game-beat-anyone-snooker-history-says-ronnie-osullivan-9449540/

science.sciencemag.org/content/359/6380/1146.full

sportmob.com/en/article/974423-Novak-Djokovic-Biography-The-Joker

sportsgazette.co.uk/it-took-me-two-years-to-feel-like-i-belonged-michaela-tabb-on-the-difficulties-of-being-the-first-major-female-snooker-referee/; snookerhq.com/2012/03/22/big-interview-michaela-tabb/

theoria.art-zoo.com/sorbonne-lecture-yves-klein/

web.stanford.edu/~jsabol/certainty/readings/Galileo-Assayer.pdf

withasideofpod.nd.edu/episodes/4-6-on-misinformation-and-truth-sand-wiches-lisa-fazio-vanderbilt-university/

wst.tv/celebrity-snooker-fans-lionel-shriver/

wst.tv/kicking-out-kicks/

wst.tv/podcast-with-neil-robertson/

wst.tv/remembering-the-hurricane/

www.bbc.co.uk/news/uk-england-lancashire-47732213

www.bbc.co.uk/news/world-asia-china-55454146

www.bbc.co.uk/sport/av/snooker/17953362

www.bbc.co.uk/sport/snooker/44409924

www.bbc.co.uk/sport/snooker/55690030

www.bbc.co.uk/sport/snooker/57077091

www.belfasttelegraph.co.uk/imported/jimmy-bottles-it-28222274.html

www.bigissue.com/culture/stephen-hendry-you-have-to-be-very-selfish-to-be-and-stay-the-best/

www.dafasnooker.com/special-interviews/qa-session-jan-verhaas/

www.dailymail.co.uk/home/you/article-9788137/Joanne-Hegarty-Yes-black-really-happy-shade.html

www.dailymail.co.uk/news/article-1305512/Krays-How-National-Service-transformed-twins-gangland-thugs.html

www.dailymail.co.uk/news/article-3591955/So-Steve-interesting-Davis-Did-really-torrid-SEVEN-times-night-affair-s-one-lover-claimed-JANE-FRYER-asks-famously-dull-snooker-ace-true.html

www.dailymail.co.uk/sport/othersports/article-1270438/Snooker-chief-Barry-Hearn-decide-fate-John-Higgins-match-fixing-claims.html

www.dailymail.co.uk/sport/othersports/article-1270862/Snooker-legend-Steve-Davis-says-John-Higgins-fix-scandal-questions-fabric-game.html

www.dailymail.co.uk/sport/othersports/article-1270983/John-Higgins-Snooker-champion-match-fixing-row.html

www.dailymail.co.uk/sport/othersports/article-1297738/Jimmy-White-admits-I-cried-day-friend-Alex-Higgins.html

www.dailymail.co.uk/sport/othersports/article-2262832/Judd-Trump-wear-spiky-shoes-snooker--cost-845.html

www.dailymail.co.uk/sport/othersports/article-4120828/Mark-Selby-driven-trauma-dad-s-death-man-Ronnie-O-Sullivan-calls-torturer.html

www.dailymail.co.uk/sport/othersports/article-4203480/Ronnie-O-Sullivan-vows-not-open-media-interviews.html

www.dailymail.co.uk/sport/othersports/article-459026/OSullivan-hit-21
-000-fine-UK-Championship-walkout.html

www.dailymail.co.uk/sport/sportsnews/article-10313877/Referees-leave-
football-droves-horrific-abuse-10-000-gone-five-years.html

www.dailymail.co.uk/tvshowbiz/article-10442243/Madonna-63-reclines
-pool-table-bites-cue-stick-billiard-themed-photo-shoot.html

www.dailymail.co.uk/tvshowbiz/article-2049454/Paul-Gascoigne-I-
downed-9-brandies-snorted-cocaine-matches.html

www.dailyrecord.co.uk/sport/other-sports/snooker/steve-davis-hails-
genius-champion-976567

www.dailystar.co.uk/sport/snooker/steve-davis-snooker-music-dj
-23908084

www.espn.co.uk/tennis/story/_/id/15031425/novak-djokovic-questions-
whether-women-deserve-equal-pay-tennis

www.eurosport.co.uk/snooker/uk-championship/2021-2022/the-most-
dangerous-player-on-tour-jimmy-white-sees-a-lot-of-himself-in-rising-
star-zhao-xintong_sto8655231/story.shtml

www.eurosport.co.uk/snooker/world-championship/2015-2016/michael
-holt-leaving-school-early-to-play-snooker-remains-a-huge-regret-in-
my-life_sto5454658/story.shtml

www.eurosport.co.uk/snooker/world-championship/2019-2020/martin-
gould-on-his-battle-against-depression-i-felt-ashamed-pathetic-and-
my-body-ached_sto7829425/story.shtml

www.eurosport.co.uk/snooker/world-championship/2020-2021/world-
snooker-championship-2021-no-one-enjoys-playing-in-a-bow-tie-and
-waistcoat-mark-allen_sto8284489/story.shtml

www.eurosport.com/snooker/ronnie-o-sullivan-exclusive-can-you-justify
-feeling-like-s-why-depression-stalks-snooker_sto8083615/story.shtml

www.eurosport.com/snooker/snooker-news-can-cause-you-a-lot-of-
damage-why-ronnie-o-sullivan-doesn-t-want-kids-to-follow-in-his-_
sto8393331/story.shtml

www.eurosport.com/snooker/world-championship/2016-2017/blood-on
-the-carpet-how-bitter-rivals-alex-higgins-and-steve-davis-created-
modern-snooker_sto6126816/story.shtml

www.express.co.uk/sport/othersport/172911/Snooker-John-Higgins-
suspended-in-match-fix-row

www.express.co.uk/sport/othersport/4709/Only-perfection-will-do-for
-me

www.fourfourtwo.com/news/paolo-di-canio-west-ham-everton
-sportsmanship

www.frontiersin.org/articles/10.3389/fsoc.2017.00008/full

www.heraldscotland.com/sport/13157311.tartan-clad-mcmanus-happy-left-flying-saltire/

www.hindustantimes.com/india/feminism-makes-love-easier-says-gloria-steinem/story-CMt7gY31ffRlpYcfetbvBL.html

www.independent.co.uk/independentpremium/editors-letters/india-vs-england-ashwin-kohli-cricket-b1802601.html

www.independent.co.uk/news/obituaries/david-vine-commentator-who-helped-make-snooker-a-staple-of-televised-sport-1332044.html

www.independent.co.uk/news/uk/this-britain/remembering-the-80s-6101125.html

www.independent.co.uk/sport/football/european/lionel-messi-more-worried-about-being-a-good-person-than-being-the-best-player-in-the-world-8192210.html

www.independent.co.uk/sport/general/others/stephen-lee-found-guilty-of-matchfixing-ronnie-o-sullivan-claims-many-more-snooker-players-throw-matches-8821493.html

www.independent.co.uk/sport/general/snooker-the-beckham-of-the-baize-it-s-better-than-being-called-ugly-i-love-it-me-56441.html

www.independent.co.uk/sport/snooker-francisco-banned-for-five-years-1618853.html

www.independent.ie/sport/osullivan-sorry-over-walk-out-26351398.html

www.independent.ie/world-news/and-finally/real-tennis-the-original-racket-sport-thats-making-a-slow-but-steady-comeback-35910327.html

www.insidermedia.com/news/national/114215-

www.irishtimes.com/sport/other-sports/ken-doherty-can-t-understand-why-stephen-lee-got-involved-in-match-fixing-1.1533528

www.livemint.com/Leisure/5zJiXoHYDYnfbZWwDEIi8H/A-conversation-with-Martin-Amis.html

www.livesnooker.com/snooker-interviews/davis-insists-snooker-doesnt-have-to-be-fast-to-be-entertainin-20180919/

www.mansworldindia.com/sports/rafael-nadal-superstitious-man-tennis/

www.mirror.co.uk/3am/celebrity-news/freddie-flintoff-dismayed-elitist-cricket-24805064

www.mirror.co.uk/news/uk-news/alex-higgins-ex-wife-lynn-on-her-life-240331

www.mirror.co.uk/news/uk-news/john-higgins-suspended-in-snooker-match-fixing-218579

www.mirror.co.uk/news/uk-news/snooker-official-this-was-boring
-623398

www.mirror.co.uk/news/uk-news/snooker-stars-are-thickest-628325

www.mirror.co.uk/news/world-news/ronnie-osullivans-night-of-passion-
and-turmoil-1681034

www.mirror.co.uk/sport/other-sports/snooker/drugs-violence-buckets-
booze-rocknroll-7036694

www.mirror.co.uk/sport/other-sports/snooker/mark-selby-hailed-mind-
charity-25991762

www.mirror.co.uk/sport/other-sports/snooker/world-snooker-chairman-
barry-hearn-6924104

www.newyorker.com/tech/annals-of-technology/why-your-name
-matters

www.nytimes.com/1978/06/04/archives/words-of-the-painter-matisse-on
-art-henri-matisse-paper-cutouts.html

www.nytimes.com/1990/02/04/magazine/martin-amis-down-london-s-
mean-streets.html

www.prosnookerblog.com/2011/04/29/psb-interview-a-chat-at-the-
crucible-with-rob-walker/

www.rte.ie/sport/snooker/2006/1214/212344-snooker/

www.runnersworld.com/uk/training/motivation/a28396561/ronnie-
osullivan/

www.scotsman.com/sport/hunter-master-comebacks-2477276

www.scotsman.com/sport/interview-interesting-twist-boring-steve-davis
-1506018

www.skysports.com/darts/news/12288/12074258/fallon-sherrock-hopes-
women-beating-male-darts-players-becomes-normalised

www.smh.com.au/sport/wild-bills-hiccup-20030123-gdg5kw.html

www.spiked-online.com/2009/01/16/the-boring-but-beautiful-game/

www.standard.co.uk/sport/interviews/steve-davis-if-ronnie-o-sullivan-
was-a-greyhound-you-d-put-him-down-6393940.html

www.thefreelibrary.com/Snooker%3A+Napoleon+tips+helped+me+to
+rule+the+world%3B+EBDON+DOES+IT+BY...-a085511450

www.theguardian.com/books/2007/aug/04/fiction.asbyatt

www.theguardian.com/books/2014/jun/01/maya-angelou-appreciation-
afua-hirsch

www.theguardian.com/media/greenslade/2010/sep/09/john-higgins
-newsoftheworld

www.theguardian.com/music/2021/apr/04/steve-davis-and-kavus-torabi-
medical-grade-music-utopia-strong-interview

www.theguardian.com/observer/osm/story/0,¦433063,00.html

www.theguardian.com/observer/osm/story/0,6903,641889,00.html

www.theguardian.com/sport/2004/apr/12/snooker

www.theguardian.com/sport/2004/apr/23/smalltalk.sportinterviews

www.theguardian.com/sport/2004/aug/13/smalltalk.sportinterviews

www.theguardian.com/sport/2004/mar/07/snooker.features

www.theguardian.com/sport/2006/dec/15/snooker.gdnsport3

www.theguardian.com/sport/2006/may/02/snooker.worldsnooker
championship2006

www.theguardian.com/sport/2009/nov/08/allison-fisher-pool-interview

www.theguardian.com/sport/2010/may/02/john-higgins-snooker-match-
fixing-kiev

www.theguardian.com/sport/2010/may/02/steve-davis-john-higgins-
snooker

www.theguardian.com/sport/2010/oct/05/ben-johnson-drugs-
olympics#:~:text = In%201988%20Johnson%20became%20
a,notorious%20cheat%20in%20sporting%20history.&text=%22I%20
said%20to%20myself%2C%20%27,I%27m%20OK%20with%20it.

www.theguardian.com/sport/2010/sep/08/john-higgins-banned-cleared-
match-fixing#:~:text = %22I%20am%20pleased%20that%20
Sport,anything%20corrupt%2C%22%20said%20Higgins.

www.theguardian.com/sport/2010/sep/20/cheating-barry-hearn

www.theguardian.com/sport/2012/oct/12/stephen-lee-snooker-
suspended-betting?newsfeed=true

www.theguardian.com/sport/2013/feb/14/stephen-lee-snooker-match-
fixing

www.theguardian.com/sport/2013/nov/25/cricket-depression-jonathan-
trott-ashes

www.theguardian.com/sport/2017/apr/04/the-spin-t20-next-generation-
big-bash-cricket

www.theguardian.com/sport/2017/jun/22/small-talk-stephen-hendry-
jimmy-white-fight

www.theguardian.com/sport/2019/apr/23/jimmy-white-interview-alex-
higgins-world-snooker-championships

www.theguardian.com/sport/2019/may/09/i-thought-the-main-issue-in-
womens-sports-was-equal-pay-i-was-wrong

www.theguardian.com/sport/2020/aug/23/i-was-the-king-of-sabotage-
ronnie-osullivan-on-controversy-comebacks-and-becoming-a-carer

www.theguardian.com/sport/2021/may/16/gods-of-snooker-how-the-
sport-went-from-dingy-hobby-to-national-treasure

www.theguardian.com/sport/blog/2010/may/03/world-snooker-championship

www.theguardian.com/sport/that-1980s-sports-blog/2015/dec/03/uk-snooker-championship-willie-thorne-1985-steve-davis

www.theguardian.com/sport/live/2022/may/02/world-snooker-championship-final-2022-ronnie-osullivan-v-judd-trump-live

www.theguardian.com/world/2017/may/11/accelerationism-how-a-fringe-philosophy-predicted-the-future-we-live-in

www.thepowerof10.info/athletes/profile.aspx?athleteid=38667;

www.thesun.co.uk/news/398333/kinky-steve-was-king-of-the-bedroom/

www.thesun.co.uk/sport/13798226/gary-wilson-snooker-bed-depression/

www.thesun.co.uk/sport/othersports/16724637/judd-trump-snooker-champion-of-champions/

www.the-sun.com/sport/3029185/tony-adams-euro-96-wreck/

www.timeshighereducation.com/news/poetry-in-motion/99086.article

www.yorkpress.co.uk/news/9275474.the-big-interview-with-willie-thorne/

www.youtube.com/watch?v=_ki9D772kqU

www.youtube.com/watch?v=oKVCkcTw-nQ

www.youtube.com/watch?v=cUqRwCEoA2E&t=2033s; Everton, Black Farce, 165-6.

www.youtube.com/watch?v=FYP655z1ryo

www.youtube.com/watch?v=IjKWhVNkunE

www.youtube.com/watch?v=InJOClzZYUE

www.youtube.com/watch?v=JqfOMLE3AmU

www.youtube.com/watch?v=Lw4sKsygBRc

www.youtube.com/watch?v=t__UPN-cTmU&t=47s

INDEX